To Sue &

With grateful thanks
for your support for
wildlife & wild places.

THE
GREAT FEN
A Journey Through Time

ALAN BOWLEY

Illustrations by Oliver Bowley

piscespublications

Published 2020 by Pisces Publications

First published 2020.

British-Library-in-Publication Data
A catalogue record for this book is available from the British Library.

ISBN 978-1-874357-96-4

Designed and published by Pisces Publications

Visit our bookshop
www.naturebureau.co.uk/bookshop/

Pisces Publications is the imprint of NatureBureau,
2C The Votec Centre, Hambridge Lane, Newbury, Berkshire RG14 5TN
www.naturebureau.co.uk

Printed and bound in the UK by Gomer Press Ltd

Front cover: **Woodwalton Fen** [Guy Pilkington]
Back cover: **Ely Cathedral** [jakubkohout.com]; **Dyke digging**; **Gordon's Mere, Woodwalton Fen**; **Bittern** [Guy Pilkington]

Contents

Dedication

This book is dedicated to my family, Ginny, Oli, Hannah and Nick. They have proof-read endless drafts, typed and organised my research and listened to never-ending monologues on history and ecology! Without their unceasing love, support and encouragement this work would never have been completed.

Acknowledgements

Several people have contributed to the writing of this book. Sue Wallis read through all the early drafts and gave much expert and wise advice. Great Fen partners and staff gave helpful comments on the text, in particular Brian Eversham, Lorna Parker, Henry Stainier, Louise Rackham. Peter Marren offered useful advice and comments and Phil Gibbard was helpful in clarifying post-glacial fenland. Arnold Cooke, Camilla Lambrick, Steve Boreham and Ben le Bas have all contributed comments on the text and Chris Gerrard was generous with his experience as the first project officer for the Great Fen.

Photographs have been generously given by Jim Asher [JA], Paul Brock [PB], David Chandler [DC], Peter Creed [PC], Phil Cutt [PCu], Chris Evans [CE], David Garner [DG], Paul Goriup [PG], Chris Grant [CG], Chris Kirby-Evans [CK-E], David Kjaer [DK], Roy Leverton [RL], Richard Lindsay [RLi], Matt Lodge [ML]. Kevin Lunham [KL], Jacqueline Macou [JM], Nigel Phillips [P], Guy Pilkington [GP], Henry Stainier [HS], Sandy Sutherland [SS], Sue Wallis [SW], Catherine Weightman [CW], David White [DW], Wildlife Trust BCN [WTBCN], The University of Bristol permitted the image of 'London, Going Out of Town', Cambridge Library allowed the use of the *Cambridgeshire Collection* photos of fenland life and Vivacity supplied images of Flag Fen. Natural England [NE] allowed use of their Flickr images and Rebekah O'Driscoll sourced several Great Fen/Wildlife Trust images. Cambridge Archaeological Unit [CAU] supplied photos of the Bronze-Age log boats. Other images were sourced through Wikimedia Commons etc. Alex Brown [WC/AB], Andrew Curtis [WC/AC], Julian Dowse [WC/JD], Alex Brown [WC/AB], All other photos are by the author.

Oliver Bowley drew illustrations at each chapter head and Hannah Bowley the 'Nature in a Flowerpot' on page 171.

Artists for Nature artists were: Carry Ackroyd, Vadim Gorbatov, Chris Rose and Jonathan Yule.

I would like to thank Peter Creed and staff from NatureBureau/Pisces Publications for their support in getting an idea into print and Kate Carver for co-ordinating support from the Great Fen partners. This has been a partnership with the Great Fen from the outset and I am grateful for their continuing support. Finally, my friends, colleagues and family who have sustained me through the hard times.

Foreword

Charting the history of one of the most evocative landscapes in the British Isles, Alan Bowley's *The Great Fen – A Journey Through Time* paints a vivid portrait of the flat country where East Anglia meets the Wash and North Sea. His expertise and knowledge flow onto pages that tell not only the story of this vast and once wild wetland, but also our changing relationships with it.

Through millennia of climate changes and rising human demands, waves of shifting influences have left the landscapes we see today very far from those experienced by successive generations of our ancestors. In charting those changes, *The Great Fen* is a masterful feat of natural history, but also of history and the story of the fen people, the events that shaped their lives, their culture and art. Through this vital fusion of history and Nature writing, this wonderful book brings a vital and timely reminder that we can make little sense of our natural world unless we understand the human lives that created it.

It charts the changing demands of people over time, from the Mesolithic hunter-gatherer economy to Victorian drainage of The Fens by steam-powered pumps. It tells of how the curve and sweep of natural landscape was replaced by the straight lines of drainage ditches, slicing across the dark Fen soils, culminating during the 1850s in the destruction of what was then England's largest lowland lake, Whittlesea Mere.

But while the momentum of modern farming, and the lucrative returns that could be derived from it, caused most of the wetlands to be lost, early environmental awakenings led a few tiny fragments of the Whittlesea Mere wetland to be spared, which are now the National Nature Reserves of Woodwalton Fen and Holme Fen.

While intensive farming drove the Fen to silent lifelessness, in these little oases the jingling songs of Reed and Sedge Warblers, the buzz of insects, and the boom of a Bittern could still be heard over the rustle of breeze in sedge and reed. It was between these two fragments of Fen that during the late 1990s Alan Bowley helped give life to a vision to create a new wetland, restoring Fen habitat across 37 square kilometres of intensively farmed land between Holme and Woodwalton, so constituting one of the largest habitat restoration projects in the United Kingdom.

Although initial reaction was not universally positive, the proposal did inspire interest among key organisations, and in 1999 a grant from WWF provided the first seed-funding to enable the elaboration of proposals between English Nature, the Wildlife Trusts, Environment Agency and others. The Great Fen was born, and as the new millennium began, so did a new chapter for conservation, and not only for The Fens, but also more widely.

This was the time when the aim of conservation explicitly moved from the protection of the last fragments of remaining wildlife-rich habitats and toward their recreation at large scale. Driven by an emerging understanding that land is not only important for food production, but also for a wide range of other essential functions, the pendulum has progressively swung toward the kind of thinking that is now visible in dozens of initiatives across Britain and beyond.

This new approach to conservation seeks to meet multiple goals from habitat creation, not only for wildlife, but also to mitigate and adapt to climate change, to reduce flood risk and enable more opportunities for healthy outdoor recreation, while at the same time as meeting economic goals, including harnessing the benefits of tourism for rural economies.

That this thinking has in the two decades since the Great Fen was first proposed become mainstream is seen in, among other things, the new mission of Natural England, which today is to support 'Building Partnerships for Nature's Recovery'. Whereas such an ambitious notion would once have seemed unrealistic, momentum toward the re-establishment of wild habitats is high profile in the work of many organisations, including The Wildlife Trusts, RSPB, National Trust and private estates, including Knepp Castle in Sussex.

The next chapters are yet to be written, but when they are penned by future historians they might well tell of a living landscape, to where people travel from far and wide to enjoy time outside in a beautiful, vibrant and wildlife-rich landscape, where beavers, storks, cranes and swallowtails might once more be seen in a wetland that has had its lifeblood restored. They might write of how during the early 21st century, in one of our most depleted landscapes, loss was turned to hope.

As well as being a pleasure to read, this painstakingly researched and beautifully written book provides optimism for the next and vital stage of our collective conservation journey through time.

Tony Juniper CBE, environmentalist, writer, Natural England Chair

Introduction

East Anglia is one of the most extraordinary and exciting of landscapes. Of all the land in Britain, its fenland basin bears the greatest mark of human endeavour. Trapped between inland hills and sea-ward marshes, a fascinating yet enigmatic landscape has evolved. From ancient dry plains, through forest, saltmarsh and reedbeds, to the drained arable fields of today, a vast wetland has been transformed into one of the greatest vegetable-growing areas of Britain.

Stretching across a 34-square kilometre area of fenland between Peterborough and Huntingdon lies the ancient drained wetland of Whittlesea Mere. This is now the site of Great Fen landscape project – an ambitious scheme to transform the area to benefit wildlife and people, which has become a model for many similar initiatives in Britain today.

My original purpose when writing *The Great Fen – a Journey Through Time* was to describe how and why such a revolutionary venture had been conceived. As I began my research, however, it became clear that as I opened one door, it led to another, each delving further into history. Finally, I grasped the truth – it was only by studying the events of the past that the need for a new approach to nature, people and landscapes would make any sense. The National Nature Reserves (NNRs) of Woodwalton and Holme Fens which lie at the heart of the Great Fen were not created by chance – they are the last traces of a long-abandoned wetland of enormous size.

Similarly, it was 400 years of drainage which created the farmland around the reserves, where now the grand idea of a new landscape is becoming a reality.

It might seem surprising that the Great Fen story stretches back to the glaciers of 12,000 years ago, but that is when the combined forces of geology and climate began to shape the landscape. Human influence was felt as long ago as 8000BC, and became increasingly significant as the population grew, technology led to more efficient farming and drainage, and arable farming became the principal land-use.

There have, however, been consequences of the food production. Although the 'vegetable basket' of the eastern silt fens remains highly productive, the inland black peat has not been so resilient. The peat resource of over 6,000 years has been almost entirely depleted in less than two centuries. Despite its initial triumph in producing high-quality food, arable farming has become ever-more expensive and unsustainable as the soil wastes away, taking with it much of our archaeological heritage. The effect on wildlife has been devastating and people have had less and less access to the wider fenland landscape. Added to this, the safe disposal of large quantities of water draining from agriculture, roads and towns has become more challenging as land levels have fallen. Reliance on pumping to the sea is both expensive and unreliable, and future climate variation is predicted to increase risks from 'flash-flooding'. It is a complicated story.

Wildlife, food production, the environment and human society have for too long been seen as separate entities, and this has not been a successful policy for either wildlife or people. This book attempts to trace a path by which the new 'joined-up' approach to the landscape can re-kindle our wonder and reverence for the natural world. It also argues that a thriving economy could and should be rooted amongst thriving ecosystems.

The present and future challenges of intensive agriculture, climate change and economic growth are great indeed. The story of the Great Fen is that by understanding our own past and learning lessons from our relationship with the natural world, we can be guided to make wise decisions as to the future.

The climatic, political and social history of the fens, then, has an important role in explaining the fenland of today. So this is not a book about ecology; nor is it a history book, or a treatise on archaeology, although all bind the narrative together. It is primarily a book about people, how they have shaped the landscape from the Mesolithic to the present day, how that affected the wildlife of the time, how people have reacted to the many changes and how this knowledge might help us today to make decisions for the future.

I have constructed the narrative so that you can pick out the areas which you find most interesting, without losing the overall message. Additional material is contained within information boxes.

The first two chapters describe the early history of human impact on the landscape and our ancestors' relationship with wildlife until the end of the medieval period. The next chapter, *The Great Endeavour*, traces fenland drainage from the 16th century – a hotly contested affair which brought violence, murder and catastrophe to the fenman in equal measure to profit for the landowners and food for the population.

This includes the story of that greatest of Victorian technologies – steam power – which powered the pumps that drained Whittlesey Mere in 1851.

If you are more interested in the way that attitudes towards the natural world changed from the Reformation through to the 20th century, *Emerging Concern* examines this in detail. My research has led me to conclude that it would be telling only half the story if I ignored the influence of the arts, philosophy and religion when considering the role of landscapes in today's society. The spiritual connection of our ancestors with the physical world around them was a crucial part of their lives and the loss of this connection in modern society is an important part of our story.

The 20th Century – From Rothschild to the Great Fen discusses the growth of modern conservation, its successes and failures, and some of the champions of the conservation movement. This is followed by two chapters on ecology – including a stroll through the fenland NNRs to look at their extraordinary wildlife.

The next two chapters describe the ecology of fenland and look in detail at the national natures reserves of Woodwalton and Holme Fen.

New Horizons details the development of the Great Fen itself. There has been growing public alarm about the decline in the quality of the natural environment and this has been reinforced by mounting unease at the gulf which separates people from the natural world around them. In reality, a properly functioning ecosystem (which the Fens could become again) has the capacity not only to enrich our mental and physical well-being, but also to provide essential services which we require, such as clean water and air, and flood control. This more 'naturalistic' approach to landscapes in the future is at the heart of the Great Fen story, and asks what we might learn from studying ancient landscapes and how they were used by humans and wildlife. This chapter also explores the evidence for 'wild-ness' in the fens of the last few thousand years and what that might mean for the future and considerations of 're-wilding' and 'restoration'.

As the debate over human-induced climate change rages across the world, the final chapter invites you to stand on the floodbank at Woodwalton Fen and consider the lessons of the past and the opportunities and challenges of the future.

The historical record

I have consulted two Greek written records of early Britain. In his *Bibliotheca historica*, the Greek historian, Diodorus Siculus, refers to the spread of the Roman empire across Europe until just before Julius Caesar's invasion of 55BC. In this work, he describes the inhabitants of south-west Britain: *"who dwell about the promontory known as Belerium* (Cornwall) *are especially hospitable to strangers and have adopted a civilised manner of life because of their intercourse with merchants of other peoples. They are the ones who work the tin, treating the bed which bears it in an ingenious manner"*. He also refers to the fact that the area between the mainland and what is now the Isle of Wight, was passable over land at low tide, which suggests that sea levels were considerably lower at that time than they are now.

Another Greek writer, Strabo, wrote a little later than Diodorus Siculus and travelled widely. He quotes an earlier explorer, Pytheus, as referring to the Britannic islands as "*the etani*", which is Celtic for the 'painted people'. He also refers to exports of hides, slaves and metals from Britain.

Two Roman accounts record their occupation of Britain. Tacitus, whose book *Agricola* is based largely on the experience of his soldier father-in-law, includes a detailed account of the Boudiccan revolt. Cassius Dio's epic *Roman History* also refers to this, and includes verbatim speeches by both Boudicca and some Roman commanders, although these no doubt rely more on the author's imagination than what actually happened!

The 'Dark Ages' are aptly named, because evidence of what occurred after the Roman exit from Britain is hard to come by. Gildas in his *On the Ruin of Britain* refers to the *Gallic Chronicle* of 452, which cites a major movement of Anglo-Saxons in the 440s, but the lack of archaeological finds to support this casts doubt over its accuracy.

Around 731, the Benedictine monk, Bede, penned his *Ecclesiastical History of the English People* and follows Gildas in portraying a time of violent conflict and catastrophe. The *Anglo-Saxon Chronicles*, also follow this theme, and are a useful account of life and times from about the seventh century until after the Norman conquest. One of most important of these is the *Chronicon Angliae Petriburgense,* which was compiled by monks of Peterborough Abbey. Despite the original being destroyed by fire in 1116, this Chronicle was continued into the tumultuous reign of King Stephen, and includes the fenland adventures of Hereward the Wake and King Cnut. The history described in the *Chronicles* may be less than entirely reliable however, as the monks had a tendency to interpret some of the violent events of the time before Christianity as more to do with a judgement from God, than a strict historical record.

More recent research has revealed more of life in the Saxon fens, and work by Professor Susan Oosterhuisen, in particular, illustrates the development of co-operative working between the fenland farmers (Oosterhuisen 2017).

The *Tribal Hidage* was compiled in Anglo-Saxon England some time between 670 and 690. It lists 35 tribes, including the *Sweordora* and the *Gwyre* of the fenland and its surroundings, and has been referred to as an early 'Domesday Book'. Its exact purpose is still unclear, but it provides valuable information on pre-Norman life and the political upheavals of the time.

The *Liber Elienis* is a 12th-century English chronicle written at the Abbey of Ely, and described the fens as full of: "*fish innumerable, eels, large water wolves, pickerel, perch, roach, burbots and lampreys*".

As society grew more sophisticated, historical records became more widespread, including *Domesday*, monastic records and drainage board archives.

Despite the value of these records, much of fenland history remains cloaked in mystery. There is particular uncertainty in relation to the impact of human activity on wildlife. Some plant and animal extinctions can be reasonably accurately placed, and monastic documents give a good indication of fish and eel populations in the early medieval era, but the number of other species and their abundance is not so clear.

The archaeological evidence

Although there are few remains of early human or non-human life within the Great Fen itself, we are fortunate to have evidence from the gravel terraces of the River Nene, and the causewayed enclosure of Flag Fen. The archaeological excavations and re-constructions by Francis Pryor and others (Pryor 2005) have revealed a detailed picture of life here, where people had to adapt to the rising waters of the late Bronze-Age. More recent discoveries at Must Farm, near Whittlesea, including complete timber boats, enable us to glimpse in detail the ways in which people lived, including some indications of their use of the deep fen for grazing. There is also much evidence of the various plant and animal species which lived alongside the people.

Investigations further afield in similar habitats offer some insights into more ancient life. Excavations since 1949 by Professor Clarke at Star Carr, near Scarborough (Clarke 1954) reveal an 8th millennium BC society in the making. Several small settlements have been unearthed around a post-glacial body of water, Flixton Lake, which was about the size that Whittlesea Mere would become 8,000 years later.

Closer to home, excavations by Oxford Archaeology East at Tort Hill near Sawtry, on the edge of the Great Fen, have revealed a Neolithic hand-axe and late Iron Age remains. There were settlements here from the Iron Age to Romano-British periods, of at least five roundhouses with a ditched enclosure. Later, a larger roundhouse was constructed replacing two earlier ones, and later still, stonework was incorporated into a larger building which itself was replaced by a timber rectangular structure in the second century. The site was probably abandoned due to flooding as the weather deteriorated, although a roadside settlement developed, which continued until the middle of the fourth century.

Within the Great Fen itself, investigations in 2002 (Hatton 2002) identified Neolithic remains in the northern part of the site, near Tower Farm, and other artefacts from later periods were found during a field survey of 2007/8 (Begg *et al.* 2008). There is also evidence of a wooden causeway across Woodwalton Fen, which may have served to link Sawtry and Ramsey Abbeys.

A feature which sets the fens apart from other landforms is the peat resource. It was a Cambridge geologist, Harry Godwin, who first described the past vegetation through his analysis of pollen found in peat cores around Woodwalton and Holme Fens. In his book *Fenland – an Ancient Past and an Uncertain Future* (Godwin 1978), he describes both what has gone before and illustrates the fragility of the peat resource for the future. Even this analysis can leave open questions, however. Tree pollen, for example, is better represented in the peat profile than grass pollen, and its dominant occurrence in the peat was interpreted as being evidence of a vast 'wildwood' occupying much of post-glacial England. A new hypothesis suggests that the lack of grass pollen may be due more to grazing animals, rather than the absence of grass. This paints a different picture of historical landscapes, where the woodland was interrupted by open grasslands and moors grazed by large herbivores.

More recently, Oxford Archaeology has examined peat cores from around Holme Fen and discovered the original course of the river Nene and the bed of the ancient Ugg Mere. Excavations at Rymes Reedbed, on the edge of Whittlesea Mere, have revealed the actual *Sphagnum* moss that flourished here for thousands of years.

Stories of the past

Although these records are immensely valuable, they leave many gaps in our knowledge of how people lived among the land and water and their effects on wildlife. This lack of historical evidence has led me to include stories of people and their actions which, while based on fact, include an element of imagination. The Roman soldier losing his money, the sunken boat on Whittlesea Mere are based on evidence found at the site; others may be a little more fanciful, but are still based on available knowledge of likely conditions at the time. Our journey through time starts with just such a story...

The heat and humidity of one afternoon in 1868 were like a hot sponge, and Jason Edwards was sweating profusely as he bent his back to cutting the peat with his iron 'slodger', stacking the turves to dry in the sun. With the next stab of the blade he heard a metallic 'clink'. Carefully scraping away the soil, he found a small glinting disc. Putting it in his pocket he carried on until his work was done. Much later, in his cottage on the edge of the fen, he remembered that disc. "Look what I found today!" he said to his wife Nancy "What, another old pipe?" says she "Naah... this is metal – find a bowl with some water, woman". Washing the disc, they slowly revealed the face of a curly-haired man and some inscription in a strange language.

The coin was later identified as a Roman coin from the time of Marcus Aurelius, Emperor of Rome from 161–180AD. The loss of the coin was no doubt sorely felt by the soldier who dropped it in his travels along Ermine Street to the encampment at Durobrivae (now Water Newton). How it arrived at Woodwalton remains a mystery, as in those days it was a brave man who ventured off the new highway into the hinterland of wild marsh and boggy pools.

In a curious reversal of history, it was a later fen worker who discovered an even more ancient glimpse into the fen history. Ralph Papworth had come to the fen in 1910 with his three brothers to grow celery and onions in the rich black peat. But since the drainage of Whittlesea Mere the soil had wasted away and was now several feet lower – several thousand years of history uncovered. In the autumn of one year shortly after the end of the Great War, he heard an ominous 'cloink' and his little tractor shuddered to a halt. Inspecting the plough, he found a hard object. Reversing away he set to with a spade and revealed a piece of wood, which stretched on and on as he dug. An hour later he had uncovered 20 feet of a huge tree trunk. This was the first of the thousands of great bog oaks (and pines) which have now been unearthed in the fens.

The landscape in which these trees grew would have been very different to the fen and bog which the Roman soldier knew. This was a wildwood stretching for mile after mile, inhabited by Wild Boar, Aurochs and bears where early humans had but a tenuous foothold around the lakes and open glades. Yet by the time of the Roman invasion, millions of trees had been cleared or become covered by peat and much of the land was farmed. Continued sea level rise then created a fenland which lasted for another 1,500 years.

The modern national nature reserves of Woodwalton and Holme Fens now lie marooned amidst the farmland peat. Drained, stripped of its peat and wounded by nutrient-rich waters discharged from domestic washing machines, Woodwalton in particular, miraculously survives as testament to the destruction of that vast fenland.

These glimpses into history are crucial to understanding the modern fen, the tiny flowerpot nature reserves, the onion fields, and the current concern for a lost world where humans and nature existed side by side. Like the onion itself, layer upon layer of history shaped by natural forces and human endeavour lie beneath the fen landscape of today. All the great events of history – wars, invasions and natural tumults – as well as the ordinary lives of the steadily increasing population with its need for food and shelter are preserved right here in what is now the Great Fen.

So the story of the Great Fen is a story of Britain, how it was formed, how it has been changed and how people from all walks of life can help to mould a future where wild places and human aspirations can thrive together.

From Ice to Iron

The ice sheets lay stretching into infinity, a freezing mass of white – boulders, ice and snow locked together a mile deep. The mass created a frosted wind which blew across the land beyond the ice and quickly drove the few surviving lemmings underground. Just a short distance to the south lay the land which would become the Great Fen, a tundra-like landscape where few animals could scrape a summer living. This is the land which we will follow across the Ages, through changing climates, war and famine, sea-flood and bog to the land we know today...

Life after ice – land and water in turmoil

There's a lot of East Anglia you can't see – the clays laid down in the Jurassic period of 100 million years ago lie buried by sands and gravels, the chalk of the Cretaceous period are covered by silts and clays. Successive glaciers have pushed and moulded low hills and ridges, 'islands' like Ely and Ramsey; meltwaters have eroded valleys and carried stones and gravels far and wide. What you now see are the silts, peats, sand and chalk which give the region its distinctive character of hills and sandy breckland, coastal marshes... and the black flat miles of fenland peat.

The story of the Great Fen starts 12,000 years ago, when the latest of a succession of ice sheets gripped much of northern Europe and reached down to the Wash and across to the Bristol Channel. Sea levels were 70–100 metres lower than today, and the parts of the North Sea which weren't buried under the glaciers would have resembled the Siberia of today. Life along the ice-edge was harsh and unpredictable. What is now the fenland may have escaped the grinding glaciers but was near enough to feel their frigid breath. Only Woolly Mammoths which had survived the big freeze, Reindeer and Lemmings, could survive on the meagre diet of lichens and mosses. Summers were short and unpredictable, but all was about to change.

Geologists call it the beginning of the Holocene – the interglacial period in which we live today. Quite simply, the ice began to melt. At first, the melting glaciers left huge lakes across the much of eastern Britain, around which herds of Giant Elk and Aurochs grazed. South of the Wash, a huge water body now known as Lake Sparks, formed for a short time behind a dam of ice (West 1993, Gibbard *et al.* 2018). When the ice dam melted, the rivers regained their original course out towards what is now the North Sea. Lake Flixton in the Vale of Pickering, just 150 miles north of the Great Fen, was a more substantial water body and there is considerable evidence of human occupation here as conditions became suitable. Further south in Holderness there were many smaller lakes. Some of these persisted into medieval times, but now only Hornsea Mere remains as a direct descendent of this ancient waterland.

As warmth breathed into the melting land, life began to flourish. Plants that had survived at the edges of the ice spread northwards and others began to colonise from the south.

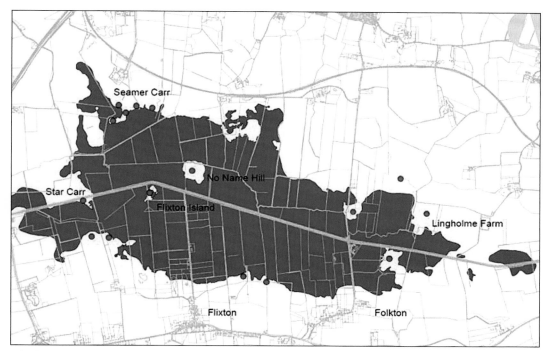

Lake Flixton [University of York]

Grasses grew over the mosses and lichens; insects, small mammals and birds moved with the new habitats, followed by herds of wild cattle, Giant Elk and horses. It was not a smooth transition – in the next few thousand years sea levels would rise dramatically, coasts shrink and expand, forests grow up and disappear, rivers swell and dry up, and volcanic eruptions cause centuries of dust and gloom. But change was unstoppable and with it came humans who were quick to exploit the new opportunities.

The human factor
The Mesolithic Age
It was a long trek over the marshes and plains. Two winters passed before the family reached the new lands. The herds were always on the move as the ice retreated in the warming air... Other travellers had moved further north, but the marshy lands were rich hunting grounds. The man was short but powerful and able to run fast to catch deer, using fragments of antler for his spear head and the older boy could fish well. After years spent on the move, they found a lake with good hunting and he built a house by a beaver dam, more than just a winter camp, where the family could stay. He set fire to reeds near the hut and cut trees so when the grasses grew up in the open glades the animals would come, and the hunting would be easier.

As Earth has pursued its uneven circuits of the sun, our ancestors endured climatic changes which had huge effects on life across the Ages. Humans and wild animals alike had to adapt – or cease to exist. Modern politics, science, technology and climate change are hot news these days, but they are nothing new. The struggles and innovations of humans have been going on for millennia and have had profound effects on the landscape.

We humans have a restless gene – even as the ice retreated and tundra gave way to soggy grasslands and scrub, the people came. There had been people in Britain before the ice, but the new Mesolithic people were more advanced, with more efficient tools. Britain was still part of the continental land-mass, the rivers of eastern England flowing into the Rhine where the English Channel is now, and those further north flowing into the plain of the North Sea. It was along these routes they walked, following the herds which were gradually advancing north as the ice-wall retreated and the land grew nutritious food.

It is important to realise that the fens did not exist at this time. According to a recent archaeological study: *"During the early Mesolithic the present fen basin was dry land drained by a series of rivers flowing out into a major outlet through the Wash"* (Hatton 2002).

As the meltwater lakes infilled, willow and birch woodland invaded the marshy ground, developing into forests much like those of north-east Europe or Canada today. Incredibly, we can catch a glimpse of this scene in fenland today. Walk to Burnham's Mere hide at Holme Fen NNR, just two miles east of the A1 motorway near Huntingdon, and you are looking out on a scene

Reconstruction of Mesolithic Hut [WC/AC]

Coniferous boreal forest may also have covered much of post-glacial Britain

Reindeer were pushed ever-northwards as the ice receded and were extinct by about 7400BC [JM]

reminiscent of that Mesolithic family camp. From the shore of the mere, the sound of the rippling water, the rustling leaves of the birch woods, the smell of damp leaves, seem to have changed little in the thousands of years which separate us from our ancestors. But during that time an estuary has swelled and died, a peat bog has grown and dried, and is now covered with the largest birch wood in lowland England. This is typical of the incessant change which has characterised the fenland for thousands of years... and continues to do so.

As the centuries rolled on and the lakes became fewer, the pioneer trees were succeeded by oak, Hazel, elm and eventually lime and Alder as conditions became warmer and drier. So rapid was the woodland advance across the warming soil that areas of dense forest had probably colonised much of Britain by 6000BC – a wildwood that stretched for miles, full of birdsong, berries, insects and flowers... or so it was thought. Early interpretations of pollen grains found from this period once led scientists to conclude that the wildwood must have covered the whole of Britain and northern Europe for centuries. It was said that a Red Squirrel could hop from the east coast to Wales without touching the ground! More recent work has suggested an alternative. Studies of prehistoric landscapes by Oliver Rackham and Frans Vera (Rackham 1976, Vera 2000) suggest that large herbivores were an essential feature of these ancient landscapes. The forest colonisation of the land left by the glaciers probably never formed the

Life in the wild

Early people built timber causeways to travel to the water. They burned reeds and bushes around the lake edge to attract wild grazing animals and collected blackberries and Hazel seeds for food. Their skin and pole huts, and later more substantial timber structures, may not have been continuously occupied, but evidence from lakeside sites, such as at Star Carr in Yorkshire, suggests they formed a central hub for hunting activities. The post-glacial lakes around the Great Fen may have been similar to this.

There were also the beginnings of a cultural or spiritual side to life where antler head-dresses suggest some sort of ritual connected with hunting.

The dried out Holme Fen bog now supports the largest area of birch woodland in lowland England

dense canopy once imagined, or if it did, it was for a much shorter period than originally thought. Instead, the new research suggests that a combination of human intervention and great herds of wild cattle and deer maintained much of the landscape as 'wood-pasture'; beavers also created clearings and pools, so that among the vast tracts of forest, there were also many open glades and larger areas. Studies of invertebrate assemblages within peat cores show that a large proportion of beetles were open grassland and scrub species, with a lesser proportion from marshland (Sandam 2014, Whitehouse, Smith 2009, Alexander *et al.* 2018, Fyfe 2018). It was, as Vera puts it, a 'kaleidoscope' landscape of varying vegetation types.

Within the area which would later develop into fenland, however, woodland may have been denser than in other drier areas, and its remains are evident in the Great Fen today. Modern ploughing and soil wastage continue to expose the great 'bog oaks' and pines which have lain asleep in the peat for thousands of years.

The people were at first nomadic, shadows constantly on the move, following the seasonal movements of the herds across the plains and through the woods. They camped in temporary huts of willow poles and deer hides, but new evidence suggests that some began to settle around lakes such as Lake Flixton. Here they lived alongside the birds and beavers of the waterside, as well the Giant Elk and Aurochs of the dry land, so access to food was relatively good. So closely was the life of the beaver linked to early humans that it may be that their lodges were used as platforms for the first houses, the felled logs being ready-made for fuel and building timber. For the first time, too, rudimentary cultivation by the once restless hunters may have led to a sense of belonging to one place. Land 'ownership' had arrived, and with it, people's desire and ability to effect more permanent change on the land.

With a more static lifestyle, the hunter-gatherers began to manage the land, using flint axes and fire to create clearings in the wildwood and burn lakeside reed to lure their prey to easy grazing and save the hunters energy. The combination of a warming climate and successful hunting tactics soon began to have major effects on the wild herds. The last reindeer may have been killed in the far north in as early as 7400BC, and the herds of wild horses reduced, but Aurochs and Giant Elk were also under pressure as the advancing woodland made the open plains less accessible. By contrast, wild boar may have become more

This bog oak has lied buried at Holme Fen for thousands of years. It is resting on the ancient clay where it grew. The peat is clearly visible above it

Konik ponies are related to the original wild horses

Giant and Red Deer, Elk and other large herbivores maintained open grasslands within the wildwood

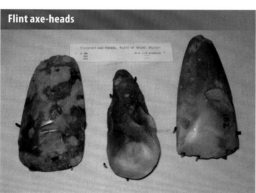
Flint axe-heads

The people of the fenland

Fenland history is an amalgam of human survival amongst the bogs and marshes, a rich culture and an astonishingly diverse wildlife. Boudicca, Hereward, the farmers, monks and 'Adventurers' all had their part to play in the story of how people and wildlife adapted and survived in the face of many challenges. Their stories speak of strong and independent societies who perfected the skills of living among the waters and harvesting an extraordinary variety of wildlife. It was their power struggles, farming and drainage technology, as much as climatic events which shaped the fens of today.

numerous at this time and bears would have roamed freely.

As the climate continued to heat up and sea level rose, the herds and the woodlands themselves adapted to ever-wetter conditions. Four thousand years into the great thaw, Britain and mainland Europe were still linked by a land now called 'Doggerland'. Once stretching all the way from Sussex to modern Denmark, the huge land bridge was a blend of swamp, marshy plains and low hills, rich with foraging, grazing and hunting for animals and humans alike. But the land had been shrinking for centuries under the onslaught of the rising sea, and catastrophe finally came around 6000BC, when a great tsunami was caused by the 'Storegga Slide' of the Norway coast. The waters roared over the sea-land and drowned it completely, creating an archipelago similar to the Britain we know today. Plants, animals and humans were swept away and those surviving on the mainland had to adjust to island life.

People adapted to the new conditions. Even in these early times some had learnt to build rudimentary boats which could cross the North Sea. Evidence from grains and seeds found in excavated sites suggest that, although essentially still hunter-gatherers, Mesolithic people in Britain had begun to trade with farming communities on the continental mainland. They may even have been experimenting with elementary farming, using their dogs to corral wild cattle and cultivating small patches of ground for spelt wheat.

As sea levels continued to rise, the rivers flowing towards the North Sea backed up and created great inland wetlands, drowning the lower-lying forests and burying the trees under the early peat which gave birth to the ancient Great Fen. These bog oaks – which were to lie

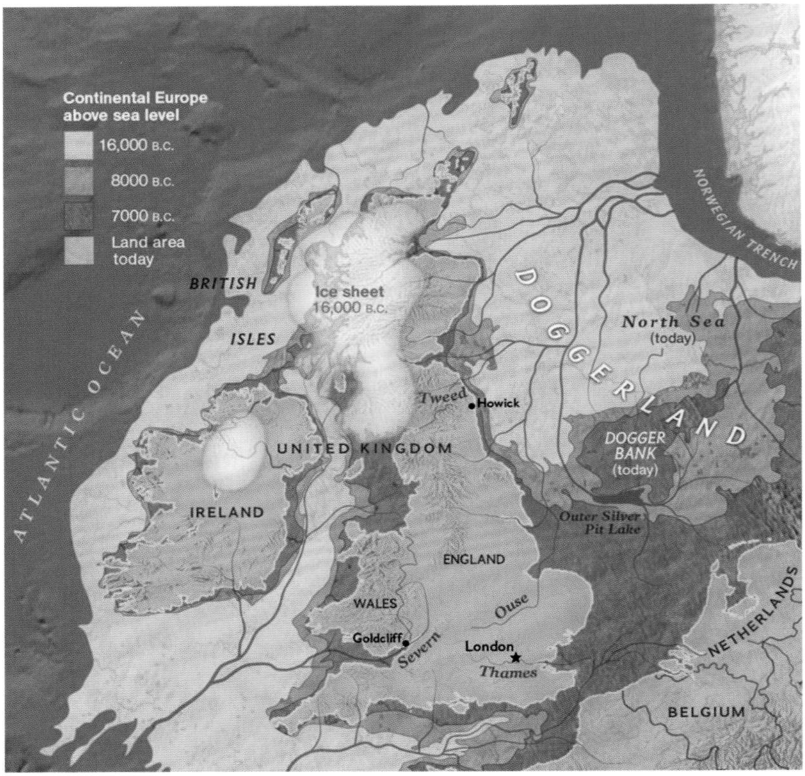

Doggerland once covered
a huge area but gradually
shrank as sea levels rose

Doggerland today

Flying over the North Sea recently, I searched in vain for an outline of Doggerland. Somewhere below the sea was a lost world which was once full of bird cries, the bark of deer and bellow of wild cattle. The only remnant now is the 'Dogger Bank', which lies submerged 150 km north of the Humber estuary and has been known for years by seafarers and fishermen as either a hazard to be avoided or a good fishing ground. Remarkably, for thousands of years the true story of this lost 'Atlantis' lay hidden beneath the waves. H.G. Wells first advanced the idea that there be a hidden island under the North Sea in his *A Story of the Stone Age*, in 1897, but it was not until 1931 that the trawler 'Colinda' dredged up a chunk of peat complete with what appeared to be an antler barb/fishing hook. Since then, further finds including a human skull have allowed archaeologists to piece together the story of this lost world.

Today the bank is a Marine Protected Area and home to a whole community of marine organisms, but may soon host thousands of wind turbines in the drive for sustainable electricity.

unknown for thousands of years – grew on the undulating Jurassic clay which became buried beneath the peat from the 3rd millennia BC. In the constantly wet conditions, fenland may have expanded, creating ideal conditions for Aurochs and other open country species like wolves, but depriving the human population of much of its land and hunting grounds. Few of the Giant Deer remained, but Red and Roe Deer roamed the open wet woodland with Wild Boar, and innumerable birds filled the wetlands. These were rich hunting for the growing human population, and when later marine incursions created silty marshes, shellfish would be added to the menu. In drier periods, woodland of birch, pine, Alder and Yew grew up, only to be buried in turn by peat and silt as the waters returned. The stories of the Great Fen journey are more varied than you might imagine.

Towards the end of the Mesolithic, around 4200BC, the erratic path of the Earth through space triggered a solar minimum and cooling of the climate brought misery. Huge storm-clouds rolled in over the land, two more tsunamis smashed the communities along the coast, driving them back across the sea or into extinction through starvation. Britain may again have become an uninhabited isle.

The Neolithic Age

The man had made the boat by hollowing out a tree trunk, about 9 metres long then setting it on fire. As the charred timber softened he scooped it out, until he had a hollow which he lined with skins. He hoped it would be deep enough to carry the family and their few possessions and would float and remain stable. Although others had gone before him, they had never returned so he didn't know if it would work. He carried a bow and few straight twigs with antler or flint as barbs for hunting. But he also packed curved antlers and wood in the boat, with which he could break the soil – for this man was a farmer and with his family would bring a new way of life to the land beyond the sea. The woman cradled a baby and another small boy huddled in the lee of their food and clothing – enough for a few days on the stormy sea. At one end of the boat was a hearth of clay, where they could cook grain and any fish they caught to sustain them on the journey, but the most precious cargoes were the sacks of seed grain and the pair of sheep – all that was left of their livestock. The man knew it was dangerous and he was afraid, but the seas had already drowned their small plot of land – they must find somewhere new or perish. For many sickening days they were blown one way and another but finally grounded on the sandy hummock, which was the edge of the drowned land where his forefathers had camped and hunted.

A bowl from a tree stump

Archaeologists from Flag Fen in Peterborough once took a section of an alder tree trunk from Woodwalton Fen NNR and created a bowl by charring and scraping in the same way as this Mesolithic traveller.

When the climate warmed again, new migrants made the hazardous journey across the North Sea to take advantage of the rich and empty lands, and with them they brought an entirely different way of existence. They found a land which was still at least half covered in dense but scattered forests, with open grasslands, fens and heath, but the new immigrants would change these 'natural' landscapes forever. They would establish an entirely different economy and way of life centred around settled farming communities; nothing would ever be

Bronze Age boat from Must Farm [CAU]

the same – if there ever had been an idyll of the natural world scarcely impacted by humans, it was about to be swept away. From now on it would be humans, not climate or wild grazers that would define the landscapes of Britain.

The new people found forests of Alder in the fenland with open grasslands and woodland clearings. The first thing they did was to excavate mines for axe-flints, such as at Grimes Graves in Norfolk, where over 400 shafts were hewn with deer antlers deep underground. Then they began to fell woodland on a scale never seen before. It is still uncertain how many permanent houses the Neolithic people built or whether they continued to live in tents and temporary shelters. One place they did live was at Fengate, just north of the Great Fen, where the timber remains of a small rectangular building were discovered by Francis Pryor in 1972 (Pryor 2010). Although Neolithic timber buildings may have been relatively few, it would require prodigious quantities of timber to build any semi-permanent shelter, and more for fuel and stakes, so even a relatively small community would need a large area of woodland to sustain it, as well as open land for cultivating grain and pasturing for animals.

The pollen record shows that the new farmers may have been helped in clearing some of the tree cover by massive destruction of the elm woods – perhaps by the same disease which would later devastate the elms of the late 20th century – creating plentiful open areas to raise their domestic pigs and cattle. Farmed land also brought the need for boundary markers such as banks or individual trees and ceremonial and religious sites needed further clearings. The wilderness was being tamed, ordered and allocated to specific needs of the human population.

Woodland clearance on the fenland may have been less than in other areas, but that is not to say the trees were left alone. It was during this time that the practice of coppicing evolved

Coppice

Lowland raised bog [NE]

Peat core – plunging your hand into history

I never fail to marvel at the sight and feel of this ancient sea-land when digging a core (picture [RLi]) through the peat. It is a soft pale grey band among the layers of thick black peat. It's like plunging your hand into history, through the very plants and invertebrates trapped in the peat into the ooze where the sea breeze still blows over the wild marshes and Curlews mew from saltmarsh.

The Holme Fen bog

On the site of the modern Holme Fen, early domes of peat bog formed a barrier against further intrusion by the sea. They would develop on this site for thousands of years, interspersed with drier periods when trees invaded for short periods. Many of these trees were oak, but others were pines and their deeply furrowed bark and reddish tinge is clearly visible in the trunks dug from the peat today.

The bog formed because it never dried out sufficiently here for other plants to get a foothold. *Sphagnum* mosses are very special. They demand water at all times and live happily in conditions which suffocate and drown most other plants. The bog devours everything in its path. Fallen trees of drier times are buried, unwary animals (or people) who step too far into the soft sponge will disappear and it will hold immense quantities of water over huge areas. Its only enemy is drought.

– cutting species such as Ash, Hazel and willow regularly to provide a never-ending supply of timber for fuel and building. Scattered around the edge of the Great Fen are several woodlands with ancient coppice 'stools'. Higney Wood is one, standing on an 'island' above the fen, where once a hermit lived. For centuries it was part of Glatton parish and mentioned in Domesday Book, before it became the property of Ramsey Abbey and absorbed into Woodwalton parish in the 18th century. There are others – Monks Wood, Riddy Wood, Lady's Wood – gradually these fragments of the wildwood all became isolated and named woods in their own right, but their ancient coppice stools may be ancestral reminders of the Neolithic wildwood.

Yet again the farmers were not to have it all their own way, because the clement weather of their early years was soon to worsen. On the edge of the modern Holme Fen is a tower hide, constructed in 2010 to look out across the site of Whittlesea Mere as the developing Great Fen changes it from arable fields to wetland. A late Neolithic farmer sitting here around 2300–2000BC would have looked out on a very different view from the one we see today, or that his grandfather would have seen. Where once there were woodlands with scattered reedbed and a growing peat-bog, now there were brackish lagoons, tidal mudflats and saltmarsh flooded by North Sea storms. The early peat deposits were being buried under marine silt, which was also deposited along the river courses and saltmarsh creeks. These deposits are visible today as raised 'roddens' where the peat has wasted away leaving the harder silt above the surrounding land. Inland, there were still remnant herds of Aurochs and deer and wolves were never far away, but the Great Fen was now a great tidal marsh. The tang of salt was in the air, fish and crabs were the staple diet for the local population; pelicans and cranes flew over the wetland and even the beavers had to move inland to find trees and freshwater for their homes.

Looking to the north, our farmer would have glimpsed his dwelling perched on stilts on the fen edge and he would not stay long away from home, for these were violent times, where competition for land and food brought neighbours into conflict. Fields and villages were abandoned and although the sea began to retreat, the silt bank which it left along the coast obstructed drainage from inland so that many areas became so wet that peat began to form once more. Settlements had to be raised and linked by causeways as hunting for fish and water birds replaced the livestock and primitive tilling of woodland glades.

One place where the people did manage to survive was at Stonea Camp, near present-day Wimblington. In later years this 'island' of the fens would become a major stronghold of the Iron Age Iceni tribe, but the thousands of Neolithic artefacts found during excavations in the 1990s indicate that this was already a significant place centuries earlier.

The Bronze Age

The boatbuilders had done a good job. The oak planks were well stitched together with string made from yew, and tree sap between the planks kept the water out. Handling the sail was difficult but he had learnt how to do it by watching the traders who had been using the new sails to cross the stormy sea to the rich pastures and wealthy kings of the islands to the west.

The boat had a strong deep keel, which kept it stable, and with his wife and children he was going to find a better life where there wasn't such competition for land. He had some good tools, too, made by melting together some sort of special stones in fire so he was confident that he could grow good crops.

Bronze axe-head found embedded in bog oak beside the Great Raveley Drain (Norris Museum, St Ives)

Beaker found at Godmanchester (Norris Museum, St Ives)

Despite the hazards of crossing the North Sea, by 2500BC yet more migrants arrived with new ideas and technologies to a rapidly changing world. With their knowledge of blending copper with tin to make bronze, the new settlers brought the ability to make strong tools which could make major inroads to the already fragmented woodland cover. The landscape changes hewn by the flint axes of the Neolithic people were a pale intimation of what was to come. Early farm systems had been on higher ground or along river valleys, where the trees were more scattered and easier to clear, but soil erosion during the wetter climate meant that future farmland would have to be won from the thicker lowland wildwood.

The so-called 'Beaker' people were the first to colonise, moving west from the central Europe and Russian Steppes to find new land and opportunities. Recent research suggests that we all carry the DNA of these people. Their characteristic pots found at Ramsey St Marys on the edge of the Great Fen, and a skeleton at Ramsey are evidence of their occupation of the fen area, with the main settlements along the terraces of the River Nene near Fengate in Peterborough. Theirs was a different society, too, based more around ownership and status. Jewellery became important and a wealthy elite emerged.

The climate favoured the growing population for a few centuries and subsistence farming based on livestock and cereal cultivation increased. Field systems which were created on the fen margins at Fengate are some of the earliest known in Britain. These were primarily for livestock, which would have been grazed deep into the fen and then moved out when it became too wet, much as happens today. So the rhythms of grazing and flooding on the washes and fenland nature reserves are rooted deep into the past. As for the early spelts and grains grown by these folk, it is worth noting that these had originated in the drier Middle East. As we shall see later, reliance on the modern-day equivalents of these dry-land crops in the fens would become an increasingly important concern, needing constant drainage to have any hope of successful harvests.

While the steady rise of sea levels presented many challenges to the farmers, it created ideal conditions for the raised bog at Holme Fen to grow in earnest, laying down the spongy peat which created this special place over centuries.

Despite the trials of the rising waters, the culture and religion of the Bronze Age people of the east was clearly important. Two or three days walk from Holme Fen is another Holme – Holme-next-the-Sea in Norfolk – where in 2049BC, two timber 'sea-henges' were built, linked by several causeways. They were nowhere near the sea at that time, but on the edge of a saltmarsh where woodland cannot have been far away as this is where the timbers for the henges were brought from. The fact that 60 different bronze axes were used to cut and shape the timbers suggest that this was an important community event, which was achieved within a relatively short space of time. Various suggestions have been made as to their purpose but their exact role remains a mystery. One possibility is that it may have been a site of human sacrifice, but is equally plausible that this was a place of pre-burial of an important

This huge stump was revealed when coastal erosion exposed the Bronze Age 'sea-henge' at Holme-next-the-Sea in Norfolk (King's Lynn Museum)

personality. The great tree stump of the main henge was set upside down and the body (or bodies) may have been lain on top for the birds and animals to strip the flesh before burial of the bones. These were deeply spiritual people, who believed that placing a body on the up-turned stump would allow the spirit to return to the earth where it originated. The human connection with the natural world was never so close and it would be many centuries before the coming of Christianity introduced the concept of the spirit returning to the heavens rather than Mother-Earth.

After about 1500BC there was also a rapid cultural change. The old communal burial sites were abandoned and life (and death) became more centred on the home. Ritual burial (often in water) of valuable objects also became more common. As people became more settled in larger communities, the beginnings of a hierarchical society evolved.

As the woodland cover reduced, so too did its wildlife, and open country species increased as more habitat became available. Ploughing began to change the face of the land, leading to the establishment of settlements and field boundaries. Hunting remained a major activity and it was more likely that which drove the last Aurochs to extinction around this time. That is not to say that overall, the diversity of wildlife declined. As woodlands became more fragmented, there may have been more edge and scrub which would have suited many warbler species; Skylarks and Lapwings would have benefitted from the open grazed fields and butterflies and other invertebrates would have access to more nectar.

From about 1200BC the climate again deteriorated in a period often referred to as a 'Little Ice Age'. Water levels rose once more and reeds, sedges and bog mosses began to cover the fields and village clusters of the earlier Bronze Age. The black freshwater peat so characteristic of the Great Fen today accreted still further, burying the creeks and saltmarsh around Holme and Woodwalton Fens; the bog at Holme grew ever higher. To the north-east of Holme Fen, the most ancient of the many fenland lakes formed – Trundle Mere – but it was not until the course of the river Nene changed around 500BC that the great Whittlesea Mere and its smaller sisters Ugg, Brick and Ramsey Meres began to form. The smell of wet peat would now replace the saltmarsh air, as new habitats of reed and sedge, moss and willow grew around the meres. You can still see the remains of the creatures that lived in and around the meres beneath the layers of peat and the calcified remains of stoneworts that thrived in those times. As the waters advanced, there was increased competition for grazing and arable land among the human population. There may also have been some conflict with invaders from across the North Sea, as archaeological finds from this period indicate that weapons of war were replacing the tree-cutter's axe.

To the north of the Great Fen is a wide area of low-lying land. About 1800BC there had been small sheep farms here, around Fengate in Peterborough and further south towards Whittlesea at Flag Fen. As the waters rose, a causeway was built around 1350BC to link the flooding pastures across the water meadows which had once been good summer grazing. The area was also probably used for salt panning, as tidal creeks still reached to within a short distance of the structure.

The causeway was an extraordinary feat of engineering. Stretching for a kilometre, it was built from 50–60,000 posts, but over the next 400 years, two million timbers were used to expand the causeway and construct a huge platform covering an area the size of a football field. This may have served as a site for ceremonial purposes, judging by the number of precious objects discovered nearby which may have been thrown into the water as an offering to the gods, as well as protecting the precious grazing from unwanted intruders. Just a few kilometres along the river Nene to the east the recently discovered settlement built over the water at Must Farm may tell a darker story. The settlement here lasted just a few months before it was burnt to the ground in an event which may suggest a violent end to its inhabitants. The preservation of the evidence of Bronze-Age life at Must Farm is extraordinary, and shows clearly the life of the time, when boats and wheels of

Flag Fen through time [Vivacity, Flag Fen Archaeology Park]

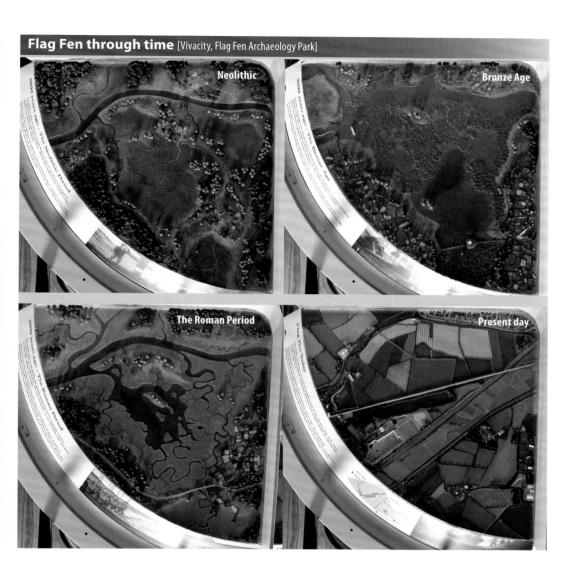

Neolithic

Bronze Age

The Roman Period

Present day

The ghosts of Flag Fen

I last visited Flag Fen on a grey and misty day in early spring. The only sound was the munching of the Soay sheep (pictured), a lone Chaffinch practising his song, and the soft yet persistent hiss of the waters spraying over the precious timbers of the causeway. In a huge shed, the bronze-age boats of Must Farm drifted in their watery graves. As I stood and glimpsed through the mist at the ugly towers of the Boongate business park, I could still feel the ghosts of the people, desperately fighting the rising waters, sacrificing their precious swords to the gods, rearing sheep and children... and hoping for better days.

local material were used as well as imported jewels. Also preserved in the peat of the wetter period are the remains of Otter, Beaver and Water Vole... crucial signposts to the life of the waterworld.

Other evidence at Must Farm stretches further back into history and is little short of spine-tingling. In the silt and clay beneath the late third millennium peat are the hoof-prints of herds of animals which once grazed an open, drier land – long before the peat began to form. Five thousand years of history is there to see and touch!

But the jewel of Must Farm are the eight wooden long boats constructed in 1500BC. Not only do these demonstrate that life was closely connected with water for transport and trade, but also that there must have been oak, lime and Field Maple woodland nearby for their construction.

Eventually the settlements along the river Nene were abandoned by communities fleeing the rising waters, leaving their distinctive Beaker pottery to be buried by the growing peat. By the time the Romans came, the ground was firm enough to build a roadway across it and all traces of the wetland people had vanished.

The Iron Age

The steady advance of the Romans across his native Gaul around 800BC had forced the man to move – they took slaves if you opposed them and he just wanted a quiet life. Also, the weather had been getting worse. Summers were shorter and wetter and the crops began to fail. In the harsh winters many animals died and starvation had taken the youngest child last spring. He had learnt how to make the new iron from people in the south and he had been told there were plenty of stones with the iron ore. He would be able to make a living by selling them to farmers who could work the land better than with the old bronze ploughs that bent too easily.

When he arrived after the long sea journey, the man would have found that the Britons already knew something of the new techniques in metal. They also had plenty of woodland to provide the fuel for the hot fires needed to melt the iron ore and the pace of forest clearance and land cultivation accelerated yet again with the new sharp axes and ploughs. It has been estimated (Rackham 1986) that a bare 50% of the original wildwood had survived the

Warham Camp near Great Yarmouth, Norfolk

attentions of mankind by the early Iron Age. But iron was not just for ploughshares. Swords and battle axes have been found more commonly in archaeological excavations from this period across England and the large number of defensive hill forts suggest a society ill at ease with itself. The role of these hillforts is not entirely clear, but certainly, they were expressions of power, carefully sited to dominate the local landscape. No doubt they were also useful refuges for local communities in case of attack, but there is little evidence that there were many instances of actual conflict and were perhaps more used for community gatherings and livestock pens.

These early hillforts are represented on the fenland by the 'marsh-forts' of Stonea Camp and Borough Fen near Peterborough. The fortifications of the ancient Stonea Camp originate from about 300BC, and along with Warham Camp in Norfolk this would later become the seat of the Iceni tribe, who would cause much conflict later on.

One particular feature of this period is the 'bog bodies'. Such was the extent of bogs and other impenetrable wetlands with rapidly growing peat, that ritual burials outside the communal tumuli appear to have been common. Although none have been found on the Great Fen, the discovery of a perfectly preserved body in peat bog at Lindow Moss in Cheshire suggests that something similar could have happened in Cambridgeshire.

A strange bog body

One tale described by the writer James Wentworth-Day refers to a body discovered in the fens but is a little far-fetched. The tale tells of a completely preserved body found in the peat at Burwell Fen. Not just a body though, this one was *standing upright* in a dug-out canoe, ready to embark on a voyage across the fen!

As well as the internal strife, this was also a time of another invasion – not of warriors and conquerors, but of Celtic art and culture. As society became more sophisticated, tribal chieftains imported precious metals for jewellery. These new styles of decoration accentuated their high standing and wealth and there is evidence of the use of coins. Some of these artefacts may have been manufactured in Britain, such as the gold torcs discovered in the Snettisham and Ipswich hoards, and which date to at least 75BC. The largest of these from Snettisham is of La Tène design and may have been associated with the Iceni royalty.

Snettisham Hoard
(King's Lynn Museum)

Conclusion

The journey from the glacier's edge to the farmland of Iron-Age Britain was one of monumental change, of climatic fluctuations, considerable immigration, and adaptation by humans and wildlife alike. For humans, it was their grit and ingenuity which triumphed over the obstacles they met. Small family groups who had found dry places to live, fished and trapped birds. These developed into tribes and larger communities who were able to exploit the riches of the fenland world with their developing technologies of bronze and iron. Such was the success of the human advance that by the end of the Iron Age the demand for fuel and building material had left an indelible mark on the landscape, and there were few places which remained entirely 'wild'. Although the fenland had not been drained, trees and bushes were almost certainly 'managed' in some way to prevent them encroaching on the fen grazing.

Wild or not, the structure of the environment in which people lived still remained immensely important to their culture and daily lives right into the Iron Age. Stories of the ancestors, of landmarks and boundaries, wild beasts and food sources were all carried down the generations by word of mouth and provided the context within which people lived. Prior to the Roman occupation, much of the knowledge of woodland, fen and grassland remained, but the more structured system of food production had probably begun to erode the deep reverence for the natural world. The landscape was becoming more of a powerhouse for the needs of the growing population, rather than the mystic world of pre-history.

Pete Marsh

The waterlogging stimulated the accretion of peat once more and the rate of peat formation is illustrated by the fate of 'Lindow Man' (Pete Marsh, as he has come to be known). The remains of this apparently ritually slaughtered young man were discovered in the peat moss at Lindow in Cheshire, where similar conditions existed from the 1st century AD as those in Huntingdonshire. The body was embalmed in the accreting peat and perfectly preserved for two thousand years! Many such bodies have been found across Europe in various stages of mutilation and the practice appears to have been common for hundreds of years.

The beetle in the bog oak

Cliff Butler and John Edwards were sawing up a bog oak when they made an extraordinary discovery. Perfectly preserved in the middle of a huge oak trunk was a longhorn beetle *Cerambyx cerdo* (Great Capricorn Beetle). This unique discovery connects us to the world of 6,000 years ago.

Until recently, this wood-boring beetle was thought to have been extinct in Britain, but has now been re-discovered.

Watch the film of the discovery on:
www.greatfen.org.uk/heritage/bog-oak

Cerambyx cerdo [www.freepik.com/pedrolunaguillen]

It is popular to consider this period of pre-history as one of a primitive existence in a world of untamed Nature. Perhaps instead we might consider how much we have to learn from the extraordinary survival and progress of humans and wildlife. The Bronze Age in particular was a time when art and culture, technology and 'civilisation' made huge strides and laid the foundations for much of our knowledge today. Here was the first 'alchemy' to transform rock into new metals, the melding of disparate groups into tribes with discrete territories, and the transformation of wild animals into domesticated livestock. This period also saw the first settled communities and a sense of ownership of the surrounding farmland.

Yet throughout these revolutions in the way that people lived, there was a constant factor. The 'wild' and the plants and animals which inhabited it were regarded with respect. Early on, this verged on reverence for supernatural forces, leading to the development of religious beliefs, such as Druidism. As knowledge increased, the use of herbs for medicine and natural materials for sustaining life became more important. Animals were hunted and killed, and later managed domestically, but there remained a close link between the human condition and the surrounding world.

There is no denying that many of the wild plants and animals which had lived in the melting ice world had suffered decline. Some of these became victim to the substantial climate changes that were occurring, while others suffered in the face of human advance. By the end of the Iron Age, the wild horses and Reindeer were long gone, followed by the Giant Deer. The Auroch herds couldn't withstand the efficient hunting and farming of the Iron Age, and the surviving bears and wolves were pushed back ever further into smaller territories. Tree clearance, burning and the munching of increasing numbers of domestic livestock were changing the face of the land and wildlife had to adapt to survive. Those that could adapt, found new habitats in the farmed and populated land where they could flourish, but other less adaptable species had great challenges to face.

Compared with our modern world, however, this must have been a fantastic wildlife spectacle. The bog oaks of the Great Fen had already been lost beneath the encroaching peat, but there were great flocks of cranes and wildfowl around Whittlesea Mere at the end of the Iron Age. Bitterns boomed from the miles of reedbeds, and the rivers and streams were full of eels and fish. Beavers appear to have been little affected by humans. Although they were hunted, they managed to co-exist reasonably well, often sharing the same resources of trees and wetland with humans.

The Romans would find little 'original' wilderness when they arrived in 55BC. What they did find was a land where sophisticated humans had changed the landscapes for their own use, but still lived amongst a rich variety of wildlife communities.

Roman invasion, salt and repression

Lucius Salvus had spent 10 years fighting in Caesar's army. When the call came to march out of Gaul and board the ships for Britannia he was nervous. He had heard that the invasion by Emperor Claudius had met some fierce opposition, even though some of the tribes had welcomed him. There had been a rebellion, too and one of the legions had been almost wiped out by painted warriors who were vicious fighters. Now this new Emperor, Marcus Aurelius, wanted to reinforce the army in Britain. Well, Lucius had heard that Hadrian's men had done well so perhaps it would be alright. Anyway, if he did a few more years he would be able to retire and live as he wanted. The troop ship was a bit scary in rough seas, but the march from the coast and through Londinium had been fairly peaceful and he was looking forward to arriving at the fort at Durobrivae where he was to be stationed. They had camped a few miles south of the town along the new road, Ermine Street. Then the centurion made him and some others go off into this half-flooded place where there must be dragons of all sorts, to get some birds and fish for the meal. But they couldn't get far. Titus got stuck in a bog and it took all of them to get him out – his armour was so heavy and Marcus had to lie flat while the others climbed over him to pull the idiot out. When he got back to camp he stank of wet peat... and found that his money purse was gone – a month's wages lost!

Julius Caesar described this new frontier as: *"one horrible forest"*. In fact, it was a land with considerable areas of developed agriculture, with fertile and managed fields that fed the population and supported an export trade for advanced, if disparate tribal societies. Iron Age farmers had revolutionised the British landscape and established small field systems and scattered communities where once there had been forest. The Romans were to take this to a different level entirely, based on urban living, organised administration and large-scale productivity for export. While coming primarily to relieve Britain of its precious metals and other resources, their 400 yearlong stay transformed both the way society was organised and the landscape itself. Material goods became important, the introduction of writing revolutionised communication and record, and drainage allowed agricultural innovation. Immense changes were coming to parts of the fens which had previously been impossible – nor would be again for centuries.

The Romans were lucky, because on their arrival the climate became warmer and drier. The land could be made more productive and capable of sustaining their preferred lifestyle. By their departure four centuries later, the fenland had flooded and for 1,000 years would be virtually uninhabitable on a permanent basis.

Caesar's ill-fated trip to Britain in 55BC was no accident. The Emperor needed a victory not only to increase his influence in Rome but also to provide materials to supply the ever-expanding Empire. There were many among the warring Britannic tribes who welcomed him. Trade across the Channel from Gaul had been going on for decades, bringing with it Roman influence and ideas. The tribal kings had developed a rich and hierarchical culture and the lure of expensive imported jewellery, amphorae of wine and weapons was great indeed. So much so that some of them had already adopted Roman styles of clothes and culture.

Boudicca Obelisk, Upshire near Epping

But neither the climate nor the majority of tribes gave Julius Caesar the welcome he had wanted and it was 100 years before the Emperor Claudius returned to complete the process of adding a new province to the empire. In the meantime, pockets of Roman influence had expanded, particularly in tribes like the Catevellauni of Hertfordshire and Cambridgeshire and their eastern neighbours, the Iceni – who would later prove to be unreliable allies to the Romans.

The Iceni had established themselves in the eastern fens sometime around the 1st century BC as part of a wave of tribes migrating from northern Europe. Under their king Prasutagus they occupied parts of East Anglia during the early days of Roman occupation with royal seats near Thetford on the Brecklands and on the coast at Snettisham. Their initial pact with the invaders had earned them the role of *'civitates peregrinae'* giving them the status of non-citizen local governors, but local Roman aggression was to turn a successful alliance into a disaster. A decree of 47AD that all tribes were to be dis-armed, infuriated the Iceni to the extent that they staged a rebellion at Stonea Camp (near present-day March). This was brutally suppressed by the local governor, Ostorias Scapula and after Prasutagus' death in 60AD their discontent was given further ammunition. Emperor Nero's procurator, Decianus Catus, dishonoured an agreement that half of the Iceni lands would pass to Rome on the king's death. Instead, Catus decided to take the lot, and his soldiers flogged the king's widow, Boudicca, and raped her daughters. This was the last straw, and gathering support from the Trinovantes of Essex, Boudicca embarked on a violent revolt which was to bring the Roman occupation to the brink of collapse.

The Britons were a force to be reckoned with, but were plagued by the inability to present a united front against invasion. Tacitus in his *Agricola* tells us:

"Their main strength is in foot-soldiers: some tribes use the war chariot as well. Formerly they were governed by kings; now they are torn by intrigues and factions between rival chiefs; nor is there anything that has been of greater service to us against these warlike races than their inability to combine for a common end. Rarely do even two or three of their tribes unite to ward off a common danger; they fight in detail, and the whole of them are thus defeated".

Boudicca proved the value of unity. She rallied other tribes and embarked on a vicious campaign against all things Roman, sacking the towns of Londinium and Verulanium (near St Albans), killing some 70,000 people. Her forces also wiped out the local IXth legion's infantry at Colchester. Boudicca came to a sticky end when she came into direct conflict with Nero's governor, Gaius Suetonius Paulinus, who met her with 10,000 troops of the XIVth and XXth legions. They eradicated her army completely, forcing her to take her own life rather than be captured.

Boudicca – warrior queen

Boudicca was of royal descent who was probably born around 30AD in Colchester, the Roman Camulodonum.

She married King Prasutagus around 43–45AD and had two daughters. Although too young to have been involved in the rebellion of AD47, she became an imposing figure. Accounts of the time from Cassius Dio describe her as: *"huge of frame, terrifying of aspect, and with a harsh voice. A great mass of bright red hair fell to her knees: she wore a twisted Torc, and a tunic of many colours…."* Cassius also suggests that she may have been queen of the Brigantes, not the Iceni, although it is clear that she was commonly accepted as the overall leader of the joint tribal assault on the Romans.

However great her ultimate defeat, Boudicca demonstrated the effectiveness of joint action against a common foe and how influential the tribes could have been if they abandoned their in-fighting. By united action they had posed a serious challenge to the emperors and could easily have changed the course of history. It may have even have been her rebellion which led Emperor Nero to consider withdrawing from Britain.

She also epitomises the fierce spirit which resides in the fens – a theme which will be repeated later in our story several times over the centuries. Despite her short-lived activity, Boudicca has lived on for centuries in art and music as the warrior-queen who united Britons against a common enemy.

Boudicca Statue, Colchester

One aspect of Boudicca's activities may shed some light on what the landscape in central England might have looked like in those days. We have no idea whether she really did have an army of 80,000 warriors (in addition to 20,000 camp followers), but there must have been large areas of open terrain for such a battle to be fought. Additionally, the two armies marched for many miles, and so would have needed vast resources of food and water, which suggests that there was access to food along the way. Although the legions carried a few days' supply it has been estimated that one legion needed 500 bushels of grain every week – that's about 14 tons!

When free from subduing the locals, the Romans developed three main industries in this part of Britannia – salt, pottery and iron – and the first two were centred in or around the fens. While most of fenland had hitherto been little occupied, the 2nd century Emperor Hadrian had other ideas. Modern fenland is the remnant of a once much bigger estuarine area, now only represented by the Wash, and in those days the saltmarsh and mudflats extended for many miles inland, earning them the

Why did Boudicca lose?

The exact site of the final battle is still unclear but may have been somewhere west of the fens along Watling Street. With an advantage of 8:1, it is difficult to understand how the Britons could have been so utterly defeated, but their sheer weight of numbers is perhaps itself one reason. The Romans had marched for many days from Wales, with the Britons in hot pursuit from London. The faster, better resourced legions finally turned to face them with an open vista to the front and woodland behind. The vast army of slower-marching Britons may have arrived exhausted, thirsty and hungry, with little time to recuperate. In addition, their practice of lining up wagons and camp followers behind the warriors played against them. When the Roman soldiers advanced in disciplined order, there was nowhere for the Britons to escape and they were slaughtered in their thousands.

Marcus Aurelius (Uffizzi gallery, Florence)

Dinario with image of Marcus Aurelius' wife (Norris Museum, St Ives)

name of *Metaris a Estuarian*. This was a perfect place to make salt and as this had become a scarce commodity across the Empire, it was both politic and profitable to exploit the fens for large-scale production. It is probable that the seat of early Iceni rebellion at Stonea Camp was developed after Hadrian's visit in 122 as a centre to control the development of the salt-panning. Salterns sprang up all over the eastern fenland and it became a profitable enterprise.

The Car dyke

The Car dyke was constructed around 125AD and was about 15 metres wide at the top and between 2 and 4 metres deep, with sloping sides and a flat bottom. Why it was built has intrigued historians and archaeologists for centuries. At least parts of the ditch may have been primarily for transport, or it may have been an early drainage channel for water from the western hills. It was an impressive structure and some of it is still in use today in the Middle Level system. Many other smaller ditches originate from this period and this may have been the first time that hollowed-out tree trunks were used as culverts to manage water levels.

There is plenty of evidence that the fens were locally drained to facilitate both the salt industry and farming and this may have been the peak of fenland activity during the Roman period. The substantial villa built at Stonea suggests that the area may have been part of an imperial estate with tenant farmers installed within it. There was a rise in the number of settlements and the population rose significantly around the salt pans.

Inland, agriculture in the silt fens was largely concentrated on supplying grain for the Roman legions and townships. Further

Samarian Pot (Norris Museum, St Ives)

west into the Great Fen area, the freshwater peat was more suited to pastoral farming and despite the lack of habitation in the deep fen, the summer-dry reedy meadows were important for grazing.

Hadrian's successors such as Marcus Aurelius did not appear to share his passion for salt-panning, probably not helped by a deterioration in the weather and lack of maintenance of the drainage channels. Much of fenland re-flooded and the population went to seek their fortunes elsewhere. The lack of maintenance also points to a decline in wealth among the owners and tenants, which may in itself have been caused by the decline in income due to flooding!

On the coast, forts were constructed at Brancaster and Caistor-by-Yarmouth in the late 2nd/early 3rd century and were soon to be followed by others along the North Sea and Channel shores – the so-called 'Saxon Shore' forts. The exact purpose of these forts is still debated. Certainly, there were constant raids from Saxons and others which needed to be deterred. However, Francis Pryor (2010) considers that they may well have been for storage of surplus products being exported via the fen waterways or those taken in lieu of taxes.

Transport was a key feature in the colonial power-base, not only allowing the legions to move quickly and efficiently, but also for export of manufactured goods. The great Fosse Way which linked the west to central areas was complete by 47AD and was soon to link with other roads such as Ermine Street and the Fen Causeway which ran for 39 km from Longthorpe in Peterborough, through Whittlesea to Denver in Norfolk. Today, walkers on the Rothschild Way route from Great Fen to Wicken might spare a thought for their ancestors who built the road from gravel.

The Fen Causeway [WC/JD]

To the north-west of the Great Fen, the area around Castor was developed on an industrial scale as a pottery, clustered around a villa on the site of what became

Roman shore fort Burgh Castle near Great Yarmouth

St Kyneburgha's church. Pottery was perhaps the reason why a garrison was established at Durobrivae on Ermine Street near Water Newton, guarding the western end of the Fen Causeway and access to the sea. 'Castor-ware' was an important export and was transported via the fen drains to the sea ports of the east coast. In those days, the coastline was somewhat different from today and there is evidence of a Roman port as far inland as Guyhirn, (on the eastern end of the Nene Washes).

While timber from the forest was probably used for firing the pottery kilns, peat was also an important resource and it has been estimated that some 4,500 tons of peat had been dug from the fens by the 3rd century (Salway 2002).

Much of the deep fenland remained stubbornly resistant to any widespread draining or habitation, particularly where raised bog was developing. Our penniless legionnaire of the 2nd century en-route to Durobrivae would have passed within two miles of Holme Fen, but had learnt the hard way about the consequences of stepping off the road into the wild bog.

Much of the wildlife probably lived reasonably in tune with the activities of its neighbours, although Roman introductions were to have significant long-term consequences. The opium poppy was introduced at this time and became the drug of choice for fenlanders escaping the rigours of the ague which haunted them for centuries. It is still widely consumed as an herbal tea. The Romans may or may not have brought rabbits to England, but fallow deer and pheasants date from this time.

The population of Britain during the Roman era rose steeply to between 2 and 3.5 million, with a good deal of 'Romanisation' of the native Britons, as well as immigrants from the empire. An equal number in the rural areas probably remained largely untouched by the new ideas and ways of living. The heated luxury of the Roman villa at Castor would have been unknown in the wetland where even the language was more Celtic than Latin. Great forests still existed around Lincoln and on the heavier clays of the present Northamptonshire, although much had been cleared and cultivated, but fenland remained largely uninhabitable and impossible to access other than by boat. Cattle and sheep might graze the lush sedge beds, but the rest was a wild and untamed land unavailable to any but the fen people. Only they truly understood its ways and could harvest its bounty of fish and fowl, reed and willow.

As the centuries passed and Roman culture became absorbed into much of Britain, the Empire itself began to unravel. Challenges from outside and rebellion from within took its toll and Rome's influence in Britain began to wane. When the legions left in 410AD, local officials were expelled, trade withered and the money dried up. It is hard to imagine the catastrophic effect on 'normal' life when suddenly the structures which had supported it were removed. Many people were doing very nicely under the administration of empire – as long as they didn't fall foul of any rules and regulations – and may have hoped the legions would someday return. That was not to be – Rome had its own problems and Britannia was on its own.

Some of the wealthier people may have managed to sustain some aspects of their Romanic lifestyle, but within a few decades most villas began to fall into disrepair. Much of the farmland, now deprived of its urban markets, gradually reverted to something close to its former state; and with no reason to maintain them, the fenland drainage channels were neglected. The legacy of cultivation, order and culture which had flourished during the occupation went into decline.

The Dark Ages
Invasion, flooding and fens

400–600AD – the Saxons and Angles
The picture of what actually occurred over the next few centuries is a faded one. The Iceni disappeared along with the infant Duroliponte (Cambridge). Sea levels rose and the

meandering fen rivers, denied their outfall to the sea, spilled over into the summer pastures creating a wetland which would remain largely unchanged for 1,000 years.

There is much debate as to exactly what happened in the years following the demise of the Romans and we may never know the true story. What infrastructure there was on the fens probably either decayed under the rising water levels or was dismantled for other purposes. Raiders from Saxony, Gaul and Denmark had been testing the Roman defences along the east coast for a long time, escaping rising sea levels at home, so the departure of the military left the country open to invasion on a grand scale – a power vacuum waiting to be filled. Until recently, it was thought that this caused a long period of violent and disruptive invasion by Germanic warriors and a subsequent desertion of the countryside, but there is evidence for neither.

That is not to downplay local fears and the effects of the bloodthirsty Saxons, Angles and Picts. In the decades after the Roman departure, the Romano-British became so rattled at the prospect of being over-run by new invaders that they appealed to Rome for help, but to no avail. Another tactic was to enlist Saxons to fend off the Picts, but that proved a disastrous policy which backfired spectacularly when the payments dried up, opening the door to a Saxon rampage through much of the east.

The picture of fenland life at this time was largely painted by historians such as H. Darby in 1940 in his *The Medieval Fenland*. Information available at the time led him to conclude that fenland was virtually abandoned in the seven centuries between the departure of the Romans and the arrival of the Normans. It was, he maintained, an impenetrable marsh separating the kingdoms of Mercia and East Anglia where wild beasts and mythic monsters roamed. Even if this had been true, the invaders would have found a cool welcome in the fens. In his *Britannia* (1586) William Camden says that the fen people: "*were in the Saxons time called* Girvii, *that is, as some interpret it,* Fen-men *or* Fen-dwellers. *A kinde of people according to the nature of the place where they dwell rude, uncivill, and envious to all others whom they call* Upland-men, *who, stalking high upon stilts, apply their mindes to grasing, fishing and fowling*".

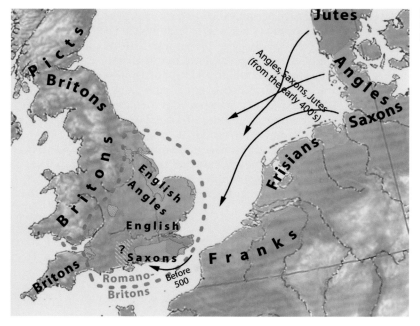

Britain 400–500AD. Anglo-Saxon homelands and settlements

More recent evidence paints a very different picture, suggesting that while there was certainly local disruption, a much more peaceful transition took place. The lack of secondary woodland points to continued cultivation or grazing in most areas and the new peoples who penetrated as far as fenland became absorbed into its ways of life. Susan Oosthuizen, in her book *The Anglo-Saxon Fenland* (2017), and others such as Peter Salway (2001) argue that the lack of archaeological finds to support a sudden and violent invasion suggests a more gradual assimilation of the new people into society. War and rampage were left to those with political aspirations. Rather than violent invasion it is more likely that during the 5th and 6th centuries many of the disparate tribes became moulded into larger kingdoms, including East Anglia.

Some of the new settlers became established along the gravel terraces of the river Nene, where the Beaker people had settled 2,000 years before, but the 'native' population persisted around the fens, consisting of several tribes with defined territories which included at least parts of the fen. Local distinctiveness persisted long into the medieval period, but was coupled with co-operative working on the land.

When the market for grain collapsed with the economic contraction after the Roman period, these fenland farmers resorted to what their land was most suited for – livestock. Despite the rising waters, over the decades and centuries which followed they developed highly skilled methods of land and water management which both sustained their families and the grazing habitat.

"Evidence from palynological research and faunal remains recovered during archaeological excavation, and place and field names, demonstrate the long-term stability of the mosaic of species that made up the varied specialised environments of the fen basin, and a long history of early medieval dairying. Documentary evidence of early rights of common indicate the deliberate, careful management of the fen landscape throughout the early medieval period, focused on maintaining the ecological mosaics that sustained rich grazing for cattle and a wide range of other fen products." Ooosthuizen 2017.

There were three key features of this success:

First, people developed an intimate knowledge of how vegetation behaved under certain hydrological conditions. Understanding the ebb and flow of water was crucial to sustaining the rich grazing which would produce the best beef and milk, from which staples such as cheese could be made. As there is no evidence for significant re-growth of trees, it follows that these farmers also knew the importance of controlling bushes (known as 'carr') and managing it for produce such as osier baskets.

Second, they were adaptable. Their area and availability of pasture varied with fluctuations in climate and water levels, so the use of land had to be flexible.

Third – and very importantly – the people had been managing the fenland from early in the Roman period. Over time this developed into a complex set of commoners' rights which protected the livelihood of those concerned, and ensured a reliable source of cropping, which would last until the major drainage of the 17th century. Many of these principles of fen and wet meadow management are still pursued on the surviving nature reserves and washlands of today.

A snapshot of the fen country during this period comes from William Camden, who tells us:
"The whole region it selfe, which in winter season and sometime most part of the yeare is overflowed by the spreading waters of the rivers Ouse, Grant, Nen, Welland, Glene, and Witham, having not loades [ditches] and sewers large enough to voide away. But againe when their streames are retired within their owne chanels, it is so plenteous and ranke of a certaine fatte grosse and full hey (which they call Lid), that when they have mowen downe as much with the better as well serve their turnes, they set fire on the rest and burne it in November, that it may come up againe in greater abundance... Great plenty it hath besides of turfe and sedge for the maintenance of fire; of reed also for to thatch their houses,

yea and of alders, beside other waterie shrubs. But chiefly it bringeth forth exceeding store of willowes both naturally and also for that, being planted by mans hand".

There were also bigger events happening, where sophisticated organisation was achieving major projects such as the creation of lodes and other big drains. A charter of 972 from Peterborough Abbey, for example, describes a dyke called *Kingesdelf*. This formed part of an artificial cut re-routing the river Nene between Stanground and Benwick and may well have been dug well before the 10th century. Similarly, *Ubbemaerelade* was cut to connect Ugg Mere with Whittlesea Mere. Another charter of 956 for Yaxley and Farcet mentions several others: *tham dicum*, 'the lode' which still exists as the modern Yaxley Lode; *dichythe*, 'the hythe along the ditch', the modern Pig Water, near its confluence with the old course of Yaxley Lode; 'the southern hythe', and *nordhythe*, 'the northern hythe', lay on either side of the Pig Water.

600–1000AD

Among all the human changes to the landscape the climate remained a potent force. Between 600 and 800 there was a marked deterioration in weather and within a few generations sea levels rose by 1.5 m. A particularly significant event occurred around 536, when a volcanic eruption or meteoric collision caused a massive disruption to the atmosphere. Summers throughout Europe became wet and cold, and sunlight absent. Perhaps it was these conditions which drove the Scandinavians from their failing crops to seek their fortune in warmer and drier lands. Added to this, bubonic plague ('Black Death') hit England around 560 and the resulting slump in population must have caused much abandonment of marginal land such as on the fen. Many generations would live through hardship until the weather improved.

Despite the obstacles and hardships, life went on. Tribes merged into principalities and these into kingdoms, whose aristocracy seemed to fare rather well and could obtain high-value goods from abroad. The glittering array of riches found in the Sutton Hoo ship burial in Suffolk probably belonged to Raedwald, the Saxon king of East Anglia, who died in 625. Resplendent in items of Celtic and Byzantine art, his grave goods illustrate the healthy trade which must have been going on at the time and the wealth of at least some Britons. 'Bling from abroad' was still a great status symbol.

By the end of the 8th century the Saxon kingdoms were relatively settled. The import of the new heavy plough sped the pace of land cultivation, heralding the open field system which was to characterise much of England for centuries. But the background to normal life was about to be shattered by violence and unpredictability.

The tribes of the fens

A feature of Whittlesea Mere is a promontory jutting out into the southern edge. Known at least since the 1146 foundation charter of Sawtry Abbey, Sword Point was the home of a local tribe of the early medieval period known as the *'Sweord Ora'*. Their territory is recorded in the 'Tribal Hidage' and may have extended north of the mere as well as to the south, where evidence shows that people from Woodwalton, Glatton, Conington and Holme had Commoners rights.

Another local tribe were the *Gyrwe* who lived around Peterborough and the fens. According to Candidus in his *Chronicle of Peterborough*, they were the people who: *"dwell in the fen, or hard by the fen, since a deep bog is called in the Saxon tongue Gyr"*. Bede in his *Historia Ecclesiastica* also refers to them: *"Ely is in the province of the East Angles, a country of about six hundred families, in the nature of an island, enclosed… either with marshes or waters, and therefore it has its name from the great plenty of eels taken in those marches"*. According to Darby, by about 600 their territory included the monastery of Medehamstede, and charters for a Conington estate in 956 and Yaxley, Stanground and Farcet in 957, put its boundaries as the river Nene, Ermine Street to the west and the 'seaxa broc' (Holme Brook) to the south.

Sutton Hoo – a king's burial

The Sutton Hoo burial contains intriguing clues to the rise of Christianity at this time. Two small spoons engraved with references to the apostle Paul were found among other pagan symbols, but whether or not Raedwold had converted to Christianity is in doubt. Some sources say he was directed to do so by Æthelberth of Kent who had supported the missionary Augustine at the end of the 6th century. Others suggest that the king's wife persuaded him to keep to the old ways. Perhaps those responsible for providing him with the necessities of the afterlife were hedging their bets!

The Sutton Hoo burial mound, Suffolk

Sutton Hoo helmet (replica)

The Vikings

The painted raven led them, flapping on the sail, Odin's spirit urging them on. There were new riches here and glory for the warriors. Every summer they had come, more boats each year. This time the man from the flooding Daneland brought his wife and child. This was to be their new land – he would strike any Britons or Saxons who dared stand in his way. The land he had found was wet and full of reeds for thatching and peat for fires. They would settle where they had camped last summer – on dry land near the woods and build a house. He could travel on the boat to fish and trap birds for food, but they would keep clear of the cursed bog at the great mere's edge where his hunting dogs had sunk out of sight last summer.

Despite their war-like ambitions, the Vikings were also closely connected with their gods and the natural world. The Raven on the Norsemen's sails was the sacred bird of Odin – 'Hrafna Gwd' – and they even took Ravens with them on their travels and used them like the dove on Noah's Ark to find land. Perhaps these birds were the ancestors of the ravens still found in the fenland until the 19th century.

The term 'Viking' is used to describe the helmeted invaders from the north, but although both of Scandinavian origin, there were two separate bands of warriors who came in the 8th century. The fair-haired Norsemen from Norway had been raiding the north-eastern coast for some decades, but it was the Danes who turned their attentions to East Anglia. A large army landed on the east coast in 865 and spread along the rivers to the rich pickings inland.

The Vikings

Local kings, such as the East Anglian Edmund (later to be Saint Edmund), attempted to buy-off the invaders, as their forefathers had with the Saxons. It was an equally calamitous policy, encouraging escalating demands for Danegeld and did little to deter the aggressors. The Danes dispatched Edmund horribly in 869 and established 'Danelaw' across much of England east of Ermine Street, including the fens. Peterborough names such as Cowgate, Westgate and Longthorpe date from this period.

The next few centuries were plagued with warring factions causing devastation to unwary monasteries and settlements alike. In 886 the Wessex king, Alfred, created a brief period of peace by defeating a fresh incursion by Guthrum, the Danish leader, but only at the cost of allowing him to perpetuate Danelaw in the east, where he converted to Christianity under the name of Æthelstan. The 'peace' which Alfred had made with Guthrum was, in effect, an exercise in buying time for the English. Following the battle, Alfred began to establish a network of 'burghs' – fortified towns within a day's march of each other – which served the dual purpose of promoting vibrant urban life but also as a bulwark against any Danish ideas of expansion.

The Danes also established nucleated settlements. Trading ports began to spring up such as at Gipswic (now Ipswich) and in the 9th century, Huntingdon was founded in the territory of the *Herefinna*.

The Battle of Holme

The next time you walk through the quiet trees of Holme Fen and survey the life of Rymes Reedbed from the Lookout Hide imagine the scene in December 902:

"Rumours had been spreading for weeks of an army sweeping through the country, burning and killing everything in its path. There was a Danish army, too, and they were somewhere south of the fens. Our unease turned to terror when a distant rumble became a roar as the two huge armies appeared over the western hills and from the great Dyke to the south. They couldn't get as far as the fen itself – it was too wet – so we all huddled in boats and reed huts hoping to keep out of the way. The battle raged all day. Occasionally bloodied warriors could be seen staggering into the bog or running as fast as they could to escape the enemy. There were bodies everywhere and eventually one army fled the field and the Danes were victorious, although there weren't many of them left. Even their king and the English prince who had wanted to be king himself was dead".

While many ordinary folk managed to avoid the conflicts of the rival kings, they could not avoid what was to happen in 902. After his death, Alfred's place was taken by his son Edward the Elder. He would later rule in an extraordinary liaison with his sister Æthflaed, but his succession was challenged by his cousin Æthelwold, who joined forces with the Danes. A series of bloody conflicts following, during which Edward, in alliance with the 'Men of Kent' laid waste to East Anglia, much as Æthelwold had done in Mercia. The fields between the Devil's Dyke near Cambridge, Huntingdon and all the way to Peterborough burned with a smoke which was visible for miles – a clear sign to the Danes and fenmen alike that trouble was on its way. According to the *Anglo-Saxon Chronicle* the final reckoning came in 902 when: *"This year was the great fight at the Holme between the men of Kent and the Danes".* Where Æthelwold actually met Alfred's allies, the Kentish army, is far from clear, but it may have been somewhere near Holme Fen. It was carnage, and although the Danes won they suffered such heavy losses including Æthelwold himself that the rebellion was effectively at an end.

A fuller account of the battle appears in 905, when the *Chronicle* tells us that:

"This year Ethelwald enticed the army in East-Anglia to rebellion; so that they overran all the land of Mercia, until they came to Cricklade, where they forded the Thames; and having seized, either in Bradon or thereabout, all that they could lay their hands upon, they went homeward again. King Edward went after, as soon as he could gather his army, and overran all their land between the foss and the Ouse quite to the fens northward. Then being desirous of returning thence, he issued an order through the whole army, that

they should all go out at once. But the Kentish men remained behind, contrary to his order, though he had sent seven messengers to them. Whereupon the army surrounded them, and there they fought."

Yet another account comes from Henry of Huntingdon:

"King Edward, having hastily collected some troops, followed their rear, ravaging the whole territory of the Mercians between the Dyke and the Ouse, as far northward as the fens. After which he resolved to retreat, and commanded his whole army to retire together; and they all withdrew, except the Kentish-men, who remained contrary to the king's order, though he sent seven messages after them. Then the army of the Danes intercepted the Kentish-men and a battle was fought."

We may never know the exact site of this battle, but the great bog of Holme Fen, which had withstood the rising sea and Roman drainage, may well have been witness to the bloodshed, while its mosses slowly grew year on watery year. Eventually both sides became weary of the wars and a peace was concluded in 906, although further raids by the Scandinavians ultimately led to the defeat of King Æthelred. His son Edmund remained king of England south of the Thames, but on his death, Cnut finally became king of all England, although his victory was to be cut short by the arrival of the Normans in 1066.

It must have been a dangerous time to be in the wrong place when the warriors were settling their scores! If they managed to avoid direct confrontation with invaders of whichever persuasion, ordinary folk and communities must have been scarred by the damage done to their farms and crops. But they had established close connections with their land and it is this continuity which had more influence on the character of the landscape than the squabbles and power struggles of the elites. The fenlanders living through these centuries continued to be defined by the landscape in which they lived and were primarily concerned with collectively managing the fenland for its grazing and rich yields of fish, eels and reed. Despite macro-politics which was moulding England into larger units, local tribal identities and independence of spirit still held firm.

The Normans and beyond

The Norman occupation was as brutal as it was successful. While the Romans, Saxons and Vikings had occupied only half the country at any one time, William of Normandy had wider aims. In the decades following his success over Harold he systematically dismantled much of Anglo-Saxon and Viking England and initiated a new way of life, culture and politics.

Moreton's Leam

One of the most influential of the medieval clerics was Bishop John Moreton. In 1480, as Lord of the Isle and head of the drainage commissioners, he ordered a straight ditch to be cut from Stanground in Peterborough 12 miles to Wisbech as part of a grand scheme to drain the marshes. This was the first recorded attempt at large-scale drainage in the fens.

King Cnut and the storm

A story in the Victoria County History tells of King Cnut's family being caught in a storm on the Whittlesea Mere and several were drowned. Cnut ordered a dyke to be cut east of the mere (Sweredsdelf) from Bodsey to Pondersbridge. The dyke still exists today.

Barnack Hills and Holes

Barnack Hills and Holes NNR lies 5 km north of Peterborough and is a wildlife mecca. Rare and beautiful plants grow in the thin limestone soil and butterflies such as the Marbled White *Melanargia galathea* and Chalk Hill Blue *Polyommatus coridon* have strong colonies here. But Barnack is an ancient quarry and stone from the holes among the hills are now to be found in abbeys and cathedrals across the region.

Not surprisingly, it was fenland that presented William with his earliest and most deadly challenge. Hereward Leofricsson (the Wake) may or may not have drawn his ancestry from Boudicca, but he was equally rebellious in defence of his rights. Like the monks before him, he found in the wild fens an ideal fortress on the Isle of Ely, where in 1070 he mounted a vigorous opposition to the Norman intrusion. By then, the East Anglian wilderness had swollen to some half a million acres – *"a pestilential region, ofttimes clouded with moist and dark vapours"* according to the Guthlac poem, and like Boudicca, Hereward posed a serious threat to the invaders. After his defeat and narrowly avoiding capture at Ely he disappears from the scene, but in the aftermath of his rebellion William set about a vicious 'cleansing' of any whiff of rebellion. In his infamous 'Harrying of the north', countless thousands were slaughtered and brought to starvation as their lands were confiscated or ruined.

William was more than repressor, though. He brought an entirely new way of life which was to annihilate much of Anglo-Saxon culture and replace it with Norman towers, castles and land-use. Having subdued any resistance, whether English Dane or Scot, he embarked

Hereward the Wake

Hereward was described by a contemporary as: *"comely in aspect, very beautiful from his yellow hair, and with large grey eyes, the right eye slightly different in colour to the left; but he was stern of feature, and somewhat stout, from the great sturdiness of his limbs, but very active for his moderate stature, and in all his limbs was found a complete vigour".*

Hereward is considered the archetypal English hero, defender of Britain's freedom from nasty Normans. Like many such legends the actual truth is neither so definite or inspiring. A recent re-evaluation of his lineage (Rex 2005) suggests that far from being English and the son of Leofric, Earl of Mercia he was, in fact, the son of Asketil Tokison, a royal Dane. Neither are 'English' of course, because Leofric himself was of Anglo-Saxon descent and only a few hundred years earlier they were the invaders!

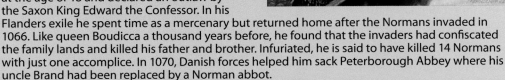

Hereward was an exuberant character from an early age, to the extent that he was exiled at the age of 18 and declared an outlaw by the Saxon King Edward the Confessor. In his Flanders exile he spent time as a mercenary but returned home after the Normans invaded in 1066. Like queen Boudicca a thousand years before, he found that the invaders had confiscated the family lands and killed his father and brother. Infuriated, he is said to have killed 14 Normans with just one accomplice. In 1070, Danish forces helped him sack Peterborough Abbey where his uncle Brand had been replaced by a Norman abbot.

Hereward took refuge on the wild Isle of Ely in his final stand against William. The fen was clearly a very wet and treacherous place at that time, because many of William's soldiers were drowned during the siege despite attempts to build a causeway – which sank under their weight. Hereward held out for some time until he was betrayed by the Abbot Thurstan who feared Norman reprisals on the Abbey, and he barely escaped into the wild fenland.

Like Boudicca, Hereward's fate is a matter of legend. Perhaps he was killed, lived as an outlaw or even made peace with William. We shall probably never know, but whether he is considered as English or Dane, terrorist or freedom fighter, his legend lives on in literature and art as a fierce and indomitable spirit who was as wild as fenland itself.

on an audit of his new realm – *The Book*, later known as *Domesday*. The survey gives us much information about the state of the settlements and prosperity of England at the beginning of the medieval period, although there are glaring omissions, particularly in fenland, which paint a misleading picture of an empty countryside (Oosthuizen 2017).

William inherited a land which was not entirely dissimilar to the one we know today. Little of the once-endless wildwood had survived until Domesday and what remained was managed for coppice and other products or as pannage for pigs. Oliver Rackham (1995) calculated that just 15% of England remained as woodland or wood-pasture, 20% as mountain, moor, heath, fen or urban land and the rest either arable or pasture. Within a hundred years of Norman occupation, even this landscape had been transformed into open fields, with just 10% of the land remained under cover of trees.

A brigand in the fen

Geoffrey de Mandeville was a particularly ambitious and rebellious baron in the reign of king Stephen during a 20-year period of extreme instability and civil war. After a chequered history of support and treachery for and against the king and his rival Matilda, Geoffrey took up residence in the fens in 1143. Commandeering Ramsey Abbey and the Isle of Ely as his strongholds he earned a fearsome reputation for general atrocities and rebellion against the king, including the building of the castle at Woodwalton. He was eventually killed during a siege of Burwell.

Domesday

Although not specifically mentioned, Holme village is probably included as part of Glatton, while Yaxley (Lacheslei) does get its own entry:

"YAXLEY the Abbot of Thorney had 15 hides to the geld. [There is] land for 20 ploughs. There are now 3 ploughs in demesne; and 38 villeins having 18 ploughs. There is a church and a priest, and 24 acres of meadow and 20 acres of scrubland."

Ramsey as a town didn't exist at this time, but at least 16,000 hectares of land was under the control of Ramsey Abbey, including fishing rights worth 10 pounds.

Monks Wood was known as Ewingswode and was described as "woodland for pannage" (grazing by pigs). An indication of the value of eels to these communities comes from an entry of the Ramsey Abbot's lands in Chatteris, which had:

3 hides less ½ virgate Land for 4 ploughs. In lordship 1½ hides;
1 plough there;
10 villagers and 5 smallholders with 3 ploughs;
2 slaves.
Meadow for 4 ploughs; woodland,100 pigs;
from fisheries
3000 eels; from presentations 27d.
Value 60s; when acquired 20s; before 1066 £4.
This land lies and always lay in (the lands)
St Benedict's Church.
In Wisbech the Abbot of Ramsey has 8 fishermen who pay 5260 eels.

William of Malmesbury wrote: *"here is such quantities of fish as to cause astonishment in strangers."*

The monastic revolution

The monastery was a long way from the mere, but the fishing platforms belonged to the Abbot and it was the monk's job to bring in 100 eels for the feast. The strange pale priest, Candidus, from the abbey of Medeshamstede was coming and the Abbot was keen to examine the chronicles he was writing.

Although Christianity had received a set-back after the Roman withdrawal, there was a resurgence after St Augustine's landing in Kent in 597. Another Roman invasion had begun, but this time one of religion, not war.

The fenland was particularly favoured by those wishing to escape the world and submit to a life of relative solitude and harshness. Aiden was the first to found a monastery at Lindisfarne in 635 and the abbey at Peterborough (Medeshamstede) was built in 655. Others

By the time the Normans established a hold on Britain, the Danelaw in East Anglia was reaching its conclusion. With the defeat of Guthrum by Alfred in 878, Scandinavian influence remained dominant in the east but subject to intense instability, with rule regularly passing from England to Denmark for at least a century. William's persistence saw the last of the Vikings deposed and his religious desire led to a resurgence of the monastic houses which were particularly dominant in the fens. Although the fenmen continued their way of life, much of it was subservient to the dictats of the friars who controlled most of the land and fishing. Following Hereward's stand against Norman incursion much land was granted to Norman families and the fenman was just as likely to be directed by one or other of these than to have his own land or be entirely free to operate under the commoners' system.

soon followed in the surrounding countryside – Ramsey, Thorney, Sawtry, Crowland, Ely. The monastic houses became major land owners and hugely influential in the exploitation of the resources of the marshes and fields. Unfortunately for them, the wealth which they acquired became a natural target for the Vikings. In 793 Lindisfarne was sacked and many monks killed or taken prisoner. In 870 the Peterborough monks suffered a similar fate. According to the Anglo-Saxon Chronicle the raiders: *"made such havoc there, that a monastery, which was before rich, was now reduced to nothing"*.

The influence of the abbeys and monasteries on the fen landscape and daily life cannot be over-estimated. It was a rich environment worth exploiting, which had been carefully managed for centuries and was essential to the monks who had to find their own food. Benedictine monks, in particular, were supposed to avoid meat except if they were ill or on special occasions, so fish, fowl and arable crops were an important feature of their lives. In an interesting twist, it was judged that Otters and Beavers were fish and so they could be eaten with impunity – except that by medieval times, beavers had become scarce enough to be a delicacy rather than a main meal. Eels were so numerous that they served as both food and currency, so the possession of fishing and grazing rights were of paramount importance and jealously guarded. Repeated destruction by Vikings and others may have damaged monastic life, but following the re-founding of many of the religious houses after 957, water management became more widespread and made a significant impact on the landscape.

In the mid-12th century the Peterborough chronicler, Hugh Candidus, described the fens around Peterborough as: *"very valuable to men because there are obtained in abundance all things needful to them that dwell thereby"* and Ramsey *"is garlanded beautifully roundabout as much with alder thickets as reedbeds, indeed, with a luxuriance of reed and rush... The same place is encircled by eel-filled marshes, by far-reaching meres and by still pools sustaining a variety of fish and swimming birds."*

The terrain they inherited has been shown from pollen analysis and peat cores to have been predominantly open herb-rich grassland and wetland, with small areas of Alder and willow carr – an environment which had persisted for centuries and would do for several more.

One example of the attention to the wetland landscape was the cutting of a dyke along the route of the present Ramsey St Mary's/Pondersbridge road to enable stone to be brought from Barnack via the river Nene to Ramsey Abbey. Monks Lode was cut to connect Sawtry Abbey to the same system. Not only did management of water provide transport, it also provided irrigation for lush grazing. Cutting bushes to prevent the succession of reed and sedge to scrub – which is so evident on Woodwalton Fen today – and clearing vegetation from ditches must have also have been widespread. Failure to do this is illustrated by later accounts of the fate of Moreton's Leam – excavated in 1480, but declared as 'decayed' in 1618 due to lack of maintenance.

As we have already seen, a few larger lodes had already been created before the 10th century, but the re-formation of the great monastic houses was instrumental in far-reaching changes on the landscape. This included the beginnings of comprehensive changes in water management – which were not always welcomed by the fen people (a theme that we will return to later in the story). The creation of the Commissioners of Sewers in 1258 in Holland, Lincolnshire was one such initiative, but the Commissioners were never particularly effective and neglect of drains and outfalls to the sea continued to cause frequent flooding during the 13th and 14th centuries.

In 1147 Monks Wood came into the ownership of Sawtry Abbey, being managed for coppice products such as firewood and thatching spars.

Later medieval times – church, invasion and plague

The order for more stone to enlarge the Abbey at Ramsey was important for the stone-hewers of Barnack. Barnack 'Rag' was much sought after for the great monastic buildings of the mediaeval period, so it was with great care and much effort that four huge stones were hewn from the quarry and loaded onto sledges for hauling to the river Welland. The boatman supervised the loading, anxious to ensure the weight was evenly distributed and set off. It was a steady sail to reach the Nene and south towards Yaxley. After a night's rest the barge set off to cross Whittlesea Mere to Ramsey. A light breeze had sprung up but the boatman was not worried. At that time of year, the great storms so typical of the mere seemed unlikely. Breasting through the rather reedy entrance to the open water a bittern flew up and away dangling is legs across the rippling water, but the ripples soon began to deepen as the barge laboured into the wind. A sudden gust sent the boatman scurrying to reduce sail but as it cleared Sword Point, tragedy struck. The wind shifted to the west and caught the sail full on. The sudden tilt of the boat put too much strain on one of the hemp ropes securing the stone and it snapped. As the stones began to slide the wind increased and the boat heeled further. Desperate to pull into the wind and correct the dangerous tilt he pushed the tiller away, but it jammed on one of the sliding stones and with a great bang the boat tipped right over. With so much weight neither boat nor boatman had a chance and they went straight to the bottom, along with their precious cargo.

In the centuries following the conquest, there was considerable agricultural advance. Horses replaced oxen which increased the rate and scope of cultivation, and there were further attempts to drain swampland. If the legend is to be believed that King John lost his baggage train in the marshes between King's Lynn and Lincoln in 1216, however, it suggests that the drainage was not particularly widespread!

A pale monk

Hugh Candidus was a monk at Peterborough Abbey in the 12th century and was responsible for compiling a history of the abbey from its inception in 655 to 1175. This is the earliest known description of Peterborough and its surroundings, including the fens. It is considered unlikely that Hugh wrote the Peterborough Chronicle, which forms part of the Anglo-Saxon Chronicles. He was particularly pale and was known as the 'pale monk'.

Following the demise of John and his absentee brother, Richard, there was political uproar, with constant strife amongst the Plantagenets culminating in the 30-year War of the Roses in the 15th century. The greatest effect on the landscape, however, came from more natural causes. The years 1315–16 saw a great famine, when poor weather caused crop failure and later livestock diseases. A few years later further disaster came from the plague. The 'Black Death' entered Britain in 1348 at Weymouth in Dorset and soon spread across the country. Within a year it had killed over 40% of the population and was to have far-reaching consequences for the economy. East Anglia was hard hit and doubtless in the damp and airless swamps of fenland the people suffered horribly. The lack of agricultural

The abbeys established around the Fens were extremely important in their effect on life in general and the landscape in particular. With their riches and power, they were instrumental in many major works of drainage and cultivation as well as becoming influential seats of learning. The abbots also spent a good deal of energy squabbling amongst themselves about the division of land and resources around them.

Benedictine

Peterborough Abbey was founded in 655 by the Mercian king Peada and was known as Medeshamstede. According to the Anglo-Saxon Chronicle, the abbey was sacked in 870 by the Vikings but re-built as a Benedictine abbey in 936. A medieval carving of 12 monks, called the Hedda Stone was made to commemorate the Viking destruction and the death of the abbot and monks, and now stands in the cathedral. Hereward did his best to destroy much of the site in 1069 but it finally burnt down in 1116. It was soon re-built from Barnack stone and subsequently developed into the cathedral which stands on the site today. In the 13th century, a painted ceiling was completed over the nave and is the only one in Britain.

According to the Anglo-Saxon Chronicle, Whittlesea Mere was given to the abbey by Wulphere, King of Mercia in 657 but after the abbey was destroyed by the Danes, the ownership returned to the king. A quarter of Whittlesea Mere was returned to the abbey in 963, which later managed to acquire the fishing rights on another quarter, but Thorney managed to have the manorial rights as well.

Ramsey Abbey was the first to be established in the eastern fens and was in its time an extremely important religious house. Modestly founded in 969 by Aylwin with a wooden chapel, the new stone building was dedicated in 974 to Our Lady, St Benedict and all holy virgins. With St Oswald as its first abbot, the Benedictine monastery was soon enriched by endowments from Aylwin, (including the Isle of Ramsey and all its pools and marshes), his wife and St Oswald – its privileges being confirmed by charter of King Edgar in 975.

In the time of kings Cnut and Edward the Confessor the abbey managed to maintain and increase its prosperity and although somewhat diminished by the ravages of the Norman conquerors the house survived complete with its English abbots until 1113. By the time of the Domesday Survey, the abbey held 24 manors in Huntingdonshire. Despite further problems – including occupation by Geoffrey de Mandeville until his death at the siege of Burwell Castle, and neglect of the abbey lands – the abbey was rejuvenated and at its height during the 12th and 13th centuries was home to 80 monks.

During the 12th century in the reign of Henry I, the abbey acquired the manor of Walton (Woodwalton) with its common rights from Walter de Bolebec and also Higney in 1134, a grange with earthworks and a surrounding ditch.

The centuries that followed saw increasing wealth and status for Ramsey. It had built up a fine library by the 15th century and was known as "Ramsey the Rich". The abbey was finally dissolved in 1539, and passed to Sir Richard Williams, nephew of Thomas Cromwell. Much of the abbey was systematically dismantled for stone to build some of the Cambridge colleges, but a part was retained and became the home of the Cromwells, until the Fellowes family took over in 1737. Now all that survives is the 15th-century gatehouse.

Crowland Abbey was probably founded after the death of St Guthlac in 715 by Ethelbald, King of Mercia, but its exact history is uncertain. Guthlac was a somewhat unlikely saint. The son of a Mercian lord, he

Medieval tile, Ramsey Abbey

led a violent and dissolute life until his mid-20s when he renounced that way of life and entered Repton Monastery. Looking for a more solitary life he took up residence in 699 on the wilderness island of Crowland where he lived for many years as a recluse. The original abbey was destroyed and the community slaughtered by the Danes in 866 and despite being re-founded in the reign of King Edred, it was again destroyed by fire in 1091, rebuilt but again much of it burnt down in 1170. Following a further re-building the abbey then prospered, it was dissolved around 1540.

Cistercian
Sawtry Abbey
The monastery of Sawtry was founded in 1147 by Simon de Senliz. This was the only house in the fens of the 'White Monks' of the Cistercian order, who lived by particularly strict rules. Unlike Ramsey, this house was not particularly large or wealthy but that did not stop its incumbents arguing with the abbeys of Ramsey and Thorney over fishing and other land rights. It is likely that Monks Lode was constructed early in its history to provide a link to Whittlesea Mere to transport stone for construction. This caused a dispute, recorded in Ramsey Abbey's Chronicles, as it gave Sawtry access to the precious fishing and other rights around the Mere. It was resolved in 1192 by the Lode being allowed to remain to transport stone for Sawtry Abbey's construction. The last abbot took up his post in 1534 after which the abbey was dissolved and much of its structure was destroyed. Any remaining stone was taken for road building on Abbey Farm in the 19th century.

Ely
The first religious settlement on the site was founded in c.673 by St Etheldreda, wife of the Northumbrian king Ecgfrith, but was probably destroyed by the Vikings in 870. By 957, we know that the Isle of Ely had found its way into the hands of the West Saxon royal house, and in c.970 – with King Edgar's approval – the monastery was re-founded by Æthelwold, bishop of Winchester, after which it flourished and became a cathedral in 1109.

Ely Cathedral [CG]

Whittlesea Mere

The *Chronicon Petriburgense*, written in the 12th century and translated by Philemon Holland in 1637, reveals more information on Whittlesea Mere's ancient fisheries: "*Now here is described the extent of these waters and marshes, lest any one through ignorance should be injured. How the pool that is called Witelsmere, with its fisheries, marshes, and waters is bounded. In the north part of the pool is a water by name Merelade going out of the river Nen, where is the northern boundary of the pool itself. This (Merelade) with its marshes, adjoins it (the mere) having at the end one fishery called Aethemuthe. In the east part are two pools called Wellepol and Trendmere. Between these pools is a narrow water two furlongs long, called Trendmere Bece, having in it two fisheries. There is also a narrow water one mile long called Falet, having in it one fishery. In that part between Witlesmere and Kyngesdelf, where is the eastern boundary is a marshy space three miles broad, having in it a narrow water called Thescuf, and a wood called Ragreholt. In the south part is a narrow water three furlongs long, called Scelfremere Bece, having in it two fisheries. At the end of this is a pool called Scelfremere, having at its southern region a narrow water called Ubbe mere-lade, half a mile long. At the head of this, that is at the end of the pool, is one fishery. Halfway in this water, is a place on the opposite side in the marsh called Aldwines Barwe, where is the southern boundary. In the west part is a narrow water two furlongs long called Trendmere Bece, having in it one fishery. At the end of this is a pool called West Trendmere. There is also in that part waters whose names are Dreig mere, Wellepool, Withibusce mere, Langemere, Keninges, and Muscle mere. There is also a water one mile long and up to the land, called Deop Bece, having in it one fishery...*"

Medieval ditch – Stonea

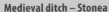

labour led to rising labour rates and arguably to the peasants' revolt of 1381. But there was a positive side and some surviving peasants could shake off the yoke of feudalism and move up the ladder to become the country squires of the next century.

Church influence remained strong on the fens with increased wealth and patronage by successive monarchs. Major dyke creations included Wheatley's drain on the western edge of Woodwalton Fen NNR, which came under the ownership of Ramsey Abbey for summer sheep grazing and hay mowing. Fishing remained an important activity and caused much strife between rival abbeys.

Despite the regular upkeep of the inland waterways, silting up of the sea-borne channels was preventing drainage to the sea, and serious floods occurred particularly in the Norfolk and Lincolnshire fens nearer to the sea, where earth banks collapsed under the press of waters.

The Reformation – fenland passes out of local control

While the great Abbeys continued their management of the fens, especially around Ramsey and Ely, fenland life continued much as usual, but political and religious events were about to change lives and the waterland forever. Henry VIII's marital difficulties and the pressing need to provide an heir, brought him into conflict with the Pope and drove him to embrace the new Protestantism of Luther. As the monasteries owed their allegiance to Rome, they became a legitimate target for the new anti-Catholic king. They were also a convenient source of wealth for the insatiable royal coffers. The entire structure of the monasteries was dismantled at a stroke and set the scene for the demolition of the delicately balanced management of the fenland. Sawtry Abbey was disbanded in 1536 and destroyed soon after, followed by Ramsey, Thorney and others. The abbey lands were sold to those who could afford it. Some were local landowners like the Earl of Bedford, but others came from outside the fen and had little understanding or interest in the old ways of life.

The dissolution of the monasteries was about to dissolve fenland itself. The waterways were abandoned, flooding became more frequent and the system began to be viewed as one in need of 'improvement'.

Wildlife

The wildlife of the fens probably remained richer on the fens than other drier areas where agriculture had been more successful. At the same time, attitudes to wildlife had become more brutal, more linked to exploitation than the almost spiritual regard of earlier generations. The harvest taken each day from the ditches and moors was bound to be unsustainable.

The abundance of fish, eels and birds referred to in early monastery records is difficult for the modern observer to comprehend. The reason for the survival of these species was not due to any altruistic notion by humans, rather the humans relied on these species for their own survival and so careful management was crucial.

The beaver was still present into the medieval period, but their numbers were much reduced. From having once been a common source of protein (beaver tail was a speciality)

From peasant to prince (almost)

The story of the de Thorpe family, the builders of Longthorpe Tower, illustrates the fortunes of some families who escaped the bonds of 12th century serfdom to become wealthy landowners in their own right. William, who died at the end of the 12th century, was a serf to the de Waterville family, but was freed to become a clerk to Peterborough Abbey. He must have become fairly well-off, because his son Thurstan held lands in the manor of Longthorpe, and his grandson William II was sufficiently wealthy to build the hall and great chamber of Longthorpe House. It was William's grandson, Robert, a distinguished lawyer, who built the tower and commissioned the wall paintings. He was finally knighted in 1320 – a successful journey from peasant to knight.

Longthorpe Tower

Population

It is impossible to view the relationship between landscape and humans without exploring population size and rates of growth or decline. Much of the development of technology employed by farmers such as the transition from the simple ard to the plough and horses replacing oxen, was related to demands for more food to feed increasing numbers of people. While some post-Roman cultivated land may have become 're-wilded' through abandonment, there was continuous cultivation during the Dark Ages, which accelerated after the Norman conquest.

Estimates of the population of Britain in the Roman period have been put at between 2 and 3.7 million (Salway 2002, Pryor 2010), almost all of whom lived in the countryside. Even this may be an underestimate, but after the departure of the legions, there appears to have been quite a rapid expansion of Saxon settlements, followed by great fluctuations in population size. A sharp drop in the 4th and 5th centuries may have been as much due to inter-tribal conflicts and invasions from Vikings. Certainly life was characterised by a battle with a cooling climate, making farming a difficult process with lower yields and an inability to support any growing population. A slow rise followed until the Norman conquest, but the population was probably still less than in Roman times. Between the Domesday Book in 1086 and late 13th century, however, the population of England may have more than doubled.

The 14th century brought the increase to a sharp halt, when famine and the plague reduced the population by almost half. By 1600, however, numbers had risen steeply to an estimated 4 million (Crane 2016).

Hungry mouths need feeding, and fenland drainage was seen as a route to increased food.

and hunted for their skins they became a delicacy only for the wealthy by the medieval period – a sure sign that numbers were in steep decline. No doubt their activities in damming waterways and causing local flooding also did little to endear them to the fen-men struggling to contain the waters for their own benefit. New evidence suggests, however, that in fact some populations managed to survive for several centuries, living without their obvious lodges in deeper rivers (Coles 2016).

Conclusion

Compared with the 10 millennia of pre-history, the 15 centuries following the Roman invasion saw monumental changes in the English landscape and the way in which people lived and related to their environment. Successive invasions, political upheaval and wars, combined with technological and social changes transformed whole regions. During the 400 years of Roman occupation, salt panning and drainage caused major changes in the fenland landscape, too, but after their departure, this probably remained the most stable of all lowland areas. Only those with intimate knowledge of the bogs and marshes could safely navigate its waterways and their way of life was known only to a few.

Worsening weather caused rapid peat formation during the Anglo-Saxon period, and the Holme bog grew considerably, but people adapted to withstand this. Understanding and manipulating water levels allowed them to establish co-operative grazing and cropping, while also creating and maintaining conditions which suited a rich diversity of wildlife.

The activities of these generations are carved through the land in a labyrinth of ditches, banks and field patterns. Famine and disease were never far away but the survivors had learnt the hard way how to live in a world of encroaching peat, bogs and floods. Fenlanders were independent and skilled at living within the resources available to them.

An emerging influence throughout this period was that of religion. Not only did the monasteries dominate fenland life, but religious thought began to influence the relationship between humans and wild Nature. Ironically, perhaps, it was the dismantling of the monastic houses on the fens, which was the catalyst for the immense change which was about to come about. It would be agricultural production for profit which would dictate the state of the fen landscape of the future, and any spiritual connection was of little concern.

Far from being the empty wildland as originally thought, the fens were a rich and productive resource that was used to the full by local farmers and communities. Throughout Saxon and Viking incursions, monastic development, ruin and revival, life in the fenland remained concentrated on the day-to-day essentials of putting food on the table in a way which perpetuated the resource in which they lived.

Increased agricultural production in other parts of Britain during the medieval period had a major effect on many species. There is no evidence for bears surviving much after the departure of the Romans and lynx were gone by the 7th century, while Wild Boar had certainly been hunted to extinction by the 13th century.

Unlike these other areas, however, the fens probably remained well populated with plants and animals. Until the dissolution of the monasteries, the fen wetland sustained a wide range of many species, and Roman introductions such as pheasant and fallow deer survived in high enough numbers to become part of the modern fauna. To what extent it remained a place of wilderness depends very much on the perspective from which it is viewed. By modern standards, the medieval fen might seem a wildlife-rich Garden of Eden, but a time-travelling Bronze Age resident of Must Farm would be aghast at the extent of drainage, pasture and cultivation.

From the time of the glaciers to the end of the 16th century, the Great Fen area had seen immense changes. From dry to wet, forest to marsh, sea to bog, it had been moulded by natural forces and human exploitation, but had remained as a wetland resource for almost 2,000 years. The lessons learned by the early ancestors had been refined into methods of wetland management which had both sustained human communities and provided for an incredible wildlife resource. It may be that the harvesting of this resource for food was leading to a decline in species, but it was positively benign compared to the brutal and sustained attack on the wetland ecosystem which was about to take place. Organised and sustained drainage would decimate the wetland ecosystem and the habitats in which plants and animals lived. It would be a wildlife disaster with few parallels, and destroy a way of life for countless fen people.

The Great Endeavour

In the centuries before the Civil War, fenland had retained much of its wildlife habitat while providing a vital resource for the growing human population. Its peoples had withstood invasion, adapted to new lifestyles and become skilled at harvesting the natural wealth of the ever-changing yet constant waterland. It was a life that was far from luxurious, but also far from the starvation which often haunted other areas of England, but ultimately, it was a life doomed to extinction.

It was a combination of factors which resulted in wholesale drainage of the fens. Changed perception of the value of a 'wild' landscape, land becoming available, the lure of increasing grain prices and wealthy individuals looking for profitable investments all conspired together. There would be many obstacles and consequences along the way, for while the 'Great Endeavour' was great indeed, it was an undertaking of immense difficulties, bringing many of its investors to financial ruin. Discontent among the native population also provoked violent conflict, but facilitated by Dutch expertise and technological advances, a process started which would continue for hundreds of years and virtually eliminate the wetland ecosystem.

If the water people expected some return to independence after Henry VIII removed the power of the monasteries, they were to be bitterly disappointed. The result was the reverse – the fabric of monastic buildings was exported to Cambridge to construct the new colleges and it was those very colleges which would be granted many of the rich fenland pickings, some of which they own to this day. Ramsey and Sawtry Abbeys virtually disappeared and the vibrant life of abbots and monks, literature, art and learning became ghosts in the mists of the abandoned marshes. Monastic land came onto the open market, encouraging wealthy business-men and favoured Tudor courtiers to get a stake in the potential riches of the fens. The wet meadows and meres passed out of local influence to the new landlords.

The dreary and unproductive 'wastes' might have seemed a golden opportunity for the investors, but they had little knowledge of how to maintain the waterways. The fabric of the system began to fall into disrepair and flooding became more frequent.

As the prospective drainers had no idea of how the system worked, they were at a loss as to how to 'improve' it for profit. Certainly, they would get no help from the local people, whose livelihood was rapidly disintegrating, so they had to wait for yet another group of 'invaders' to show them how it could be done.

Whittlesea Mere memorial plaque [SW]

Portrait of Henry VIII by Hans Holbein (1540, Galleria nazionale d'arte antica, Rome) [Wikipedia Commons]

Martin Luther by Lucas Cranach

Following Martin Luther's declaration against the excesses of the Catholic church in 1517, the rise of the 'pro-testants' in the Netherlands brought vicious retaliation from the establishment, prompting mass-killings and religious persecution. Thousands of Walloons and Flemish fled to England and were welcomed by Henry VIII. Many settled in the fens, where Sir William Russell – who had been involved with the Dutch wars against Spain – enlisted their help to drain part of his estates in Thorney. His son, the 4th Earl of Bedford, would have far wider aspirations.

The General Sewers Act of 1531 and the Statute of Sewers of the following year attempted to give some impetus to the drainage, but neither achieved a great deal. Towards the end of Queen Elizabeth 1's reign, however, the General Drainage Act of 1600 signalled a point when *"draining the great level began to become a public care"* (Walton p41). One of the greatest obstacles was that the fen commoners had no money to contribute to any grand works (or indeed would want to). With no central funds or sufficient revenue from the Commissioners, the only alternative was for landowners to raise the money themselves. So began the rise of the 'Adventurers' – wealthy investors who would be rewarded with drained land which would hopefully generate enough income to recompense their initial outlay... and more. The idea was prompted by King James 1, who became frustrated by the lack of progress, particularly after the disastrous flood of 1603, and *"would not suffer any longer the said land to be abandoned to the will of the waters"*. It also introduced the concept of the 'Undertakers' – those who would be contracted to actually carry out the works. Little appears to have been achieved by James' intervention, except for Sir John Popham's 1605 scheme to drain 6,000 acres of land near Upwell by cutting a 9 km drain from the Nene to the Well Creek at Nordelph (Popham's Eau). Other projects in the Isle of Ely and Upwell also achieved some relief – particularly Sir Charles Tindell's scheme at Waldersea – but there was always local opposition, especially if there was any foreign involvement.

Dutch courage

Jan van Boelen was just 16 and was serving as a gunner's mate on board the Dutchman *Patientia* when the fleet of ships was attacked by the British off Portand Bill in 1653.

"It was a long battle over several days and at first I thought we would be victorious, but then we had run out of shot and were captured by the English. We were taken ashore and imprisoned. Conditions were terrible and there were many Scottish prisoners there from the English Civil War, too, who received appalling treatment. Then one day we were ordered to march. It took forever, and my shoes were in shreds when we arrived in a country not unlike my native Zeeland. It was winter, and the mists were freezing and we had little shelter. We were given long-handled shovels and told to dig some new drains. Can you believe it? – there was a rumour that the man who had designed all these huge dykes was a Dutchman! Anyway, we dug for all we were worth but some of them tried to get away. I saw one man shot in the back, then they just threw him into the bank and covered him up. It was brutal. And the locals! Well if you got left in a small group you had better watch out, because they hated us and what we were doing and they attacked us lots of times. In one place they put up a gallows and said they'd hang us!"

James' successor, Charles I, was also short of cash. Although at first disinterested in the fenland, he soon realised the potential profit in draining some of the royal estate in Hatfield Chase in Yorkshire (around what is now Thorne Moors NNR). This crucial step in the drainage story introduced the most influential of all the drainers – Cornelius Vermuyden, whom Charles engaged in 1626. The Hatfield drainage scheme was a success, but was not received well locally due to its Dutch finance and execution. Riots and murder ensued, not to mention law suits by commoners who had lost the rights to their land. Other schemes were also attempted – like those of the Duke of Arundel – but lacked the skill of the Dutch engineer and were less effective.

Vermuyden's work encouraged the Commissioners of Sewers to propose the drainage of the Great Level, prompted by veiled threats from the king that he "*should not be constrained to use his regal power*" if work didn't proceed without delay. Vermuyden was contracted for the job, but his demand for a large area of land as payment and the opposition to him as a foreigner soon persuaded the Commissioners to approach Francis Russell, the Earl of Bedford, instead. The agreement with Bedford was concluded at a meeting of the Lynn Commissioners in 1630 and was dubbed the 'Lynn Law'. The Earl was not about to commit himself unreservedly, however, and the agreement included a phrase that if: "*by sudden waters, which shall not lie longer on the lands than in convenient time the same may pass away again, shall not be held or esteemed to be a not draining thereof*". In short, the scheme would guarantee summer dry ground only. Nor was he intending or able to bear the entire financial burden, but engaged to share the cost through an Indenture with 13 other investors (many

Cornelius Vermuyden

Cornelius Vermuyden was born in 1595 in Zeeland and trained as an engineer. He came to the public eye after his works to embank the Thames and was the leading figure in the draining of fenland for about 40 years from 1626. Despite his undoubted skills as an engineer he lacked a full understanding of fenland ecology and particularly the fact that as the peat dried the land level would fall, creating fresh drainage needs for the future and compromising fen drainage for centuries. Although rising to great eminence, he lost his considerable wealth because of the costs of drainage. Despite being knighted in 1629 and later becoming a British citizen, it seems that he died in obscurity at Westminster around 1677. (Rotherham 2013)

Cornelius Vermuyden by Michiel Jansz. van Miereveld (1567–1641)

from outside the fens). As these Adventurers were able to assign their share to others there were eventually up to 200 investors involved, many of whom had no connection with the fen whatsoever, merely seeing it as a road to profit. Ironically, the earl did not have the expertise to plan the work, so Vermuyden re-entered the scene.

Francis Russell, 4th Earl of Bedford by Henry Bone

The work was beset with problems from the start. Vermuyden's plans were not universally accepted, and were challenged by another Dutchman, Jan Westerlake, who proposed a cheaper and possibly more effective alternative. Second, the opposition which had bedevilled the Hatfield scheme was repeated in earnest by the Cambridgeshire men.

Despite the problems, the initial scheme was considered complete by 1637, but it was to be a short-lived celebration. Within a year, disappointment at the lack of winter dry ground and the disproportionate amount of land allotted to the Adventurers and Undertakers led to the scheme being declared defective. At this point the king himself took a hand – in part to avail himself of more land which might make a profit – and Vermuyden was again engaged to further the works. In order to help this along he drafted his *'Discourse'* on drainage in 1638 which, amongst other things, hotly opposed the embankment of more drains, introducing instead the idea of sacrificial washlands which would dissipate the water in times of flood. He also proposed the division of the levels into North, Middle and South. The Civil War and Charles'

Oliver Cromwell's house in Ely

execution interrupted further progress but Cromwell himself kept the idea of drainage alive during his tenure as governor of the Isle of Ely. In 1649 Vermuyden found himself with yet another contract in the 'Fenland Project', which was essentially intended to make the summer grounds winter-dry.

By the 1650s opposition from local people was at its height, whipped into action (if they had needed to be) by Oliver Cromwell, who maintained that King Charles was backing the scheme for his own profit entirely and cared little for their welfare. From 1651, opposition was further fuelled when Cromwell sent thousands of prisoners-of-war from the Scottish and Dutch campaigns to dig the drains in filthy conditions. This ended many a life in the slime and ooze of the dykeside banks, where attempting an escape meant certain death. Even in the towns, opponents complained that the decline in water levels was adversely affecting navigation and their trade routes to and from the sea.

Ironically, it was Cromwell who disrupted the drainage efforts when his forces broke the dams to flood some areas in order to isolate the king's troops during the Civil War. During this time the 'Adventurers' regained control and the second part of the drainage of the 'Great Fen' began. This huge project included cutting the 40-foot drain from Ramsey to Welches dam and improvements to Bevill's Leam east of Whittlesea Mere, but it brought several of the Adventurers to financial ruin. Much of the land produced nothing like the return which had been expected and some newly-drained land was sold to pay off debts. Nonetheless the works were considered sufficiently successful for a thanksgiving service to be held in 1652.

The legacy of Vermuyden is beyond dispute, but he had also made two crucial mistakes. He did not appreciate the way in which the restricted outfalls to the sea would impede successful drainage, and failed to recognise the effect that of lowering the water table would have on the peat level. In 1664 Colonel Dodson, warned that the peat would shrink, but imagined that this would be a short-lived phenomenon and could be solved by deepening the drain bottoms. The reality was that as the land level fell, the peat banks of the drains became ever-more unstable and were repeatedly overtopped by high flows, flooding the lower-lying land.

Beyond Vermuyden

Not only was the engineering difficult, but the works continued to be opposed. In 1632 Robert Castel from Glatton staged a fierce rebellion. *"We weren't goin' to let them take away our grazing lands. When they tried to drive our cattle away and dig new drains, me and my missus and a whole lot of Holme villagers we set on them with our scythes and pitchforks. We drove our sheep onto the fen. We tried to get the people in Yaxley and other places to petition the king to stop the drainage but it weren't no use. We've worked these fens for hundreds of years but all they want now is to drain them and kill off all the birds and fish and grow lousy Dutch crops for their own profit"*.

Local discontent reached such a pitch that in 1653 an edict was issued to deter *"those who do assemble together in a riotous manner and by violence dispossess the Adventurers for draining the great levels of the Fenns"*. Costs also spiralled – the Fenland Project since 1630 may have cost anything up to half a million pounds – the equivalent of perhaps £150 million today – and even the new Duke of Bedford (the 5th Earl) had to sell land to honour his debts. The new sluice at Denver collapsed under the weight of water in 1713 and would not be reinstated for 30 years, and doubts remained as to the sanity of attempting such work at all. Writing as early as 1622 Camden wonders *"was it right to meddle at all in that which God hath ordained"* and in 1665 Fuller reminds his readers that *"many have burnt their fingers in these waters and instead of draining the fens have emptied their own estates"*.

Despite all the set-backs, the reclaimed land did help Britain to become a net exporter of grain by the end of the 17th century and in 1663 the General Draining Act established the Bedford Level Corporation. Unfortunately, ineffective management, the destruction of their

Dyke digging

London offices in the Great Fire and lack of money hampered the corporation's activities to the extent that by 1688 there were further complaints of the deterioration of the system

Technological advance

Despite all the work of Bedford and Vermuyden, by the close of the 18th century much of the fenland was again covered by water. In 1794 Charles Vancouver considered that there was *"a deplorable state of drainage"* and *"miserable state of cultivation"* in Cambridgeshire. Writing a report to the Board of Agriculture in the same year, William Donaldson's opinion of 6,000 or so acres of common land fen in the Soke of Peterborough, is a useful illustration

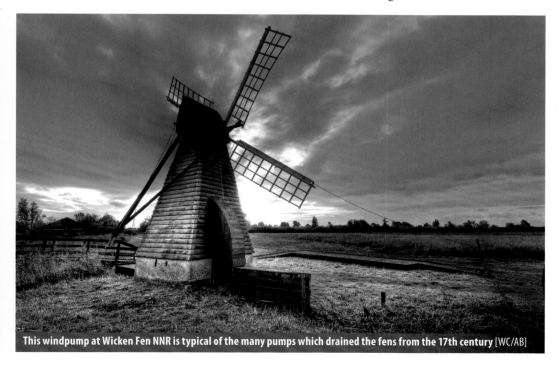

This windpump at Wicken Fen NNR is typical of the many pumps which drained the fens from the 17th century [WC/AB]

of the opinion by this time. Donaldson maintained that the commoners were not really interested in getting best value from the land, and recommended that it should be divided up into private farms "*of proper size*" and cultivated, which would increase its value ten-fold and bring additional employment to the area. He doesn't venture exactly how this could be achieved but insists that "*bringing the commons and waste lands under cultivation... will certainly promote or maintain an increased population*". He also considered that the benefits of employment and food production could be: "*effected without being attended with any bad consequences whatsoever*". This was the reality of opinion by this time. Those outside the immediate environs of the fen really could not see anything but profit and increased food production as a product of the drainage. The consequences for wildlife was not an issue and there was considerable prejudice against the fen people, who were regarded as wild and opposed to change.

Clearly something had to be done. Schemes like the straight cut in 1721 to the north of Moreton's Leam to improve flow along the river Nene were just not enough to guarantee dry farmland. It was technology which came to the rescue. The first wind-powered pumps were encouraged by an order of the Corporation in 1678 and soon would be seen everywhere across the flat landscape. By 1748 Thomas Neale wrote "*I myself, riding... from Ramsey to Holm, about 6 miles across the fens, counted forty in my view*". The turning sails were never out of sight, like the great wind turbines which are springing up across the fens today. Marvellous as they were, however, the wind-pumps led to another problem. The amount of water which could now be delivered into the main drains often overwhelmed their capacity to carry it, and coupled with the constricted outfalls to the sea, caused havoc. The problem had simply been moved from the local farms to further down-stream.

The effect of the restricted outfalls had been ignored for years, but soon became a serious issue. Conflicting opinions of how to solve the 'outfall problem' raged for years and the situation did not improve until major projects like those of Sir John Rennie. He rebuilt the Denver sluice in 1825 and advocated other improvements, combined with better 'puddling' of the banks with clay.

One major obstacle which still stood in the way of effective drainage was the unreliability of the wind. Although the medieval banks had been replaced by deep channels, and outfalls to the sea were gradually improved, water could still only be moved from low-lying fields to higher-level lodes by pumping. The only way to pump was using wind-power, and the wind does not always blow, particularly after storms which are often followed by calm weather! We can imagine the excitement when it was realised how the newly-discovered steam power could be applied to water pumping. Proposed as early as 1789, the first pump to be operational was in 1817 at Sutton St Edmund near Wisbech, followed in 1820 by another at Bottisham Fen. Perhaps it was this pump which spelt the end for the Large Copper *Lycaena dispar* butterfly which was last seen here in 1851. Five years later, two scoop-wheel pumps at Deeping Fen were capable of draining 25,000 acres!

Mr and Mrs Gotobed

Over the next few years, the lazy sails of windpumps were replaced by the belching smoke of steam-pumps. For 40 pumps driven by the wind, one steam engine would suffice. It was no mean feat to install and work one of these beasts. The scoop-wheel system involved very heavy machinery and the wheel itself could be 8 metres across, so considerable space and expertise were needed to operate the system.

Despite the steam power, a more efficient system was clearly needed to match the increasing demand for dry land and it was a further technological advance which would write the final chapter in the drainage story. The centrifugal pump, was perfected by John Appold (Appold's Impeller) and won him a medal at the Great Exhibition of 1851. Local squire William Wells of Holme was much taken by the idea and had one transported to his fenland estate at Holme. Whittlesea Mere was seeing its last days.

What if…?

In my 24 years as warden of the fenland NNRs I often used to wonder how they might have been had the mere not been drained. What if the thousands of hectares in between had stayed wet, the peat still 3 metres above my head and the eels too numerous to count? What if the splash of water was a Beaver hauling logs rather than a Coot with a stick? What if…

The battle for Whittlesea Mere

The zenith of Whittlesea Mere as a lake and surrounding wetland was probably in the early medieval period, but works to divert the river Nene and ecclesiastical drainage had begun to reduce the input of fresh waters. By the time of William Wells, the waters had been receding for centuries. The Saxon farmer, with his herds on the summer meadows and the bounty of fish on the Mere, would have been horrified if he had seen the waters of the 17th century. Bodger's map of 1786 shows an area of about 3.5 × 2.5 miles in extent (about 7,500 acres (3,000 ha), but when major drainage began in 1850s, Wells considered the Mere itself to be no more than a tenth of that area just 2 feet 6 inches (750 cm) deep (Wells 1860).

Although the greatest lake of the lowlands had been reduced to no more than a large puddle by the Victorian era, it had been witness to a long and colourful phase of our history. Created during the wet phase of the Iron Age, the waters had seen the Romans come and go, and sustained the lives of generations of fen people. It had born King Cnut across its treacherous waters (whilst drowning some of his party), resisted the best attempts of the Dutch drainers, and hosted regattas and skating events well into the 19th century. In 1774, Lord Orford's famous voyage along the waterways of East Anglia brought him to Whittlesea and Trundle Meres, where he is perhaps the last person to have navigated into the ancient Trundle Mere, which was drained in the 1840s. He met with various adventures on the way,

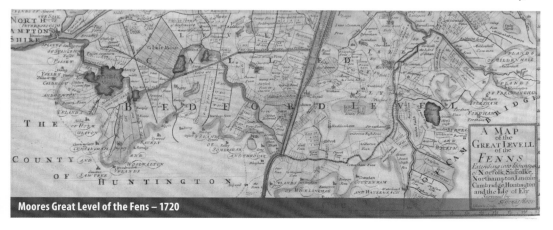

Moores Great Level of the Fens – 1720

some of which are humorously recorded by youngsters from King's Lynn in a Utube video (**www.utube/lordorfordvoyage**).

Previous schemes, using the Nene to drain the Mere, had been proposed by John Rennie, but problems with the outfall and its distance from the sea had mitigated against them.

In 1844, the Middle Level Act had enabled Wells and his partners, including the Lord de Ramsey, to raise £200,000 for the drainage (a further £230,000 would be found for later works). A long cut was made, intending to lower levels and increase fall, but the problems this created for navigation made this ineffective. In 1851 a new ditch was made – Marshland cut – and lowering the ditch beds was successful in persuading the waters to flow and empty the mere by gravity, but in winter it filled up again!

Much has been made of the opposition of the fen people to the drainage of the 17th and 18th centuries. The independent life of fisher and punt-gunner, reed and peat-cutter was replaced by ploughman and corn merchant and it must have been a time of great change and heartache for those who for generations had so been intimately reliant on the bounty of the fens.

Skating

The early 19th century witnessed some cold winters and skating was a popular past-time, including fierce competitions. Turkey Smart was the first of several generations of fen skaters who honed their skills on the frozen waters.

An 1827 newspaper article in the Huntingdon, Bedford & Peterborough Gazette described a skating competition on the Mere:

"A skating match is run. Prize of a pig and a hat. Berry of Ramsey wins the pig and Germain of Whittlesea the hat. Prizes given by John Heathcote Esq. Mrs Gossip of Holme gave a sovereign for another race won by George Richardson of Yaxley."

(www.yaxleyhistory.org)

By the time of the Wells scheme, however, there seemed to be little dissent among the local people. Thousands turned up to witness the last waters seeping from the lake bed, and many came armed with baskets and carts to remove the eels and fish (largest 52 lb Pike – not very large!). Yet still there were still some visionaries who warned against the loss of the wetland. Even the agriculturalist Albert Pell questioned the validity of the drainage:

"The meres are bright, not with water, but with spring green and… with autumn gold. Spacious and substantial farm-houses and buildings have replaced the decoy and the charcoal-burners' camp, while the wattle and daub hut, with its thatched roof snug and picturesque, has disappeared for a modern brick substitute, answering indeed to the idea of decency and salubrity, but at the cost of rustic beauty and some domestic comforts."

Charlie Scholes with punt gun

Peat stacking

Willow eel traps

Imagination cannot do better than Wells' own description of the day when the mere waters were let out:

"The fading light of a blood-red sunset fell on the vast multitudes of figures scattered in all directions over the dreary waste of slimy ooze, it left on the mind the same sort of impression as is left by some of Martin's ambitious pictures". (John Martin, 1789–1854, was an English Romantic artist famous for his fantastical paintings).

Despite the conversion of the bright waters to a 'slimy ooze' it soon became clear that the waters would return without further measures. After consulting with engineers Easton and Amos, Wells purchased a 25 hp engine Appold pump which was transported along the new railway to Holme in December of 1851 and then duly installed at the eastern end of the Mere. The following November, ambitious plans for the new farms on the site of the Mere were shattered when heavy rains caused such a rise in dyke water levels around the mere that their banks burst and the bed was flooded– the waters were re-born! Such was the power of the pump, however, that within three weeks all was restored and the waters would never again return to their home of centuries. Because the drain feeding the pump had become

Holme Post

Before the Mere was pumped dry, William Wells had the foresight to install some timber piles to record peat shrinkage after drainage. It is rumoured that one of these may have survived for almost 100 years, but clearly it was thought that the timber would rot away, so a cast-iron pillar was fixed onto timber piles driven into the underlying clay in 1851/52. It has been disputed as to whether or not this was a post from the Great Exhibition of 1851 as it does not appear on any plans of the structure, but it may have been from an internal exhibition and there are others still holding up roofs in barns nearby. The post still stands today, although it was supplemented in 1957 by a lamp-post which is secured on a concrete foundation.

The Wells Dynasty

William Wells senior was a Chatham ship-builder who inherited the estate of Holme in 1769 from his wife's uncle, Thomas Truman. The estate remained in the family for almost a century, when it was sold to Lord de Ramsey. It was William's great-grandson, born at Holme in 1818 and also named William, who became an ardent agriculturalist and drained Whittlesea Mere.

The author at the original Holme Post. This was once the lowest place in Britain bu the land to the west is now even lower!

He was Liberal member of Parliament for Peterborough for some time and became president of the Royal Agricultural Society and also chairman of the Middle Level Commissioners. William was convinced of the need to drain the Mere and took pains to record both the method and the result of his labours.

He wrote extensively of the drainage, both in the Journal of the Royal Agricultural Society and in the Illustrated London News (1860). He referred to this account as: *"a record of the blotting out from the map of England of one of its largest inland sheets of water, and of the conversion of its bed into the site of thriving farms, as well as of the operations now being carried on for the reclamation of the peat-bog which surrounded the mere…"*

He delighted that, after drainage:
"on arriving by the Great Northern Railway, the chimney of the steam engine, which now maintains the drainage of the mere...is plainly visible three miles off towards the south-east".

silted, the pump could only work for short periods so the feeder drain was then deepened and smaller ditches from the mere bed were dug or renewed – some of which pierced the heart of the 3,000 year-old Holme Fen bog.

To stabilise the peat soil, it was decided to mix it with clay – 'dry-warping', which had proved successful on reclaimed land in Ireland. As the Whittlesea Mere clay was buried beneath 7 metres of peat, it was necessary to import it, so a steam-operated railway was installed to carry clay to line the ditch and then mix it into the Mere bed.

The following summer saw the bed crack and the bog surface collapse as the water continued to flow into the outside drains. Those of us who have witnessed the machines labouring in the newly-created wetlands where the waters of Whittlesea once flowed (Rymes Reedbed and Kester's Docking) might spare a thought for the labourers who tilled the emerging farmland by hand, as the surface could not support the weight of a horse. Their labours paid off and within three years pioneer crops of coleseed (much like modern oilseed rape) and Italian rye grass had been replaced by crops of wheat and oats.

A more intractable problem lay in the cultivation of the bog, but by 1860 no tenant had been found who was prepared to take the considerable risk of bringing this into production, so it was never farmed. Through thousands of years of growth and drought, sea lapping at its feet and the rise and fall of the mere, the great bog survived. A mighty birch wood has grown up over the dried-out mosses, but the original surface is still there, so there is potential to re-wet it. Perhaps the last 200 years of woodland are but another short chapter in the great bog's life.

Wells considered that the total area released from the Whittlesea Mere's waters for cultivation was 3,000 acres (1,200 ha) plus another 2,000 acres (800 ha) around the margins which would benefit from the drainage. He calculated that it produced £12,350 worth of crops including livestock, whereas the fishing, reed and sedge from the old Mere produced less than £100.

Fen tygers

Nobody seems to know when and where the term 'fen tyger' first emerged, but its use symbolises the often fierce and always independent nature of those who made the homes around the waters. Sly (2010) considers that the fen people are made up of a variety of ancient tribes and immigrants over thousands of years. In 1896 William Henry Wheeler described them as:

"Although their condition was very miserable, they never the less enjoyed a sort of wild liberty amidst the watery wastes, which they were not disposed to give up. Though they might alternatively burn and shiver with ague, and become prematurely bowed and twisted with rheumatism, still the fen was their native land, such as it was and their only source of subsistence, precious though it might be".

The most extreme were the freedom-fighters like Boudicca and Hereward, whilst others quietly got on with their lives in the face of Saxon rampage, Viking pillage and Norman feudalism. They perfected the technique of living from the bounty of the waters and grazing the meadows where they learnt to control the water to best effect. In most peoples' eyes, however, it was the tygers' resistance to the drainers which is most colourful. The draining was set to destroy the very essence of their being and it is little surprise that they did not take it lying down.

As early as 1646 the 'anti-projector' (projector = undertaker) movement had orchestrated furious opposition to the drainers' view that: *"all the fens is a meere quagmire, and that it is a level hurtfully surrounded, and of little or no value"*. In truth, the movement argued, it gave employment and sustained large numbers of people through gathering *"reeds, fodder, thacks, turves, flags, hassocks, segg, fleggweed for fleggeren collars, mattweed for churches..."*. So deep were the feelings that in 1674 Swavesey residents had threatened to erect a gallows for the benefit of the hapless ditch diggers there, and in 1722 drainers were attacked by 1,000 angry residents of Wisbech. *"What is coleseed and rape"* they argued *"but Dutch commodities and trash and trumpery?"*.

Although complaining about the taxes due to the Middle Level, Wells concluded that: *"... the satisfaction of contemplating the changed aspect of the district, as well as the improved condition of the neighbouring poor, both in respect of constant well-paid employment and better health, is alone a never-failing and substantial interest for the capital expended"*.

Wildlife

When Queen Elizabeth I breathed her last in 1603, she left a fenland where wildlife still maintained healthy populations of birds, invertebrates and mammals. Cranes and White Storks, Swallowtail butterflies, Eels and Otters still abounded in the marshes and meres, and flowering plants provided abundant nectar. The balance of survival, though, was always unequal, so it is debatable to what degree the wildlife could have lasted even without the drainage. Certainly, the shift towards external markets with their insatiable demand placed an

Common Cotton-grass *Eriophorum angustifolium* [NE]

intense burden on populations, and there were signs of a decline in many species even before the Norman invasion, such as the beaver. Even though wildlife diversity was far richer than it is now, the 16th-century fen was a pale imitation of what it had once been.

Swallowtail *Papilio machaon* [PB]

White Storks *Ciconia ciconia* [PG]

Conclusion

There can be few other endeavours in which technology and human determination has destroyed an ecosystem and way of life so comprehensively as the fenland drainage, but we need to understand the context in which it happened.

On the one hand the 'Great Endeavour' was an undertaking of unmatched bravery, ingenuity and foresight. The commitment of a small number of people transformed a huge wetland into a land of corn and vegetable production which was a rival to any in the Empire. Despite financial, social and technical obstacles, the Adventurers and their Undertakers had stuck to their guns and achieved the seemingly impossible. In their eyes, a 'wasteland' had become a 'wonderland'.

On the other hand, the fenland drainage is tinged with more than a little sadness. Ironically, sadness for the investors themselves, many of whom lost everything in the enterprise and ended up deprived of their estates and fortunes in a project which had proved just too ambitious and not worth the promised returns. Even Vermuyden himself never really reaped the reward he might have expected.

Sadness too, for the 'fen tygers', whose entire way of life was swept away by the removal of the resource which had sustained them for centuries. For them it was a catastrophe not unlike the slaughter of millions of bison which brought the First Nation peoples of North America to their knees. The riches of the fen wetlands had been destroyed by people who failed to understand the wider consequences, and appeared to care little about the fate of the wild fenmen.

Lastly, sadness for the unimaginable richness of an ecosystem which would undoubtedly be a World Heritage Site if it had survived. For thousands of years, communities of wild animals and plants had adapted to natural climatic changes. Some had not survived, but many had withstood or adapted to the human impact on fenland. Humans and wildlife had evolved an almost symbiotic relationship with the marshlands which supported a level of biodiversity rarely seen today.

So, what drove them to do it? We may lament the loss of wildlife in the path of rapacious fortune-hunters, but it really was not that simple. The engines of change in human society have always been the same – population growth, economic vitality, politics and technology – and these were all part of the drainage story. Politics had caused centuries of wars, invasions and change of culture, but fenland life remained largely unaffected. Even the monastic dominance, which led to agricultural improvements and drainage, produced reliable supplies of food and other materials without destroying the resource itself. It was increasing demand for both food and economic return from external investors which brought a sea-change to fenland. Regarded by few as a rich resource, it became widely seen as an embarrassment to a developing nation and one which could be changed for the better. The needs of society as a whole were far more important than an isolated and misunderstood population of fierce 'tygers' living among the spirits and demons of the watery wastes.

There was also a growing view, often supported by the Church, that humans were in control and were justified in any endeavour which favoured their species. Life was often harsh, and attitudes to both Nature and humans reflected this. As we shall see in the next chapter, a more enlightened view would grow steadily into the first of the environmental 'campaigns' of the Victorian age, but for fenland it was too late.

In short, the drainage had simply been a natural response to what was widely considered as a noble enterprise for the greater good. Of all the events of fenland history, it was the drainage which has most influenced the shape of the fens today. The desire to extract maximum production from the peat ignored the lessons of the past, where the wetland resource had supported countless generations. While it may have promoted a few centuries of food production, it ultimately led to the destruction of a whole ecosystem and the soils which supported it. This was the background to a new awareness – Nature was not an inexhaustible resource, and without it our own existence was in peril.

It is in that context that we should consider later developments, examine the long-term effect of the destruction of the wetland ecosystem and enquire as to what really is the objective of the modern Great Fen, where there is growing clamour on the one hand for a return to 'wilderness', and on the other for ever-expanding economic growth.

Travellers, Poets and Campaigners

"It is such a country as a man would wish to see once for curiosity but would never desire to visit a second time. One view sufficiently imprints the idea" (Gilpin 1769).

"They have a beauty of their own, these great Fens, even now when they are dyked and drained, tilled and fenced, a beauty as of the sea, of boundless expanse and freedom" (Kingsley 1866).

Well nothing much changes. When I first came to fenland in 1991, chief warden Maurice Massey introduced me to the local saying: *"anyone can appreciate the mountains, but it takes a man or a poet to love the fens"*! There's truth in that. It may take years for the essence of the wide-skied fenland to work on the soul... or it may never happen at all. The flat, endless miles, the towering clouds, the 'lazy' wind – they expose the heart of your character. This is no 'chocolate-box' tourist destination. For landworkers – whether farmer or conservationist – it's hard and unforgiving; too wet and you sink, too dry and the soils blow away. For people in the towns and fenland villages, water is never far away and the spectre of the 1940s floods live on in many a hamlet. For some it saps the spirit, for others the freedom is liberating and

The fenland was not to Gilpin's taste

the wildlife – where you can find it – exhilarating. The unmistakable reek of wet peat, the continual hum of life in the reed and sedge beds, the autumn orange hue of the bog myrtle is a unique experience.

Love them or hate them – the fens have forever held people in their thrall. Breeding both wild people and wild creatures, they have been fought over, loved and cursed in equal measure. Why else would Angle, Saxon and Norseman spend so much energy fighting to gain the moors and bogs, meres and saltmarsh; hermits and monks retreat from the distractions of the secular world and 'Adventurers', (who we met earlier), risk all for the imagined riches from drained fenland?

As we have seen, fenland has been an ever-changing scene and its wildlife and people have changed with it. The view of the wild by a Mesolithic hunter or Bronze-Age warrior would be very different from that of a Norman peasant working the water meadows. The drainage investor wished for fields of corn for his money, not reedy swamps and bird-filled meres, the modern conservationist dreams of a Garden of Eden where humans and nature live in harmony. These changing views are important, because this is the background against which we view the fens today and ponder how they might look in the future.

Celia Fiennes is often cited as the first to describe the pre-drainage fens, but people would have always had opinions of their surroundings, long before the written word. We can only imagine how the earliest people felt – fear maybe. Children of Nature they may have been, developing an almost supernatural relationship with the native lakes and woods – but there was danger too, with wild animals lurking everywhere. As the axe and plough began to transform the wild into something more familiar, people would have had greater confidence in survival, but also a deeper empirical knowledge of the plants and animals which sustained them. This intimate knowledge went hand-in-hand with a respect and worship of the wild and its 'gods'. This resulted in the sacrifices of precious objects to the waters such as at Flag Fen, as well as the more gruesome human ritual killings like 'Pete Marsh'. Superstition flourished around the traditions of the shamans of course, and the ripening folklore of the fens was as much based on fear as any realistic experience. The Whittlesea 'Straw bear' is one such survivor of legend. On Plough Tuesday, which follows Twelfth Night, a boy or man would tour the town and dance for treats, all the while clad from head to foot in straw to resemble a bear. The origins are lost in time but have recently been revived after falling out of favour in the 20th century.

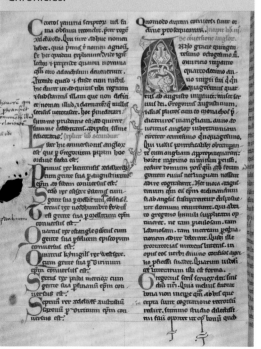

Henry of Huntingdon

Henry of Huntingdon was born in Lincoln. After succeeding his father to the Archdeaconry of Huntingdon in 1110 he embarked on his life work of the *Historia Anglorum*. He lived in Little Stukeley, a few miles south-west of the fen edge. Some of his earlier poetry praises the wild fenland beyond the confines of town and monastery. He started writing his *Historia* after 1123, drawing on both his own observations and earlier works such as the Anglo-Saxon Chronicles.

The 7th century warrior-monk, Guthlac, was one of the first to leave us a written account. Retreating to the marshes around Crowland, his dreams were populated by fenland demons battling with the new Christian ideals. Guthlac described it as: "*... a most dismal fen of immense size... it is a very long tract, now consisting of marshes, now of bogs, sometimes of black waters overhung by fog, sometimes studded with woody islands and traversed by the windings of tortuous streams*" Colgrave (2010).

Henry of Huntingdon wrote extensively in poetry and prose, particularly his *Historia Anglorum*, in which he sees the fens as: "*Beautiful to behold, washed by many flowing rivers, adorned by many meres, great and small and with many woods and islands*" (Greenway 1996).

Other medieval chroniclers were also euphoric about the 'delectable' Ramsey spring meadows. In the 12th century, they were: '*just as if painted with flowers which are looking at you merrily*' and '*Many fertile meads and pastures*' encircled Peterborough. William of Malmesbury delighted how '*the Plain [at Thorney] is as level as the Sea, which with the flourishing of its grass allureth the Eye, and so smooth that there is nothing to hinder him that runs through it*".

After the dissolution the monasteries and several serious floods, new landowners took a very different view of the 'unproductive wastes'. Rather than rich sources of food, materials and wildlife, they were seen as unused assets which, when drained, could produce healthy profits and food for a growing nation. It was at this time, 1697, that Celia Fiennes came riding her horse through the muddy lanes of England and glimpsed one of the last undrained wildlands – Whittlesea Mere and Holme Fen.

At the same time "*Ffrom Huntington we... Came in Sight of a great water on the Right hand about a mile off wch Looked Like Some Sea it being so high and of great Length: this is in part of the ffenny Country and is Called Whitlsome Mer, is 3 mile broad and six long. In ye Midst is a little jsland where a great Store of Wildfowle breeds, there is no coming near it; in a Mile or two the ground is all wett and Marshy but there are severall little Channells runs into it wch by boats people go up to this place. When you enter the mouth of ye Mer it lookes fformidable and its often very dangerous by reason of sudden winds that will rise Like Hurricanes in the Mer, but at other tymes people boate it round the Mer with pleasure. There is abundance of good ffish in it. This was thought to have been Sea some tyme agoe and Choak'd up and so remaines all about it for some miles a ffenny Marshy Ground for those little Rivers that runns into ye Sea some distance of miles.*"

An equestrian historian

Celia Fiennes was the daughter of Nathaniel Fiennes, a puritan and staunch Parliamentarian. She was born near Salisbury and moved to London in 1691. In an extraordinary feat for a woman of the time, she rode across much of England between 1684–1712 and visited the fens in 1697. Her impressions from her journal were later published in 1888 under the title *Through England on a side-saddle in the Time of William and Mary*. In the introduction to the published work, the Hon. Mrs Emily Griffiths says: "*The writer's diligent and attentive observation of details concerning the various counties through which she passed…seems worthy of notice and preservation…(and) gives a good idea of what England was like 200 years back*". In somewhat of an understatement she goes on: "*Celia Fiennes' diary almost takes the position of an historical document*". Legend has it that she may be the lady of the nursery rhyme 'Ride a cock horse to Banbury Cross', but there is no evidence for this.

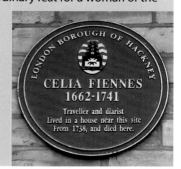

A century later, Daniel Defoe saw the fenland as quite mysterious and felt sympathy for those trapped within the confines of the fen vapours! When he visited the fens in 1723 as part of his "*A Tour in Circuits through the island of Great Britain*" he says:

"As these fens appear cover'd with water, so I observ'e too, that they generally at this latter part of the year appear also cover'd with foggs, so that when the Downs and higher grounds of the adjacent country were gilded by the beams of the sun, the Isle of Ely look'd as if wrapped up in blankets, and nothing to be seen, but now and then, the lanthorn or cupola of Ely Minster.

One could hardly see this from the hills and not pity the many thousands of families that were bound to or confin'd in those fogs and had no other breath to draw than what must be mixed with those vapours, and that steam which so universally overspread the county. But the people... live unconcern'd and as healthy as other folks, except now and then an ague, which they make light of...".

These two journals were remarkable in being the first attempt to record and categorise the landscape of England, rather than the religiously-biased accounts of Henry and Bede. They do not make much attempt to explore the attitude to, or indeed the existence of, raw nature being more concerned with the condition of fine houses and farmed estates. They concluded that while most people lived and worked close to the land, the fens in particular were wild, uncharted and inaccessible to all but the most intrepid traveller.

In the late 16th century, William Camden describes fenland as:

"Besides al this, the herb scordium, which also is called Water Germander, groweth plentifully here hard by the diches sides: but as for those fenny Ilands, Foelix, a writer of good antiquity, hath depainted them forth in these words: There is a fen of exceeding great largenes, which beginning at the banks of the river Gront, arising somwhere with sedge plots, in other places with blackewaters, yeelding a duskish vapour, with woods also among the Isles, and having many winding turnes of the banke, reacheth out in a very long tract from South to Northeast as farre as to the Sea" (Camden 1586).

The writings of Defoe and Fiennes were more travelogues than social comment, but were set against the anthropocentric view of the Tudor and Stuart period. This view maintained that all Nature had been created solely for the use of the human race and this was enshrined in religious teaching. Francis Bacon wrote at this time:

"Man, if we look to final causes must be regarded as the centre of the world insomuch that if man were taken away from the world the rest would seem to be all astray without aim or purpose".

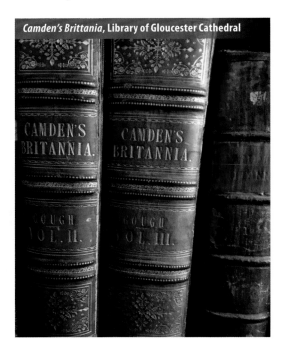

Camden's Brittania, **Library of Gloucester Cathedral**

The Venerable Bede

Bede spent the greater part of his life as a monk in the Benedictine monastery at Jarrow. Among many other works on biblical subjects he is mostly remembered for his *Historia Ecclesiastica Gentis Anglorum* (*The Ecclesiastical History of the English People*) which was completed in 731. It is considered that this was primarily a work documenting and commenting on the fortunes of the early church in Britain, so its historical accuracy is not always guaranteed.

Some years later the poet William Somerville would write:
   "The brute creation are his property, Subservient to his will and for him made".

The Enlightenment – changing views

It is at this point that changes in religious and scientific thought began to have a profound effect on the way that Nature was regarded. The development of the 'scientific' view of the natural world grew out of, not in spite of, biblical teaching and interpretation of the 16th and 17th centuries. There had been early beliefs, which developed over the centuries as humans became more aware of themselves as cognisant beings and of the world around them. This included all sorts of superstitions, such as fear of dragons, worshipping gods of the water, and all manner of less than desirable activities like human sacrifice. But the end result was an intimate relationship with the natural world.

By the Middle Ages it was considered that God and Nature were indivisible. Peter Harrison (2012) explores the process by which modern science developed out of existing and new religious thought. For example, Isaac Newton's scientific achievements of the 17th century were a product of his inherent belief that God had created laws of Nature. When Alexander Pope declared...
   "Nature and Nature's laws lay hid in night
   God said: 'Let Newton be!' and all was light".

... he was acknowledging that the Laws were already in place, what Newton did was to uncover them. The prevailing view until then was that laws of morality may belong to humans but the laws of nature were quite different, with inherent properties of their own. What Newton did, followed by Descartes, Boyle and other scientific philosophers and innovators, was to demonstrate that all things were subject to the same physical and chemical properties. The fact that the earth revolved around the sun was not the heresy that caused Galileo to confront the Inquisition, it was bald fact which explained the movement of celestial bodies. Rather than the development of scientific discovery being an obstacle to religious faith, it actually underscored it – the pre-existing Laws of Nature were intimately involved in all living organisms and so there was a closer connection between humans and other species than previously imagined. As Galileo explained, there were two 'Books' – one was the Bible and the other was the Natural World. Nature was not to be understood terms of allegorical interpretations of the Bible, but for its own importance. Plants and animals existed not for the use of humans, but in their own right.

After the Middle Ages, it was not until the Renaissance that ideas began to change and feed into the great movements of the 17th century that produced geniuses like Sir Isaac Newton. When the Rosicrucian movement was born in the early 17th century, it called for what we would now call a 'holistic' form of knowledge, bringing together religion, science and the arts. It never really caught on, but it might be argued that it was a missed opportunity to bring about a more holistic way of thinking, and that now the time has come for a renewed attempt to do so.

Science

William Turner was a physician and sometime clergyman from Northumberland, who was also a gifted naturalist. In 1544, he published *A Short and Succinct History of the Principal Birds noticed by Pliny and Aristotle* (Evans 1903) and went on to become the first to write a study of the healing properties of plants. His *A New Herball* was published in three volumes between 1551 and 1568, and was remarkable not only in its detailed and accurate descriptions of plants, but because it was written in English. This made it accessible to a far wider audience that the usual Latin tomes of the medical or scientific professions.

A century later, it was another Englishman, John Ray, who went on to classify plants according to their specific characteristics. Ray had been inspired by a treatise on plant morphology by Joachim Jung (*Isagoge Phytoscopia 1687*) and his early studies around the Cambridge fens are recorded in his *'A catalogue of plants growing around Cambridge'* (1660). Here, he developed his ideas of species; for the first time moncotyledons and dicotyledons were separated using features such as petals for identification and classification (*Historia Plantarum* 1686–1704). So influential was his work that Gilbert White considered:

"*... our countryman, the excellent Mr Ray, is the only describer who conveys some precise idea in every term or word, maintaining his superiority over his followers and imitators in spite of the advantage of fresh discoveries and modern information.*"

The Swede, Carl von Linne (Linnaeus), developed this work still further when he published his *Systema naturae* in 1735, the first time that a systematic account of the plant and animal kingdom was widely available. Linnaeus's work laid the foundations for further investigations of the natural philosophy. Theories of evolution were further explored by Jean-Baptiste Lamarck, and in 1844 Robert Chambers had anonymously published his *Vestiges of the Natural History of Creation* (Secord 1994). These were to be crucial supporting evidence to Chares Darwin's theory of natural selection.

Philosophers were also exploring the effects of the new 'profit-motivated actions of both agriculture and industry. In 1883, in his *Dialectics of Nature*, Friedrich Engels warned:

"*Let us not, however, flatter ourselves overmuch on account of our human conquest over nature. For each such conquest takes its revenge on us... at every step we are reminded that we by no means rule over nature like a conqueror over a foreign people, like someone standing outside nature – but that we, with flesh, blood, and brain, belong to nature, and exist in its midst, and that all our mastery of it consists in the fact that we have the advantage over all other beings of being able to know and correctly apply its laws.*"

The 'Enlightenment' had been defined by a decline in religious explanations of the world, with the emphasis now being on 'fact' and 'scientific proof', but the first years of the Victorian Age were marked by resurgence of religion. Even Darwin, though rejecting outright the concept that species were 'created', still maintained that a Creator had after all a hand in the process, although his belief was to wane with the years.

This debate as to the spiritual and physical connection of Man and Nature is significant part of the wider debate about the future of the natural world and our part in it. It emphasises that the whole history of our relationship with other species has itself evolved from the deep knowledge of Nature which our ancestors had. Modern reliance on science to explain all, while excluding the role of the arts, faith and spirituality, highlights that we have forgotten much that was once known. Perhaps this national amnesia is the reason that 20th century conservation failed to inspire whole generations to value the natural world.

Early awakening

Gilbert White's *The Natural History of Selbourne* in 1789 was the first and arguably

Plate from the *Butterflies and Moths of Europe*, 1882 W.F. Kirby

the most influential of all literary works on natural history and has never been out of print. In describing and analysing in minute detail the habits of the wildlife around him, White established Selbourne as the cradle of ecology, in a work which was essentially scientific but was also accessible to a wider audience. He was an ardent experimenter in his efforts to discover the mysteries of plants and animals – including shouting at bees through an ear trumpet to prove whether or not they could hear!

The quickening pace of philosophical and scientific thought led to more than a changed perception of the mechanisms of the natural world; it heralded a completely new idea. Landscapes had a beauty and value of their own, outside their practical role as provider of the necessities of life. William Gilpin was the first to introduce the concept of the 'picturesque' to the general reader, and encouraged visitors to the Lake District to view the grandeurs of Nature, as of more than scientific interest. Once thought of as dangerous and full of demons, they were now an inspiration for the beauty of the

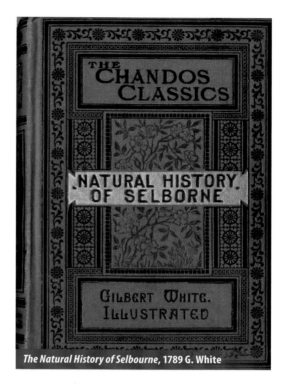

The Natural History of Selbourne, 1789 G. White

Earth, although perhaps sometimes a little too wild for the more genteel. Not all landscapes were quite so favoured it must be said, and Gilpin remained acutely dismissive of the 'dreary' fens.

With this new appreciation came the emergence of writers and artists who drew inspiration from nature and 'wild' places.

Poets and painters

John Constable was the first to abandon the classically-inspired landscape artists like Claude, and concentrate on his native Suffolk. His accuracy of form and attention to the detail of 'ordinary 'life took painting to new heights, with studies such as the *Haywain*, and he became a master of capturing the atmosphere of the world around him. Constable's genius was revealing the glories that lay behind the commonplace, where ordinary folk were going about their business in a beautiful landscape. These were not scenes of lazy days by the river; the

carts and mills were part of a busy industrial scene and the air would have been full of the cries of the carter's boys and tramp and smell of heavy horses. Yet amongst all that was the simple truth of light and shade, reflection and colour. His cloud painting has always seemed to me the most fascinating of his skills – the rain is about to fall or the sun to emerge from astonishing billows of greys, whites and blues which draw you into the scene. William Mallord Turner took this a stage further with his abstractions of light

Flatford Mill by John Constable

and atmosphere, which was also a record of the new technologies such as the steam trains, in his painting, *Rain Steam and Speed* of 1844.

Dedham Vale by John Constable [Google Art]

Like Constable, William Wordsworth expressed deep affection for his native land and had a penetrating eye for detail in the landscape. His greater gift, however – if he needed one – was to recognise the spiritual links which humans had with wild nature. The 'Two Book' approach of Galileo – that the values of Nature and Spirituality are linked – is firmly embedded in Wordsworth's poetry. In *Ode, Intimations of Immortality from Recollections of Early Childhood*, he says:

> "There was a time when meadow, grove, and stream,
> The earth, and every common sight,
> To me did seem
> Apparell'd in celestial light,
> The glory and the freshness of a dream".

Later in the same poem he regrets the innocent child drawing away from the state of perfect harmony with Nature:

> "Our birth is but a sleep and a forgetting..
> Shades of the prison house begin to close around the growing boy
> But he beholds the light, and whence it flows,.."
> At length the man perceives it die away
> And fade into the light of common day".

In a later poem *The world is too Much with Us* he says that this distraction from nature leads us to forget its power:

> "little we see in Nature that is ours
> Getting and spending we lay waste our powers".

In his wanderings in the wilderness, Wordsworth developed his conviction that the natural world was neither just a pleasant backdrop to human life, nor purely means for agricultural production. Here, he says, is the living proof that all life is connected. This vision of the position of humans within the natural world is of immense importance because it is the backdrop to understanding mankind's journey from the wildwood and boundless fens to the constructed landscapes of today. This is the path which led to the fragmented countryside of today. Society has forgotten the link between humans and Nature.

While writing about the Lakes, Wordsworth has some salutary words for those who find the fens a 'difficult' landscape to love. It is, as Keegan *et al.* (2006) states, all about learning, to look with a more perceptive eye:

> "... what we have loved,
> Others will love, and we will teach them how"

The Prelude, (1850).

This idea was taken up by later writers. In his 1896 novel *Clara Hopgood*, Mark Rutherford has one of his heroines says:

*"during the greater part of the year the visitor to Fenmarket would perhaps find it dull and depressing, and at times, under a grey, wintry sky, almost unendurable; but nevertheless, for days and weeks it has a charm possessed by few other landscapes in England, **provided only that behind the eye which looks there is something to which a landscape of that peculiar character answers**. There is, for example, the wide, dome-like expanse of the sky, there is the distance, there is the freedom and there are the stars on a clear night...".*

The 19th century saw the fen landscape appear in other literary works. In 1848, Elizabeth Gaskell, in her novel *Mary Barton*, highlights the plight of the industrial workers of Manchester who, despite their deep knowledge of the botany of the surrounding hills were cut off from the countryside by the poverty and grime of their workaday lives. Gaskell's novel highlighted the huge changes which were going on in Victorian urban and rural landscapes. Industrial powerhouses like Manchester were enslaving the workers, who despite rebellions such as the Chartist movement, had little say in their own lives, let alone the countryside. Gaskell's heroine escapes to the wilds of Canada, but many did not, and it is the plight of these people which her book highlights, and which led others such as William Morris to become convinced of the perils of capitalism. Here was further evidence that the natural world and people's well-being and self-respect were interlinked.

Like Wordsworth, John Clare celebrated the scenery of his native Northamptonshire and nearby fens. Living a few miles north of Peterborough and the Great Fen, Clare not only described the surrounding fens and farms, but was acutely aware of the threat to the rural way of life from the Enclosures. The loss of common land was changing the open countryside and denying access to the common man. His *Poems Descriptive of Rural Life and Scenery,* published in 1820, was a cry from the heart and he lost his sanity to the relentless march of 'progress'. Worse still, the Enclosures drove many agricultural labourers into the towns to work in the very factories which were to further mar the countryside. Clare knew his plants and was one of the first to accurately describe the flowers around

Whittlesea Mere in the precious years before its drainage. We can only imagine the poet's reaction when the waters disappeared in 1851. Clare is part of the landscape and the wildlife in it, and the pain he feels at the drainage and Enclosures is apparent in his poem *The Fens*:

"*Wandering by the river's edge,*
I love to rustle through the sedge
And through the woods of reed to tear
Almost as high as bushes are

There's not a hill in all the view,
Save that a forked cloud or two
Upon the verge of distance lies
And into mountains cheats the eyes."

But then:

"*Green paddocks have but little charms*
With gain the merchandise of farms;
And, muse and marvel where we may,
Gain mars the landscape every day—".

Charles Kingsley, in his *Hereward the Wake* took a somewhat romantic view:

"*Overhead the arch of heaven spread*
more ample than elsewhere, as over the
open sea; and that vastness gave, and still
gives, such cloudlands, such sunrises, such
sunsets, as can be seen nowhere else within
these isles."

John Clare [John Clare Trust]

Later authors were also not blind to the beauty and importance of the marshland. In his *Romance of the Marshes* (1911), GK Chesterton says:

"*It is a matter of taste... whether marshes are monotonous; but it is a matter of fact and science that they are not monochrome... Now exactly where you can find colours like those of a tulip garden or a stained-glass window, is in those sunken and sodden lands which are always called dreary... swamp and fenlands in England are always especially rich in gay grasses or gorgeous fungoids... In these splendid scenes it is always very easy to put your foot through the scenery. You may sink up to your armpits; but you will sink up to your armpits in flowers*".

The celebration of the wonders of Nature, however, began to assume a more alarmist aspect, as technological ability increased with the discovery of steam and other industrial processes. The thirst for urban living generated rapid house-building, and protest against wanton destruction of the beauty of Nature led to a new cast of actors entering the stage.

One of the most influential of the 19th century writers was W.H. Hudson. Hudson grew up on the plains of Argentina, before moving to England in his thirties. He became well known amongst writers and is credited with being one of the first 'nature writers'. Hudson was convinced of the power of Nature and was a founder member of the RSPB, writing guides to the birds of both Britain and Argentina. He also wrote several novels, of which the best-known is *Green Mansions*, as well as non-fiction. *Far Away and Long Ago* (1918) describes his wild upbringing in Argentina but perhaps his most influential book was *The Shepherd's Life*, written in 1910 with vivid descriptions of raw nature. His final work was *A Hind in Richmond Park*. Although not as popularly known as some authors, he influenced writers like Ernest Hemingway and Joseph Conrad and is credited with inspiring the 'Back-to-Nature' movement of the early 20th century. His effect was, as Robert Hamilton describes: "*Directly, his effect was not startling; but indirectly, through the spread of his ideals, he is responsible for a great change in the attitude of modern Englishmen. He has made us conscious of nature...*" (Hamilton 1946).

Campaigns and campaigners

The new focus on the environment beyond farm or factory floor soon awakened concern. Newly-recognised beauty could be lost to the effects of industrial expansion and urban sprawl, not to mention wholesale drainage of the wild fens. Steam was the greatest catalyst; the boon of fast and cheap rail travel and efficient water pumps was more than countered by smoke-belching and dangerous factories, where people toiled for hours on end with little fresh air or exercise. The drainage of the Whittlesea Mere was symptomatic of a countryside which was in retreat on a scale never before imagined, and with it the freedoms and independence of rural life.

It was not just the natural environment which was at stake. The new-urbanites saw much of rural practice as cruel. The control of weeds and predators had been a necessary part of farm life to protect vital crops, but other pursuits such as cock-fighting and bear-bating had no place in a more enlightened world. In 1824 the Society for the Prevention of Cruelty to Animals (SPCA) was formed, and received royal patronage in 1837. Much of their early work was centred around the conditions for ponies working in the coal mines which were providing the power for burgeoning factories and homes. In 1869 the Wild Birds Act had passed through Parliament in response to the slaughter of sea birds along the Bempton cliffs and in the same year the Norfolk and Norwich Naturalists' Society was formed. Conversely, the Georgian and Victorian obsession with game shooting continued to have a major effect on the wildlife of the countryside and by the middle of the century thousands of game-keepers were ruthlessly persecuting birds of prey and other 'vermin' such as stoats and weasels.

It might be a century before Joni Mitchell would warn "*... you don't know what you've got 'til it's gone*" (Mitchell 1970), but there were some far-sighted and revolutionary personalities of the Victorian Age who had already realised that. It was their energy and foresight which stood in the face of the wholesale destruction of wild nature.

The Victorian campaigners

The destructive power of Victorian technology was breath-taking to a generation used to gradual change and manual labour. Much of Hainault Wood in Essex was cleared in just a few weeks in 1851 and Whittlesea Mere drained – to equal applause and consternation. The agriculturalist Albert Pell called the drainage of the Mere "*an act of vandalism*" and it might be argued that these two events spawned what we now recognise as the conservation movement.

Charles Waterton was the foremost of a new breed of naturalists, and travelled the world collecting specimens and researching natural history. In the 1820s he returned to his estate of Walton Hall in West Yorkshire and here, from 1826, created what might be considered as the first modern nature reserve. He also campaigned against pollution and brought a successive action against a nearby soap works for the effect of their emissions on nearby trees.

One of the first artists to raise the alarm about the industrial assault on the environment was the cartoonist George Cruikshank. In 1829 he depicted the effects of the march of industry and unchecked housing development in his etching *London going out of Town or*

LONDON going out of Town. — or — The March of Bricks & mortar. —

London going out of Town or The March of Bricks and Mortar by George Cruickshank [University of Bristol Library]

The March of Bricks and Mortar. In 1866, alarm at the unchecked sprawling of London had resulted in the Metropolitan Commons Act, without which the great network of London Parks would not exist.

The concerns of art world were further emphasised by William Morris who was collaborating with Octavia Hill to protect the countryside from the worst excesses of railway building, long before the foundation of the National Trust. At the same time, the critic John Ruskin became ever more convinced of the connectivity between Nature, Art and Society.

Morris was a giant of the crusaders of the new industrial age. Starting life as an architect and then designer he became increasingly concerned about the morality of capitalism and industry and their effect on the natural world and the poor. He neatly summed up the journey that nature and humans had made to reach the conditions of his time:

"England was once a country of clearings amongst the woods and wastes, with a few towns interspersed. It then became a country of huge and foul workshops and fouler gambling-dens... Was not their mistake once more bred of the life of slavery that they had been living?—a life which was always looking upon...'nature'... as one thing, and mankind as another. It was natural to people thinking in this way, that they should try to make 'nature' their slave, since they thought 'nature' was something outside them."

It is important to look beyond Morris as a 'proto-environmentalist'. He was concerned not merely with 'Nature' for itself, nor with the capitalist view of profit, nor nature subjected for human use, but that they are linked (O'Sullivan 2011). He investigated the causes of this degradation and crucially, how it might be put right. 'True' wealth, he argued, was the wealth of Nature, which had largely survived the activities of our forebears and which would provide for humans into the future – as long as it was conserved and used wisely. The wealth of the material world, on the other hand, was a false wealth:

"... I will forever refuse to call (articles of folly and luxury) wealth: they are not wealth, but waste. Wealth is what Nature gives us, and what reasonable (people) can make out of the

gifts of Nature for (their) reasonable use. The sunlight, the fresh air, the unspoiled face of the earth, food, raiment and housing necessary and decent;... works of art,... all things which serve the pleasure of people, free, manly and uncorrupted. This is wealth".

"Shall I tell you what luxury has done for you in modern Europe? It has covered the merry green fields with the hovels of slaves, and blighted flowers and trees with poisonous gases, and turned the rivers into sewers; till over many parts of Britain the common people have forgotten what a field or a flower is like...".

One of the most influential of all the Victorian campaigners for the environment was John Muir. Born in 1838, Muir moved to the United States of America when still a child, but his influence on the conservation movement was pivotal to the whole concept of creating protected 'wild' areas and the importance of wild Nature to humankind. His legacy lives on through the John Muir Trust, which was founded in 1983 and strives to protect wild places in Britain.

Others took up the theme. After working to improve the lot of the working poor in London, Octavia Hill collaborated with Hardwicke Rawnsley and Sir Robert Hunter to form the National Trust in 1895. The Society for the Protection of Birds was established in 1891 by Emily Wilkinson and Eliza Phillips, receiving its royal charter (RSPB) in 1904. In 1912, Charles Rothschild formed the Society for the Promotion of Nature Reserves (SPNR), later to become the County Wildlife Trusts. He might be described as the first 'New Naturalist', who was able to match his enthusiasm with his money. He purchased Wicken Fen in 1899

William Morris

William Morris was born in 1834 and grew up in the countryside around Walthamstow. He showed an early interest in forests and gardens and the flowers and birds which surrounded his home.

As a young man he quickly abandoned ideas of entering the priesthood and trained as an architect, having been inspired by visits to Europe with his friend, John Ruskin. After developing his design skills with his wife whilst designing the interior of their new house in Kent, he embarked upon a career of design, forming a company in 1861 with his friends, Rosetti, Philip Webb and Burne-Jones, which lasted in various forms until 1940.

Beneath his skill and passion for art and design, Morris became increasingly concerned at the human and environmental cost of the rapid industrial and urban growth of the Victorian period. He outlined his views in lectures and writings and became convinced that the desire for profit-at-all costs was destroying the natural beauty of the Earth and enslaving its workers in appalling conditions.

William Morris by George Frederick Watts

"Mankind, in striving to attain to a complete mastery over Nature, should destroy her simplest and widest-spread gifts, and thereby enslave simple people to them, and themselves to themselves, and so at last drag the world into a second barbarism... a thousandfold more hopeless, than the first." (The Beauty of Life 1880)

He became a founder member of the Society for the Protection of Ancient Buildings and published his utopian view of the world in his 1890 *News from Nowhere*.

and Woodwalton Fen in 1910 – two of the very first nature reserves in England, setting the pattern for a century of nature reserve creation and management.

The bold initiatives of the 17th and 18th century poets and thinkers were tantamount to revolution. Whilst it may be argued that this was the cradle of socialism, it was also a significant recognition of the relationship between humans and Nature. The accelerating loss of Nature in the face of modern economic development is perhaps the consequence of the breaking of that relationship.

It was these many and varied events which formed the bedrock of the conservation organisations we recognise today. Importantly, it was not just the naturalists' view of the threats to wildlife and wild places, but the recognition of the spiritual and aesthetic value Nature, both for its own sake and for the value it held for the well-being of the 'ordinary folk'; this is one of the pillars of the Great Fen vision today.

Conclusion

The centuries following fen drainage were pivotal to the change in outlook towards landscape in general and the fens in particular. It was partly because many people now lived in urban areas, separated from extracting their livelihood directly from Nature. They had the luxury to regard it from afar, as something to be either vilified or admired. Travel books and efficient transport offered opportunities to make day visits to far flung places, while the burgeoning natural sciences encouraged the amateur naturalist to take to the field. Darwin's explanation of evolution emphasised the connection between Nature and humans, but artists and philosophers had already come the same conclusion. The attitude of the religious establishment – once the defender of the ascendancy of Man over Nature – also changed, as it must if it were to maintain any authority in new era. Crucially, the value of Nature for

The birth of the National Trust

Octavia Hill was born on 3 December 1838 in Wisbech and died in 1912. Robert Hunter introduced her to the Commons Preservation Society and with the Rev. Hardwicke they went on to found the National Trust in 1895. Hill was a pioneer of 'cultural philanthropy' and was convinced that exposure to art and beauty could improve the life of the poor. She founded the Kyrle Society in 1875 (named after the 17th/18th century philanthropist John Kyrle) 'for the diffusion of beauty'. The Society planted trees and flowers in urban areas, promoted aesthetics in the decoration and building of houses and was strongly supported by William Morris. She was the author of *Our Common Land* in which she outlined the urgent need for all people to have access to the open air and countryside.

Flatford Mill, Suffolk

its own sake, as well as its beneficial effects on society, appealed to scientists, writers, artists and philosophers alike. The world of waters and woods, moors and bogs did not exist for the benefit of the human race, but were an essential part of an environment in a world where humans and wildlife were intimately linked.

The value of the writings of Wordsworth and Clare was not that they described pretty landscapes and evoked the smell of roses. They cried out that these places and their wildlife were as much a part of the human condition as the constructed world. They were, in fact, more important because it was on these that people relied, not just for food and water, but for spiritual fulfilment as well. Today, research tells us that mental health is greatly affected by the environment, but in the 18th and 19th centuries the artistic and literary visionaries felt this instinctively. At the same time scientists and naturalists discovered more and more connections between all species, including our own.

While enlightenment brought awareness of the beauty of the natural world, the thirst for a closer knowledge of its plants and animals brought its own dangers. Over-collecting became a serious issue and may have been at least partly responsible for the loss of species, such as the Large Copper butterfly, from the fens in the 1870s.

The Victorian campaigners were the first of a long line of activists who have fought to re-instate the balance between human progress and its effects on the landscape. Conservation had been invented and would eventually lead to the need for schemes like the Great Fen.

The philosophers and artists of the 'Awakening' left us with an important message. Nature and human well-being are not separate entities. They have always been and always will be interlinked. The value of one equals the value of the other and each depends on the other, and can be expressed through art, literature and music. It was a key feature through which campaigners like William Morris elevated the status of Nature and one which was re-learned during the process of developing the Great Fen. It is one which we will return to later.

"We have enough examples of this habitat already"
Member of the Nature Conservancy Council 1985

"This is just gardening"
Senior NCC manager 1987

"I would like to see Woodwalton and Holme Fen joined together again"
Miriam Rothschild c 2006

The historical perspective

There have been several accounts of the history of conservation in the 20th century (e.g. Sheail 1998, Marren 2002) so only a brief overview is given here, concentrating on the fenland between Huntingdon and Peterborough.

'Conservation' is often regarded as a modern concept, but in reality, it has been developing for centuries. As land-use became more intensive, so did the appreciation of the value of the world outside human endeavour. In the fens, drainage for arable production had met with opposition from the outset, principally from those whose livelihood had depended on the fens and marshes. Draining the land not only meant the end of their way of life, but for wildlife as well.

In many ways, all the issues and events of the preceding millennia are compressed into the 20th century. A growing population, increased agricultural efficiency, and the drive for constant economic growth did not sit well with nurturing the natural world. In fenland, drainage became ever more efficient as steam was first replaced by diesel to run the pumps (the first were at Methwold and Feltwell in 1913) and later by electricity. The pressure on the remaining undrained areas became so intense that it seemed there would soon be no trace left of wet fenland.

We owe a great deal to the visionaries of the 18th and 19th centuries because without their action, the landscapes of England would be much the poorer. Drainage of fenland may have been an ecological disaster which Georgian and Victorian campaigners were unable to prevent, but it galvanised them to challenge further threats to the natural world, as seen in the last chapter. In doing so, they laid the foundations of conservation which the 'new naturalists' like Charles Rothschild and Arthur Tansley, Herbert Smith and Sir John Fryer, would carry so enthusiastically into the new century. It was this which led directly to the modern 'conservation' movement, the establishment of nature reserves, and the path which protection of Britain's natural resource would take over the next century.

In 1899, Charles Rothschild purchased Wicken Fen near Cambridge, gifting it to the newly formed National Trust (NT) a few years later, and in 1910 he acquired a large part of Woodwalton Fen near Ramsey. Unable to pass the reserve to the NT, he formed the Society for the Promotion of Nature Reserves (SPNR) in 1912 and Woodwalton became its first reserve in 1919.

Rothschild and others saw the threat that population growth and new technologies posed to wild places and their plants and animals. Recognising that accurate description of 'natural' habitats was the most effective way to argue for their protection, he published a list of 284 vulnerable wildlife sites in 1915, which were "worthy of preservation". In his speech to the Royal Entomological Society the following year, he urged the establishment of wildlife reserves from this list. Today, half of these sites still exist as nature reserves, although others have not survived.

It has been suggested that the drive of nature conservation faltered somewhat after Charles Rothschild's untimely death in 1923. One reason may have been that there appeared to be little threat to the countryside, and what nature reserves did exist were seen primarily as: *"outdoor workshops for the study of plants and animals"* as W.B. Crump had put it. In fact, the inter-war years saw a dramatic increase in the pace of urban spread, such as the piecemeal

Wicken Fen

Charles Rothschild

Although heavily involved in the family banking business, Charles Rothschild and his older brother, Walter, were naturalists at heart. Born in 1877, Charles travelled the world collecting specimens for Walter's museum at Tring (now part of the Natural History Museum). His specialism was fleas, an interest inherited by his daughter Miriam, who produced a catalogue of his collection of fleas which was later bequeathed to the British Museum. His collection of pressed irises was presented to Kew.

He moved to his grandfather's estate at Ashton Wold in Northamptonshire at the end of the 19th century, and gathered round him some of the most eminent scientists and naturalists of the Age.

After his death in 1923, his daughter, Miriam, said of him *"he always made other people feel clever"* (Rothschild archive).

developments along the cliffs at Peacehaven in Sussex, and had absorbed a further 2% of the countryside by the Second World War (Sheail 1998).

Happily, the enthusiasm and expertise of the early 20th century continued to prevail amongst many scientists. One was a Cambridge botanist, Arthur Tansley, who undertook a major survey of the British vegetation and formed the British Ecological Society in 1913, with others such as W.G. Smith. This was the first ever society devoted to the scientific study of the natural world.

As Victorian industrial expansion had prompted opposition, so did the urban spread of the 1920s. Those who could see beyond the lure of quick profits and unfettered house building began to organise themselves into coherent groups. The Council for the Preservation of Rural England (CPRE) was formed in 1926, and increasing scientific interest led to the British Trust for Ornithology (BTO) in 1932. The inspiration of the SPNR also bore fruit, as it expanded into county-based Wildlife Trust organisations, the first of which was the Norfolk Naturalists' Trust, which established its first reserve at Cley marshes, on the Norfolk coast, in 1926. Later, these bodies would expand into a national Wildlife Trust movement, which had its first meeting in 1960. Credit for this achievement is largely due to Ted Smith, who went on to chair the Woodwalton Fen Joint Advisory Committee for many years.

The need to protect natural areas from the onslaught of agricultural and urban development after the end of the Second World War had been foreseen during the conflict itself, and considerable progress was made in planning for life in peacetime. In 1939, Tansley had published his epic 'British Islands and Their Vegetation' (Tansley 1939) which provided a valuable background for establishing protected wildlife areas. A 1941 conference of Rothschild's SPNR (now under the guidance of Herbert Smith) considered submissions by H.M. Edelsten and Sir John Fryer. Both men later worked on Woodwalton Fen and argued the case for conservation of nature from a position of scientific knowledge and field experience. The Nature Reserves Investigation Committee (NRIC) was set up in 1942 and the debate for a strategy for nature conservation continued to develop.

After a long and tortuous process, Parliament passed the Town and Country Planning Act in 1947. Whilst creating a planning system intended to regulate urban spread, the Act also established a National Park Authority and the world's first government agency for nature conservation – the Nature Conservancy (NC). The Conservancy received its Royal Charter two years later, but in the face of the post-war emphasis on agricultural and urban growth, its ability to act effectively was far from certain. As it was, the persuasive voices and scientific credibility of 'giants' such as Tansley, Fryer, Max Nicholson and Julian Huxley established NC as a force to be reckoned with. The rest of the century would be studded with conflict between nature conservation, economic growth and intensive agriculture, but without the NC and its successors, habitat and species loss would undoubtedly have been significantly worse. Despite the constraints which successive governments of all hues placed on NC, and the particular emasculation of its successor bodies, it achieved some remarkable progress in site protection in the face of immense changes to the countryside. Ultimately, the contraction, fragmentation and loss of wildlife habitats would lead to the urgent need for a bold new direction, such as the Great Fen, but that would take another 50 years. During that time, the Conservancy would designate and manage a swathe of wonderful wildlife refuges and fund much research into conservation techniques and species dynamics. Seventy years after the creation of NC, there are almost half a million hectares of nature reserve and other 'protected sites' in England – a testament to the determination of both the government agency and voluntary bodies against a tide of pressure from other land uses.

The agricultural effect

Agriculture has been central to the success of humans throughout our journey through the post-ice millennia. It is no surprise, then, that it remained a crucial factor in 20th century life. By the end of the century, continued drainage had contributed to the 50% loss of global wetland for agriculture and forestry (Davison *et al.* 2014) and in the English fens the proportion was far higher. Here, the impacts from the earliest days of drainage mushroomed with advances in pumping and farming techniques. Government initiatives to increase food production after the shortages of the Second World War included more mechanisation, research into greater yields and larger-scale production. Industrial expansion, commercial forestry and urban spread completed the suite of activities which endangered whole landscapes and their wildlife. Little value was placed on wetlands and their important role for absorbing floodwater, which would later have expensive and damaging consequences.

Throughout the following decades, the decline in wildlife mirrored improved drainage and advances in farming techniques. Admittedly, the back-breaking work of hauling out thousands of bog oaks, mixing clay to bind the peat and extracting maximum productivity from the ancient soils resulted in increased yields. The fens earned the reputation as the vegetable basket of England, where potatoes, sugar beet and carrots became the mainstay of the local economy and the farmers became skilled practitioners. The costs, however, were huge. Ever-increasing amounts of inorganic fertiliser, pesticides, and expensive pumping regimes not only put a strain on farm budgets but began to affect soil and pollinating

Women's Land Army training, Somerset, c.1940

Evacuees digging potatoes, Pembrokeshire, 1940

invertebrates. Peat could not withstand exposure to the elements and short cropping regimes. Since 1851, five metres depth of black peat has disappeared through wastage – a combination of shrinkage, removal with crops, wind-blow and oxidation. Few places retained more than a sift of the 'black gold' over an increasingly acid sub-soil, and at 2 cm wastage every year, the Neolithic soils beneath peat would soon be fully exposed across the region.

The role of soil invertebrates and pollinating insects is well known, but the damage to their populations from modern farming techniques has only recently been recognised (Mathews *et al.* 2012). In 2014, a study by the University of Sheffield, which was widely reported in the media (*Farmers Weekly, The Independent* 2014) suggested that Britain had just 100 harvests left before soil degradation made food production impossible. So, it was not just the effect of intensive production on sites of nature conservation interest which was of concern, it was the very fabric of food production itself and the variety of bacteria and invertebrates which supports it.

In fenland, efficient management of water was essential to sustain high productivity. The Middle Level commissioners invested heavily in a high-capacity pumping station at the eastern end of the river Ouse and worked tirelessly to maintain the banks and drains evacuating water from the low-lying fields.

Even the places set aside for nature were not immune to cultivation. As we have already seen, significant areas of Woodwalton Fen were both dug for peat and ploughed for a considerable period until Rothschild's intervention. More recently, the reserve has been used to dump floodwater in order to facilitate farmland drainage. Many Sites of Special Scientific Interest (SSSI) also remained in agricultural production, albeit with some restriction of fertilisers and other intensive techniques.

Children in flood, Walpole St Peter

Irrigation [NE]

Modern combine harvester

Modern farming next to Stonea Camp

St Germans pumping station

1930s pump

As agricultural advances intensified, it became the norm for conservationists to blame farmers for losses of wild places, and farmers to resist attempts to curtail their activities in producing food for a hungry generation, but the fate of many farmers was far from ideal. In a long-running study, the Countryside Commission reported:

> "Perhaps the most important change has been in relative income. Indexing the average UK Farming Income as 100 over the period 1950–59... it peaked at 138 in 1973, declined to a low of 34 in the late 1980s, rose to a high of 91 in 1995 and has declined to only 10 in 2003... the industry as a whole has clearly suffered from a very significant decline in relative and absolute profitability since the start of this study".

Set against this was the significant increase in technology:

> "The reduction in labour availability has been accompanied by fairly dramatic increases in the rates of work achievable with more powerful and larger machines. Thus the average rate of ploughing... was about 2 ha/day in 1970, but 6 ha/day in 2005; fertiliser spreading – 12.5 ha/day in 1970 and 30 ha/day in 2005: sugar beet harvesting – 0.75 ha/day in 1970, 3.5 ha/day in 2005" (Natural England 2006).

Farmers were fully engaged with making a living and increasing production. Subsidies and other inducements favoured the large 'agri-businesses', and far outweighed the conservation budget. Many smaller farmers, however, simply could not afford to manage land for conservation, and any financial help they did receive was firmly centred on increased efficiency. Agriculture was producing high quality affordable food, but the longer-term consequences for the soil, wildlife and society as a whole were not acknowledged. Where there were calls for a more sustainable approach they were largely ignored.

The conservation effect

Set against the backdrop of a rapidly growing and market-driven economy, the task of the budding government and voluntary conservation bodies was great indeed. The first achievements of the new NC were the establishment of NNRs, of which Holme Fen

Forestry Commission

The creation of the Forestry Commission (FC) in 1919 was intended to meet the for need trees after the First World War, when woodland cover was at a very low level. Activity increased after the Second World War, but focussed on planting for fast-growing conifers. Although much planting was on open land, the replacement of many survivors of the ancient wildwood with coniferous forest was a disaster and it may take generations to redress the balance.

The 1968 Countryside Act encouraged the Commission to make its forests more accessible to the public and it now concentrates its effort more on conservation, research and advice.

was one of the first in 1952, closely followed by Monks Wood (1953) and Woodwalton Fen (1954). Many have followed, and there are now over 200 NNRs across England, with 35 in East Anglia alone. It was a similar story for the National Parks, the first of which was established in 1951 in the Peak District and Lake District. By the year 2000, their combined area covered about 8% of England in eight locations, including the Norfolk Broads.

The years that followed were plagued by tension between government-sponsored agricultural improvement (including drainage), and poorly financed initiatives for conservation, which were centred around defensive measures rather any strategic plan. This was typified by the procedure for notifying SSSIs created under the 1949 Charter, which was entirely voluntary. As the NC had no powers to enforce compliance or prevent destruction (particularly if the work was deemed of agricultural benefit) the scheme proved to be seriously flawed. The 1968 Countryside Act appeared to offer a way to break the deadlock, by encouraging farmers to restore a balance between production and conservation. It raised hopes of better protection for SSSIs because for the first time, NC was given the power to enter into Management Agreements with SSSI owners, so that at last there would be a financial incentive to set against agricultural grants. Poor funding. however, (NC was expected to meet costs from its existing budget) meant that for five years no Agreements were made at all, and when they were, results were often less than effective. SSSI protection proved to be minimal, and in the wider countryside destruction continued apace. Despite the fact that by the early 1980s, 6% of Britain's land surface was SSSI, the lack of finance and authority of NC and its successor the Nature Conservancy Council (NCC), severely restricted their value for wildlife. Grants for agricultural efficiency, on the other hand, continued to encourage damage and loss. On the fenland peat, there were few SSSIs anyway, and pump-drained arable production remained paramount. The lessons of peat wastage resulting from drainage, which the 17th century Adventurers had learnt at such cost, appeared to have been completely forgotten, and the peat continued its steady decline.

In the 1960s, pesticides became a particular concern. It was work led by Prof. Norman Moore at the Monks Wood Research station on the edge of the Great Fen, which highlighted the dangers from organo-chloride insecticides to birds in particular, through deaths and breeding failure (Moore 1965). I remember him telling me how he would walk up the lane

Tansley Stone, Kingley Vale NNR

to Woodwalton Fen and see dead finches scattered over the ground. Following his research, substances like dieldrin and DDT were withdrawn, but chemicals remain an important part of the agricultural armoury to control invertebrates and weeds to this day.

1981 was a turning point for the NCC, when the Wildlife and Countryside Act came into force. No longer could damage be caused to SSSIs in the name of agricultural efficiency without informing NCC, and

there were significant improvements to species and habitat protection. It ushered in a period of intense activity within the organisation, as the entire series of SSSIs had to be re-notified. Despite the Wildlife and Countryside Act (or perhaps because of it), however, the relationship of conservation and the agri-business remained antagonistic. Well-meant initiatives like European Year of Conservation in 1970 achieved few measurable results, and the conservation movement was battling a formidable set of obstacles where the valuable role of the natural world was overshadowed by the attractions of economic growth. There had been some gains for wildlife in new habitats such as those created by gravel extraction, but generally butterflies and bats, meadows and marshes were seen as a minority interest with little relevance to the hard facts of the modern economy. By 1972 in East Anglia alone, half the hedges had been removed since the end of the Second World War (Sheail 1998) and drainage was becoming ever-more efficient. During the 1970s, grant-aided schemes were draining 100,000 hectares every year (Baldock *et al.* 1980) and there seemed to be no reprieve for wild places anywhere in England, let alone the beleaguered fens.

The essential value to society of an ecologically stable environment was just not recognised and so it was easy for decision-makers to dismiss it as irrelevant. Landowning organisations such as the National Farmers' Union (NFU) and Country Landowners Association (CLA) were pitted against a disparate (but increasingly vocal) collection of government and

Halvergate Marshes, Norfolk [NE]

voluntary conservation bodies with few resources. It was a 'them and us' situation, where everyone believed they were doing the right thing, but which resulted in an atmosphere of mistrust and conflict.

Inevitably, perhaps, the increased power of the NCC through the Wildlife and Countryside Act brought bitter recriminations, and in the wetlands the clashes of competing interests were particularly fierce. Iconic wetland such as Amberley Wildbrooks in Sussex, the Somerset Levels, and Romney Marsh raised intense conflict between farmers and conservationists. Even when the proposed drainage was prevented, as was the case at Amberley, it caused further rancour and led to unease in some quarters at the perceived power of the NCC. In 1984, the battle to halt the ploughing of the Halvergate Marshes in Norfolk became so intense that the prime minister, Margaret Thatcher, directly intervened. The outcome of Halvergate did, however, seem to offer a glimmer of hope, and arguably turned the tide on a seemingly intractable problem. Payments for positive action to maintain the grazing marshes led to the Broads Grazing Marshes Conservation scheme which was widely supported by farmers, conservationists and the government alike. Out of conflict, suspicion and mistrust emerged a degree of consensus.

Further north, another battle was raging. The supply of peat for horticulture had become big business (the meres at Holme Fen were excavated in order to create wetland habitat but the dug peat was sold for horticulture). Thorne and Hatfield Moors in Yorkshire had long been on-stage as part of the wetland drainage drama. It was here that Charles I instructed Vermuyden to drain his estate, and it was here that a major horticultural company began to extract peat on a grand scale in the 1980s. It started a national debate with recriminations traded freely.

Eventually, English Nature purchased much of the site in 1994 and a long programme of restoration began. Although controversial, the Thorne Moors story was another illustration of the changing fortunes of the conservation voice. It demonstrated again that there could be dialogue about the relationship between big business and the delicate environment. As it turned out, these victories came at a price for the national NCC. After a particularly vigorous stand taken by the organisation over afforestation on the bogs of Caithness, led by the redoubtable William Wilkinson, the national body was broken up in 1991. English Nature (EN) emerged as England's wildlife

What's in a name?

English Nature (EN) replaced the Nature Conservancy Council (NCC) in 1991, but was again re-structured in 2006, when the Rural Development Service, the Countryside Agency and EN were merged into Natural England (NE). While it appeared that this was a sensible blending of differing countryside interests, it also served to dilute the direction of conservation, and depleted the ecological expertise within the wildlife arm. Resources were also severely curtailed and the morale of staff damaged by what many saw as a departure from the core role of protecting the nation's wildlife. This was symptomatic of the effect of government changes of policy. Writing in 1987, Duncan Poore (director general of NC from 1966–73) despaired of continual government re-structuring of its nature conservation arm *"the British government has a fatal proclivity to tinker with its most imaginative institutions"* (Poore 1987) while NCC Chairman Sir David Serpell (chairman of NCC from 1973–77) declared *"a besetting weakness of this country is the belief that changes in machinery are tantamount to improvements in policy"*.

Conservation conflict

I remember being pinned against a wall by angry fen farmers when the Great Fen first launched, but my fate was nothing as to the chairman of the NCC, Sir Ralph Verney, and other conservation leaders. In 1981, they were hanged and burnt in effigy on the Somerset Levels by angry farmers who wanted to drain the remaining wildlife habitats for arable cultivation. A neat reversal of the time in the 17th century when the fen tygers erected a gallows to frighten the hapless labourers digging the fen drains!

watchdog, with similar bodies in Scotland and Wales. Only by concerted last-minute efforts did a national co-ordinating body emerge in the Joint Nature Conservation Council (JNCC).

With few visionaries to promote a holistic approach to the use of the countryside, the interests of agriculture and forestry on one side and conservation on the other became polarised. The essential value of an ecologically stable environment was poorly understood and so easy to dismiss as irrelevant. Landowning organisations such as the National Farmers' Union (NFU) and Country Landowners' Association (CLA) were pitted against a disparate but increasingly vocal collection of government and voluntary conservation bodies. It was a 'them and us' situation where everyone believed they were doing the right thing, but which resulted in an atmosphere of mistrust and conflict. The situation by the mid-1980s was untenable.

A new direction

Despite the scything of its powers, the new EN developed a series of incentives designed to bring some relief to an increasingly troubled countryside.

The 1981 Act was followed by the establishment of Environmentally Sensitive Areas in 1986, Countryside Stewardship in 1991, the Wildlife Enhancement Scheme (WES) in 2004 and Environmental Stewardship in 2005, all backed by European funding. These schemes were plagued by problems, especially the earlier ones which were vulnerable to excess claims as they included an amount for 'profits foregone'. Some large-scale farmers were thus not only able to capitalise on generous and ill-conceived European subsidies for over-production, but also to make considerable incomes from the estimated loss of profit from the restrictions of management agreements for conservation. In at least one case on the Kent marshes, a farmer used these payments to improve the land for wildlife, but this was not the norm and was in any case hugely expensive for the tax-payer. On the Nene Washes to the east of the Great Fen, a similarly expensive scheme prevented drainage and ploughing, but it was also costly because of the compensation element and benefits for nature conservation were slow to develop.

Increasingly, 'agri-environment' agreements have been targeted at positive works but remain complicated and onerous to administer.

The relevance of protected sites

The response of conservationists to the impact of agriculture and urban development was to put wildlife into reserves and pull up the drawbridge. It was often not a simple matter and the campaign could become brutal and personal, but there was little alternative. While this policy was a valiant and often successful attempt to maintain some areas of vibrant wildlife in SSSIs and nature reserves, the result was that they became separated from the 'rest of the countryside'. These were special areas which were not part of the farming and business community. There was also a widely held view that these were 'examples' of habitats and that was sufficient. Therein laid the problem. If just a few scattered examples of habitats were deemed sufficient, then nature conservation was doomed to be a side show, while the rest of the world moved on in an entirely different direction. What was not appreciated was that it would prove almost impossible to maintain the original diversity of these fragments. It was a classic example of what

Professor Bill Adams calls the 'stamp-collecting' approach to site protection (Adams 1996) – the sense that a few patches of each habitat were sufficient.

I had experience of this myself. As a warden on the South Downs in the 1980s I had been outraged at the comments of a visiting NCC board member that the number and size of nature reserves should be restricted – for just those reasons stated above. A later charge by a senior NCC manager that nature reserve management was just 'gardening' served to underline the point that these small sites were simply not fit for purpose. 'Examples' of declining habitats were certainly never going to provide a sustainable future for wildlife, and while 'gardening' might be on a grand scale, it could not guarantee lasting and 'bona-fide' wildlife communities. Most reserves were simply not big enough, did not relate to the wider landscape, and did not impact significantly into peoples' lives. They tended to be the preserves of naturalists, and as such were irrelevant to wider society. I often refer to the present reserves in the Great Fen as 'flowerpots', because even constant intervention and tinkering with species management cannot replicate the conditions which once prevailed. No amount of internal management can alter the fact that the Holme Fen bog has been destroyed by drainage, and Woodwalton is marooned within clay-lined flood banks (see boxes).

Nature in a flowerpot

Woodwalton Fen NNR is a classic example of the challenges of 'wildlife gardening' – worse still, an isolated flowerpot.

The ecological dilemma here centres on the impact of drainage for agriculture, and its geographical isolation. The cause of – and remedy for – the reserve's damaged ecology lies outside its borders. Selecting the site in the 1970s to act as a flood alleviation system effectively turned it from a live 'sieve' with free-flowing water, to a static 'bucket'. Together with high-nutrient water entering the site, and difficulties of removing standing water, maintaining optimum hydrology and water quality has become a major issue, because of the failure to forsee the effects of flood storage and consequences of long-term irrigation of the site with the effluent from washing machines. Add to that the separation of many species from other populations and the overall diversity of life has begun to decline, which internal management can do little to alleviate.

Due to the dedication of a succession of naturalists, wardens and volunteers, there have been some spectacular wildlife successes, but this fragment of the Whittlesea Mere wetland now bears little resemblance to the richness of that ancient world. Its long-term future can only be guaranteed by an outward-looking policy of better water management and quality, combined with links to a species-rich wider countryside.

Scaling the barricades

Legend has it that early wardens were under instructions to consider the reserve a fortress. One of the Rothschild family was an ex-marine and if he could steal over the barbed wire and onto the reserve at night... there would be trouble for the wardens in the morning!

This was for many years a mysterious 'island' at the end of Chapel Lane which was only accessible by dedicated naturalists. People lived for generations at the other end of the lane and scarcely knew it existed! How then, could they possibly be expected to join in campaigns to support a place they scarcely knew and were only able to visit under strict supervision? Yet it was believed to be the right policy. With so many threats to this vulnerable place, surely it was better to keep it secret and allow its fen workers, who knew and cared for it so passionately, to care for it in their own way?

A more enlightened policy in recent years whereby visitors are made welcome has shown what a positive effect access to such a wonderful wetland can have on people's lives. Volunteers, schoolchildren, families, scientists and faith groups have become friends and defenders of this special place, laying the foundations of the Great Fen vision of inspiring care for the planet by inclusion and education.

While there were certainly drawbacks of the protected sites approach, the successes of conservation in the 20th century were, in some cases, quite extraordinary. Peregrines *Falco peregrinus*, Marsh Harriers *Circus aeruginosus*, Bitterns *Botaurus stellaris* and Avocets *Recurvirostra avosetta* all recovered from a seemingly irrecoverable low population sizes. Numbers of Swallowtail butterflies and Fen Orchids *Liparis loeselii* held firm in the Norfolk Broads and the understanding of the ecology of fenland in particular broadened widely.

Access to nature

As the decades wore on there was increasing pressure for more access to the countryside. National Parks were large but not always easily accessible, most nature reserves had restricted access and were generally vulnerable to damage, while farmland was jealously guarded. One aspect of the 1968 Countryside Act as to create areas of countryside which would be accessible to the public. Local Authorities and others were given the ability to establish 'Country Parks', where recreation would be the primary use, but where wildlife was also important. Around the Great Fen, Ferry Meadows and Barnwell Country Park near Oundle are good examples.

The Countryside and Rights of Way Act 2000 (CROW) redefined both wildlife legislation and countryside access. It required public bodies to take habitats and species into account when planning their work. As far as access was concerned, it introduced the so-called 'right to roam'. This declared some areas of land open to access under certain conditions, particularly high-level moorland. While some conservationists considered it was a potential disaster for breeding birds such as Curlews (and still needs to be closely monitored), it was an important departure from the previous widely-held view that people should only be allowed onto nature reserves under sufferance. Natural England declared many of its NNRs as open access.

While unrestricted access to areas of high landscape or biodiversity interest can be damaging (particularly if dogs are included), it can be argued that the denial of access to such beauty lies at the heart of the failure of the conservation movement to prevent the wholesale destruction of so many wild places in the 20th century. If ordinary folk cannot enjoy wildlife and be able to see it at first-hand, how can they appreciate its relevance to them? If they don't regard Nature as important, then why should they support moves to protect it or vote for politicians who would defend it? If the natural world does not impact their own well-being and that of their children, why would they be moved by cries of horror about the loss of butterflies? The recognition of this fact is a core feature of the Great Fen, which we will explore in more detail later in the book. Engagement with local people is essential if they are to appreciate the value of the natural world to their daily lives. A countryside rich in biodiversity is not a minority interest – it is the bedrock of a healthy society and a potential major contributor to a thriving economy.

River Great Ouse flowing towards King's Lynn

River Ouse at St Ives

Addressing the issue of access is central to the success of both small sites and large landscape areas like the Great Fen. If the public is to appreciate the wonders of a landscape, they must be able to enter at least some of it in order to experience its value. At the same time, uncontrolled access can too easily destroy the essence of the wild which people have come to see. The arguments have long been debated. John Dower was warning of the threat from increased leisure and tourism in the 1960s:

> "Three great waves have broken across the face of Britain since 1800. First the sudden growth of dark industrial towns. Second, the thrusting movement along far flung railways. Third, the sprawl of car-based suburbs. Now we see under the guise of a modest word, the surge of the fourth wave which could be more powerful than all the others. The modest word is leisure". (Dower 1965, p. 123).

Train in fenland floods at Littleport, 1947

This fear of greater access was somewhat ironic, as the driving passion of William Morris and other proto-conservationists a century earlier, had been to free the working man from the penury of labour so that he could enjoy the countryside. Now, as Dower saw it, the danger was that he would destroy what he had come to see! There is no question that open access has the potential to degrade sensitive landscapes, but denying people the opportunity to experience first-hand the natural world does little to ensure its long-term protection.

Balanced against the negative aspects of increased access, however, is the positive effect which direct access to Nature can have on people. The increasing influence of the voluntary conservation bodies lies in the extraordinary growth of their membership – much of which results from direct exposure to nature in some form or another. It is these people who have been so instrumental in raising the profile of our natural heritage and led to action for change.

The RSPB was formed (as SPB) in 1889 and by 1960 had 10,000 members. Just two decades later on its centenary, membership had risen to 500,000 and in 1997 passed one million. The National Trust grew from an initial 100 members in 1895 to one million in 1985 and by the turn of the 20th century had reached almost three million (it is now over four million). The Wildlife Trust movement grew from a roomful of pioneers and one reserve (Woodwalton Fen) in 1912, to 800,000 members a century later. In a slightly less genteel vein, organisations such as Greenpeace and Friends of the Earth (FoE) began to take direct action against what they perceived as unacceptable activities such as oil prospecting and whaling.

A friendly Chair

Such are the changing fortunes of the conservation message and the influence of campaigning organisations, that long-time director of Friends of the Earth, Tony Juniper, was appointed Chair of Natural England in 2019!

It is this unstoppable tide of interest and concern among the general public which has been of enormous benefit to the progress of conservation, and begun to influence policy-makers in Parliament. The 20 years since the inception of the idea of a 'Great Fen' has seen further strengthening of moves to mitigate the loss of countryside and much of this is due to increasing awareness in society of the importance of the natural world. Whether or not the more relaxed approach to access enshrined in the CROW Act proves to be of overall advantage to inspiring people to care about the non-human remains to be seen. John Dower's concerns remain as valid as those of William Morris – the challenge is how we can balance one against the other for the benefit of ourselves and our wildlife neighbours.

The power of the pen, the flash of the lens

It was not just members of conservation organisations who came to the rescue of the natural world. As in past centuries, it was artists and writers who would publicise the plight of the countryside and its wildlife, but it now included high quality TV coverage. Pioneers such as Hans and Lotte Hass and Jacques Cousteau set the scene, which David Attenborough has taken to new heights and proved an influential catalyst for change.

Literature was also significant in revealing both real cost of intensive agriculture but also the wonders of nature. In America, Rachel Carson's *Silent Spring* (Carson 1962) was hugely influential in highlighting the effects of pesticides and was a major reason for my own entry into nature conservation. In England, Marian Shoard's 1980 *The Theft of the Countryside* (Shoard 1980) was equally praised and castigated, while Richard Mabey's *The Common Ground* (Mabey 1980) took a more measured approach in reviewing the conflict between conservation and other conflicting pressures.

Earlier authors had highlighted the plight of threatened and iconic species. Henry Williamson's *Tarka the Otter* revealed the life and hardships of a once common species. Hunted for centuries, the Otter population went into sharp decline with the advent of a more efficient countryside, water pollution and river engineering. Williamson's book earned him the accolade of one of the foremost natural history writers of the century, and was followed by Gavin Maxwell's more personal account of his experiences with captive Otters in *Ring of Bright Water*. In the same year that the Nature Conservancy came into being, Kenneth Allsop's tale of the first breeding of Little Ringed Plovers *Charadrius dubius* on a reservoir in Middlesex, *Adventure lit their star* (Allsop 1949), demonstrated that some man-made landscapes could benefit wildlife.

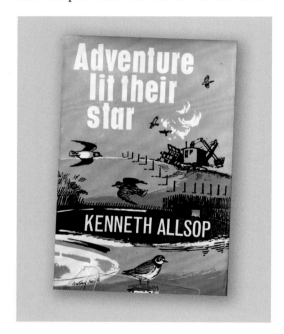

A longer-term addition to the awakening of interest in and knowledge of the natural world was the *New Naturalist* series, published by Collins. Beginning with E.B. Ford's *Butterflies* in 1945, the series has gone onto publish over 140 volumes and has been a major feature of both natural history writing and book collecting.

Conclusion

The course of nature conservation in Britain throughout the 20th century was not an easy one. Beset by new agricultural technologies and government support for greater food production, voluntary and government agencies alike fought what seemed at times to be an ever-losing battle. Wetlands were severely affected and the entire wildlife resource of the Cambridgeshire fens became reduced to just four sites, which were themselves under constant pressure from drainage, pesticides and lack of recognition of their role in wider society.

It is tempting to look back and place the blame for the decline in wildlife and wild places against governments, farmers, or indeed conservationists themselves. But that would be to ignore the very real situation which two world wars presented, the technological advances of the Age and the growth in both population and living standards. Like the drainers of the 17th and 18th centuries, farmers were responding to the demands of society and to a great degree these were met. Cheap, high quality food became the norm and the hidden environmental costs were not challenged until comparatively recently. The initial slaughter of wild birds and invertebrates by DDT and other pesticides was brought to halt, but pesticides of a more targeted nature have remained a foundation of modern food production and soil degradation has become a serious issue. Even the green pastures of livestock country are often green in colour only, and offer few opportunities for wildlife to find home or food.

It was not just the physical demands of the post-war generations which influenced landscapes. The spread of computer-based life and urban living seemed to create a deep gulf between humans and the natural world. Of the 300-odd generations who have lived throughout the period of our story, those of the 20th century have experienced increasing isolation from Nature and forgotten much of the wisdom of their forebears. Opposition to the relentless pressure which an ever-growing economy exerted was not popular, and economists and ecologists had to work hard to quantify the benefits which Nature can bring to society.

Considering these obstacles, it is remarkable that so much of our wildlife survived. The nature reserves and SSSIs owe their existence to the tireless efforts of naturalists and growing public concern about the loss of green space. They are wonderful places, and the increasing knowledge of habitat conservation and creation has protected many precious species. Careful scientific research and applied conservation management has also broadened our understanding of the complexities of the natural world and highlighted the role which we can play in sustaining or destroying it. In the next chapters we will explore the value of fenland wildlife, take a walk through the NNRs of Woodwalton and Holme Fens, and ponder how entire landscapes might function if we took a more enlightened approach to the 'natural capital' which they contain.

If these sites had not been saved from destruction, we would have no template against which to measure the increasing uniformity which now characterises much of our countryside, but protecting individual sites has not been enough. By the end of the 20th century, Nature was largely confined to unsustainable islands and did not feature as a central issue either in the mind of society, or in Government policies. At times, there seemed to be little appetite to defend the non-human world from the unstoppable pursuit of economic prosperity, or indeed an understanding of the consequences.

Although the global consequences of climate change were only beginning to be understood, there was growing awareness of the plight of the natural world, reflected through TV, film, art and literature. People became more aware both of its wonders and the threats to its existence, but opinions about the countryside remained deeply polarised. As the century drew to a close, however, the voices of individuals and organisations alike began to become more strident about a new approach, where Nature would not be confined to isolated sites, but was part of everyday life.

In the coming chapters, we will see how the impetus for large-scale change grew and came to early fruition in the Great Fen of Cambridgeshire.

The Ecology of the Fens

The Nene and Great Ouse are lazy rivers. High above the fens they trickle from springs in the Northamptonshire hills. The trickle becomes a stream and the stream a river that ambles for hundreds of kilometres before reaching the sea. The Nene changes both its name (Nen to Nene) and character as it meanders through its broad valley. It by-passed Whittlesea Mere centuries ago when a straight drain was cut towards Wisbech, forgetting the Mere and its glories. From the Dog-in -a-Doublet sluice north of Whittlesea, the river blends with the tides and feeds the bird-filled Nene Washes, before squeezing between the two 'lighthouses' out into the Wash. To the south, the Ouse flows for over 200 kms, and waters the ancient meadows of Portholme in Huntingdon, before passing through Ely and Downham Market. Near Ely, the 17th century diversion drains of Vermuyden and the Earls of Bedford contain the nature reserves of the Ouse Washes. Eventually, its fresh peaty waters give way to the salt-marsh and waves of the North Sea.

Without these rivers, drifting and flooding through the great Anglian plain, the fens would not exist. Without the sluggish waters, reeds and marshy meadows, fish and birds would have not have existed here, and the tales of bogs and eels, beavers and fen tygers would never have been. The slow pace of the rivers created the damp grasslands and wet peaty pools along their way, but was also one of the main problems for the drainers – the flow was so lethargic that the outfalls to the sea easily silted, so pumps and new drains often made the flooding worse.

River Nene, near Oundle

River Great Ouse

In my years on the fenland nature reserves I lost count of the times when visitors asked me *"What did the fens once look like?".* My answer was always the same: *"it depends what period you are thinking of!"* The point being that the story of the fens has been one of continual change. Once dry and half-frozen, they became grassy and wooded, then reed and sedge invaded as the climate became wetter. Livestock grazed summer fields as the peat formed over thousands of years, deep bog overtook the wettest areas, only to collapse and disappear as humans drained and farmed the land. Whittlesea Mere may have once been a wonderland of water and birds but it didn't exist before 500BC and was gone before Queen Victoria had got used to wearing her crown!

Different people have very different views of today's fenlands. For some they are vast skies and open landscape, for others black peat fields of potatoes, carrots and celery, for others a wildlife spectacle with Bitterns and butterflies. So it's useful to describe exactly what these various terms mean. What is a fen, or a bog or a marsh and why are they important?

The Oxford Dictionary describes a **fen** as:
A low and marshy or frequently flooded area of land:
1.1 The flat low-lying areas of eastern England, mainly in Lincolnshire, Cambridgeshire, and Norfolk, formerly marshland but largely drained for agriculture since the 17th century.
1.2 Ecology: Wetland with alkaline, neutral, or only slightly acid peaty soil.

A **bog**, on the other hand is:
An area of wet muddy ground that is too soft to support a heavy body 'a peat bog'
1.1 Ecology: Wetland with acid peaty soil, typically dominated by peat moss.

Whereas a **marsh** is:
An area of low-lying land which is flooded in wet seasons or at high tide, and typically remains waterlogged at all times.

The Joint Nature Conservation Council (JNCC) takes a rather more scientific view:
Fens and marshes are characterised by a variety of vegetation types that are found on groundwater-fed (minerotrophic) peat, peaty soils, or mineral soils. These may be permanently, seasonally or periodically waterlogged. Fens are peatlands which receive water and nutrients from groundwater and surface run-off, as well as from rainfall... Marsh is a general term usually used to imply waterlogged soil; it is used more specifically to refer to fen meadows and rush-pasture communities on mineral soils and shallow peats. Swamps are characterised by tall emergent vegetation. Reedbeds (i.e. swamps dominated by stands of common reed Phragmites australis) are also included in this type.

Fen
Lowland Fens are minerotrophic peatlands (i.e. their nutrients come from ground water as well as rain water), that are at least periodically waterlogged. Although they are underlain by peat, decomposition tends to be relatively high and so the peat depth is shallow and there is no peat dome (as with raised bogs). These fens may frequently form complex mosaics with a number of associated habitat types, including wet woodland (fen carr), reedbed, lowland heathland and lowland meadow.

Two broad types of fen can be distinguished. Topogenous fens, where water movement is generally vertical and soligenous fens where water movement is predominantly lateral.

Woodwalton Fen falls into the second category, although as we shall see later, the severe effects of drainage and adjoining land-use have left the site in a very artificial state. JNCC makes a further distinction, which is between 'Poor' Fen and 'Rich' Fen:
Poor fens with their low to moderate fertility and are acid water (pH <5) occur mainly in the uplands or in association with lowland heaths. Rich fens are fed by alkaline, mineral-enriched,

Woodwalton Fen

calcareous waters (pH >5) and are mainly confined to the lowlands. The vegetation is normally relatively species-rich and includes mire vegetation dominated by a range of Carex sedges.

Woodwalton Fen sits roughly in the rich fen category, but lacks many of the normal associated species, such as *Sphagnum* bog-mosses, Bogbean *Menyanthes trifoliata* and Common Butterwort *Pinguicula vulgaris*. What Woodwalton does have is mixed tall-herb fen communities. Here, characteristic plants like Common Reed *Phragmites australis* grow alongside Comfrey *Symphytum officinale*, Hemp-agrimony *Eupatorium cannabinum*, Marsh Bedstraw *Galium palustre*, Purple-loosestrife *Lythrum salicaria* and Yellow Loosestrife *Lysimachia vulgaris*. Other less common species include Marsh Pea *Lathyrus palustris* and the rare Narrow-leaved Marsh-orchid *Dactylorhiza praetermissaa* subsp. *schoenophila*. There are more than 20 species of *Carex* sedges, some of which are scarce or rare, including the Star Sedge *Carex spicata* and the hybrid *Carex × evoluta*. Milk-parsley *Thysselinum palustre* is rarely found, which will no doubt prevent any visions of re-establishing the beautiful Swallowtail butterfly, but the recent re-discovery of Marsh Lousewort *Pedicularis palustris*, proves that Nature can still hold surprises – even after almost 100 years absence! Saw-sedge or Great Fen-sedge *Cladium mariscus*, on the other hand, dominates one or two areas where the fertility is rather lower, sometimes accompanied by Purple Moor-grass *Molinea caerulea*. Thanks to records kept by the Marchioness of Huntly and the poet John Clare, we know that the Great Fen was once rich in more exciting flowers like Grass-of-Parnassus *Parnassia palustris*, Common Butterwort and Bog Asphodel *Narthecium ossifragum*.

Holme Fen has few areas of fen, and so lacks many of these species as they have either been shaded out by the woodland or lost to dry conditions. It does, however, have some species which are not found elsewhere such as the Fen Woodrush *Luzula pallidula* and the tall fenland subspecies of Heath Dog-violet, *Viola canina* subsp. *montana*.

Lowland raised bog

JNCC describes this type of vegetation as occurring: *on elevated deposits of peat and receive mineral nutrients principally from precipitation. They are referred to as ombrotrophic (rain-fed) mires.*

This habitat is very acidic and nutrient-poor. It is also poorly drained and water-logged. This inhibits the decomposition of plant material, resulting in an accumulation of peat, which, over thousands of years, can become many metres thick.

These peatland ecosystems develop primarily, but not exclusively, in lowland areas... The resultant waterlogging provides anaerobic conditions which slow down the decomposition of plant material, which in turn leads to an accumulation of peat. Continued accrual of peat elevates the bog surface above regional groundwater levels to form a gently-curving dome from which the term 'raised' bog is derived.

Although primarily a northern and wetland habitat in the UK, remnants occur in some southern and eastern localities, for example Somerset, South Yorkshire and Fenland. The vegetation of lowland bogs is very distinctive and includes a range of specialised wetland plants, which varies depending on the pattern of surface pools, hummocks and lawns. Usually various colourful *Sphagnum* bog-mosses predominate. These are highly absorbent and produce a characteristically 'spongy-feel' to the bog surface. Other typical plants include Bog Asphodel, Bogbean, Bog-myrtle *Myrica gale*, *Eriophorum* cotton-grasses, and Cross-leaved Heath *Erica tetralix*, among others.

The flora of a raised bog is greatly affected by peat-cutting and drainage, which dry the bog out, encouraging purple moor-grass and heather and allowing birch and pine trees to invade. This is exactly what has happened at Holme Fen NNR, which is in the unique position of having retained its original bog surface but lost most of the characteristic species due to drainage.

Why are fens important?

The occurrence of these different vegetation types can vary from an intricate mixture to large areas of uniform habitat, typically reedbed. During the long evolution of the fenland landscape from the Bronze Age to the early Victorian period, there were undoubtedly vast areas of peat and its dependent communities. Today, only fragments remain due to drainage, which has not only directly reduced wildlife populations to negligible size, but also caused the inexorable decline of the peat resource itself. A report for RSPB in 2009 (Holman 2009) gave

Banded Demoiselle *Calopteryx splendens* [NE]

Gadwall *Anas strepera* [NE]

a shocking analysis of how much peat has been lost since drainage. It identified just 12,500 hectares of peat over 1 metre depth in the fens, which is half of that which was estimated just two decades earlier (Burton and Hodgson 1987).

Today's special fen wildlife can only thrive where the peat itself survives and this explains why the current scattered and fragmented location of nature reserves from the Broads to the Great Fen is so unsatisfactory. Areas such as the Great Fen, Wicken Fen and the Washes of the Nene and Ouse are the only spots in Cambridgeshire where peat of any significant depth remains and so it is only here that bog and marsh, Swallowtail butterfly and Fen Violet *Viola persicifolia* survive. Large scale and inter-connectedness has been replaced by small 'gardens' or – even worse – 'flowerpots'. Intensive management can temporarily maintain some 'semi-natural' habitat, but the chance of a small insect, mammal or plant making its way from one reserve to the next is zero.

As the wetland has been reduced to fragments, so many of its important functions have become reduced or lost completely. This includes storing flood waters, absorbing carbon dioxide, pastoral farming and recreation. To understand these impacts we need to understand how the system works.

Chemical importance

The East Anglia fenland has developed on peat which has built up over about 6,000 years. As all living creatures contain carbon, the slow accretion of peat from the preserved remains of plants acts as a significant store of this chemical, known as a carbon 'sink'. In wet conditions, this carbon remains 'locked up' in the peat, but if the peat dries and is exposed to the air, such as after drainage, the carbon oxidises and is released into the atmosphere. In large quantities this can alter the relative percentage of carbon dioxide and can be a major factor in climate change. It has been estimated that about 325,000 tons of CO_2 could potentially escape into the atmosphere each year from the Great Fen if the entire peat surface was exposed – the equivalent of emissions from about 70,000 cars! (Open University 2008, Evans *et al.*, 2017).

Physical importance

Apart from storing carbon, fens and bogs have a huge capacity for storing water and as such are well suited to preventing flooding. Conventional drainage aims to collect water and dispose of it as quickly as possible. This means that the carriers for the water – the dykes and rivers – have to be large enough to carry enormous quantities of water in times of heavy rainfall. If they are not large enough or are blocked in any way, then flooding can occur which can cause loss of life and livelihoods. By diverting the water into fen, the flow is 'attenuated', which can help to prevent flooding. Under the right conditions, it can also provide a habitat for a significant variety of plants and animals.

Biological importance

An astonishing variety of life can be supported in a functioning peatland ecosystem because of the number of different habitats within it. Water, reeds, meadows and carr all support their own species, but also with much over-lapping. Each habitat supports the other to form an intricate web of life – whose inter-connected strands make up a living organism. When some of the strands of that web are removed, it damages the way in which the other parts function. This is what happens when the fen wetlands are drained, the web is broken and begins to

Reed Bunting *Emberiza schoeniclus* [NE]

malfunction. The surviving fragments became less able to withstand outside pressures such as hunting or further drainage and may become dysfunctional beyond repair.

The fragments which have survived in the Great Fen are the two NNRs of Holme Fen and Woodwalton Fen. Theirs is a remarkable story, because it illustrates not only the damage caused by the drainage of the Whittlesea Mere wetland, but also the ability of some species to survive catastrophic changes to their environment. It also demonstrates the resolve and ingenuity of successive scientists, wardens and volunteers to conserve the best of what they have inherited.

The various plants and animals to be found in fenland can be loosely grouped into communities. Meadows, reedswamp, water and woodland all have their own characteristic features, but these can also merge into one another, such as the reeds growing out into open water. These communities are also greatly affected by management, which has been a key feature of the fens for thousands of years.

Aquatic communities

There are no large lakes left in the fens, apart from the Norfolk Broads, but there are many kilometres of ditches, with ponds and small meres which provide a home for many different types of wildlife.

Plants of the more open water such as pools and drainage dykes include the pondweeds *Potomageton* spp. and water-milfoils *Myriophyllum* spp. Plants which can survive in less open water include Lesser Water-parsnip *Berula erecta,* Bladderwort *Utricularia vulgaris* and Frogbit *Hydrocharis morsus-ranae.* One species which grows well in both the water and

Hairy Dragonflies *Brachytron pratense* [PC]

Broad-leaved Pondweed *Potomageton natans* [PC]

surrounding reed zone is the Greater Water-parsnip *Sium latifolium* and Woodwalton is a major site for this scarce plant.

Open water in the fens can be a very temporary affair. Shallow depth and the addition of organic matter from decaying plant remains or silt from run-off can transform a small pond to a marsh and then to dry ground with scrub. The early human inhabitants of the fens quickly learnt that cutting of bushes and clearance of silt was essential to maintain the open water which they relied on, and it is just the same in nature reserves today. The dynamic nature of the aquatic environment creates a constant supply of new resources for its wildlife.

The animal life of the fen waterways is very rich and many invertebrate species rely on the water for some stage of their life-cycle. Forty-three per cent of endangered and vulnerable wetland species in Britain are found in East Anglia (Lott *et al.* 2002). For example, more than half of Britain's species of Odonata (dragonflies and damselflies) have now been recorded at the Great Fen. Some larvae spend several years rampaging up and down the ditches before they emerge into the sunlight, so the network of ditches and surrounding vegetation provide a home for larvae and adults alike. The rare Tansy Beetle *Chrysolina graminis* has recently been re-discovered at Woodwalton. Until 2018, this was thought to be one of only two surviving populations of this species in England, but a further population has now been found on the Ouse Washes, about 20 km further east in the fens. There are some impressive water beetles in the ditches, too, including the fenland King Diving-beetle *Dytiscus dimidiatus*.

There are important regulating factors for these communities. The amount of available dissolved oxygen, whether or not the water is flowing and how much nutrient and dissolved calcium it contains, have major effects on aquatic life. Open water species like the pondweeds can quickly disappear if the water surface becomes overgrown and shaded, or its chemical nature altered by fertilisers. In fenland there is often little flow and in the reserves of the Great Fen, no flow at all – unless it is pumped. This was not always the case. Woodwalton was once open to the Great Raveley Drain (the main drain which flows past the site carrying drainage water from the 'highlands' as well as from the surrounding fields). Between 1968 and 1975 the reserve was embanked in order to provide a flood water storage reservoir. This engineering separated the reserve from the fen drains, with water flow only possible when sluices were opened or by pumping. The resulting lack of regular flow, and intake of nutrient-rich water have contributed to a dramatic change in the aquatic flora. Plants which are rooted into the ditch bottom, such as the water-milfoils and pondweeds, have declined as silt has accumulated. Free-floating species, on the other hand, have maintained their status and several of the Woodwalton ditches are covered with Lesser Water-parsnip and Bladderwort. in the summer. Other species are less welcome. Duckweed *Lemna* spp. blooms when nitrogen and phosphorous levels rise and can block light from reaching the ditch bottom and cause oxygen levels to decline. This leads to an overall decline in species diversity in the water body.

Tansy Beetle *Chrysolina graminis* [GP]

King Diving-beetle *Dytiscus dimidiatus* [CK-E]

Lustrous Bog-moss
Sphagnum subnitems [PC]

Bog communities

The only 'bog' in the Cambridgeshire fens is at Holme Fen and this has been severely damaged by drainage. The raised dome which once existed did not rise up of itself from the deep. It was the wetland around it which prevented water from seeping away and allowed rainfall to continuously feed the bog. These are conditions which many plants cannot tolerate – with the exception of bog-mosses of the *Sphagnum* genus, of which there are many different species. Some have bright red leaves, others drooping, whilst others still are bright green and quite upright. Until the 1970s there were at least seven different species at Holme Fen, and until 2018 it was thought that just three had survived. Blunt-leaved Bog-moss *Sphagnum palustre* is one of these which has persisted because it is more tolerant of the dry conditions. In 2017, however, local botanists discovered the first plant to be seen since 1959 of the Lustrous Bog-moss *Sphagnum subnitens*. These mosses grow in just one location on the reserve and are so vulnerable that specimens of the more common species have been taken to a botanic garden so that one day it may be re-established in other areas of the reserve if conditions become suitable. These mosses may also be used in the new 'wetland agriculture' project for the Great Fen.

Fen communities

Bogs and open water have their own special inhabitants, like the *Sphagnum* mosses or diving beetles, but often the edges of both vegetation-types grade into 'fen'.

Although much reduced, fenland still supports an astonishing array of wildlife. Reeds, sedges and rushes often dominate, but there is also a huge range of flowering plants; orchids, Common Valerian *Valeriana officinalis*, Ragged-Robin *Silene flos-cuculi* and violets *Viola* spp. can turn the fen of a summer's day into a magnificent sight.

The *Fens Biodiversity Audit* published in 2012 (UEA 2012) revealed that 13 Global Red Data Book species live here, including Black-tailed Godwits *Limosa limosa*, Otters *Lutra lutra*, the Barbastelle bat *Barbastella barbastellus*, Desmoulin's Whorl Snail *Vertigo moulinsiana*, and White-clawed Crayfish *Austropotamobius pallipes*. Astonishingly, the humble Eel *Anguilla anguilla*, once the mainstay of the fen economy, is now listed among these globally threatened species!

Soldierflies

Banded General *Stratiomys potamida* [PC]

Flecked General
Stratiomys singularior [NP]

Three-lined Soldier
Oxycera trilineata [PC]

Reed Warbler *Acrocephalus scirpaceus* [DG]

Another 82 species are special to the Fens. These purely 'local' species include the flowering plants Fen Ragwort *Jacobaea paludosa*, Fen Violet, invertebrates like feather-winged beetles, a snail-killing fly and the Cambridge Groundling Moth *Scrobipalpa pauperella*. In addition, there are 2,630 species of fly, including rare soldierflies and hoverflies, 2,159 beetles of which 92 are rare water beetles, and more than 1,500 species each of moths and plants. On the darker side, the report highlights the fate of many species which have been lost. Over 500 rare species have not been seen in the last 25 years, and of these, 100 species have been lost from the Fens altogether.

The fens have always been famous for their invertebrates, particularly butterflies and moths. The two fenland specialist butterflies are the Large Copper and the Swallowtail. Sadly, the Large Copper is now extinct in Britain, but the Swallowtail still survives in the Norfolk Broads, although attempts to re-establish it at Wicken have so far proved unsuccessful. In the days before drainage when Victorian field naturalists were very active, there was a huge variety of moths on the wetland. The Marsh Moth *Athetis palustris*, Rosy Marsh Moth *Coenophila subrosea*, and Reed Tussock *Laelia coenosa* are just some of the species which are seen no more. This is mainly due to drainage, but some may also have been victims of over-collecting, such as the Large Copper butterfly – of which more later.

Reedswamp

Although part of the fenland vegetation-type, reedswamp has its own unique features. Probably the most iconic of fen habitats, the reeds have supported humans and wildlife for thousands of years, but by the late 20th century, neglect, drainage and clearance had reduced them to a critical level. Not only did this affect the reed-cutting industry, it spelt disaster for birds such as the Bittern. These birds are entirely dependent on reeds growing very close to water where they can find fish, frogs and other food, whilst having shelter and nest sites. When the reed declines, the birds have nowhere else to go. There are several other birds which epitomise fenland habitats. The extraordinary Bearded Reedling (or Bearded Tit) *Panurus biarmicus* has the ability to vary its diet from summer insects to winter seeds by a change in the structure of its gut. Reed Warblers *Acrocephalus scirpaceus* and Sedge Warblers *Acrocephalus schoenobaenus*, Cuckoos *Cuculus canorus* and Marsh Harriers are all to be found where conditions are suitable, but all are vulnerable to the habitat drying out, or becoming invaded by scrub.

Woodland and 'carr'

It might be supposed that woody vegetation would not be welcome in a fen, but this is not always the case. Woodland and scrub (it is called 'carr' in the fens) is a very valuable wildlife resource as long as it is strictly controlled (Woodwalton was almost lost to trees and bushes until recently). One of the specialists of this habitat is the Black-and-yellow Longhorn Beetle *Rutpela maculata*. The larvae of this splendid creature live in the trunks and bark of old trees and feed on the rotting bark and the adults are important pollinators, visiting flowers across the fen. Birds such as Treecreepers *Certhia familiaris* feed exclusively on the trunks (always going up, never down) and others such as Long-eared Owls *Asio otus* and Hobbies *Falco subbuteo* nest among the branches. At Holme Fen there are many niches for bats

Black-and-yellow Longhorn Beetle *Rutpela maculata* [PC]

such as Noctules *Nyctalus noctula* in the older birch trees and this is one of England's best sites for fungi, with over 500 species having been recorded.

Acting together, the features outlined above represent a comprehensive and inter-connected land and waterscape, which can support human and non-human activity to great effect. Problems only arise where the balance is disturbed and the interactions between physical, biological and cultural features can no longer function together.

Wildlife through the ages

It is not just the reduction in size, but fragmentation, changes in edge effect and local climate which cause problems. A shift in predator-prey balance and loss of feeding and breeding sites also make it difficult or impossible for individuals to thrive on a long-term basis. While the natural dynamism of the Earth's climate has caused many changes in the natural world over the period of our story, in the fenland it is human activity which has been particularly significant. As humans became more established, cleared trees and farmed the land on a grand scale, wildlife communities either adapted or faded away altogether, particularly after the great 17th-century drainage.

It might come as a surprise then, to learn that human activity is not always bad for wildlife. The great forests of oaks and pines in ancient fenland may have been home to many birds and beetles and offered foraging for Wild Boar *Sus scrofa* and Aurochs, but large areas of similar habitat suit a relatively narrow suite of species. The woodland clearances from the Neolithic onwards created or expanded a variety of environmental 'niches' which could be filled by many new species. In fenland, the variety created by fenland grazing, reed and peat-cutting sustained thriving wildlife communities both on the water and the land. Even in modern fenland, farmland can support species like breeding Skylarks *Alauda arvensis* and wintering

Lapwings *Vanellus vanellus* as long as there is sufficient account taken of their needs. The RSPB has demonstrated this in their management of 'Hope Farm', where the farmland bird index has moved in the opposite direction to the national index because of provision of spaces like 'skylark plots' in the wheat fields, and field edge management.

Some species have played a particularly significant role in our story of humans' relationship with Nature. Eurasian Beavers *Castor fiber*, Bitterns and Eels have been part of the Great Fen journey for centuries and deserve a special mention.

Eurasian Beaver *Castor fiber* [DW]

The Beaver's story

Beavers have been a major influence in the wetlands for thousands of years and exploring their fortunes through the Ages reveals how our relationship with them has changed.

The Eurasian Beaver is known from the archaeological record for millions of years and has survived Ice Ages, climate fluctuations and human predation in a remarkable fashion. Throughout the increasing impact of drainage, farming and settlement they maintained their numbers until the industrial age of the 19th century caused a decline throughout Europe.

The relationship between ourselves and beavers over the centuries has been variable. Beavers preceded our ancestors in the post-glacial landscape of Britain, spreading from their strongholds around the Rhone in France and the Danube. Their lodges may have provided ideal crossing places for humans over wetlands and could have provided platforms for the earliest hunting camps, as well as ready-cut timber for construction. For the beavers, logs cut by humans would also have been useful for their own foundations and we can imagine an early landscape where both humans and beavers were having an equal effect!

Beaver remains from Mesolithic sites such as Star Carr in Yorkshire, suggest that from earliest times they were a useful source of meat and fur and later the castoreum – a fatty deposit from their scent glands – became valued as a medicine.

The Beaver effect

Beavers live in dens, which begin life as burrows in the river bank, with a sleeping platform above the waterline. As the water level rises in response to their dam building, they need to provide dry quarters above the waterline and that is when they build their lodges. Lodges are mainly constructed with logs from trees felled by their sharp incisor teeth, sticks, clay and stones, depending on local material. A consequence of the dam building is that mini-wetlands are created, with pools and swamp vegetation. This creates ideal conditions for a wide range of other wetland plants and animals and is why the beaver is considered by ecologists to be a 'keystone' species.

Neolithic farming probably introduced more competition for land and water, but may have had little effect on wild beavers. It was more likely the shifting availability of habitat caused by sea level rise which affected their distribution. On the one hand, sea flooding into previously dry inland areas held up the outflow of rivers and created inland lagoons and swamps which would have suited the local beavers very nicely. On the other hand, the loss of coastal habitat and the marshes of Doggerland would have reduced available habitat for both humans and beavers, which may have led to competition for the remaining land.

It may have been a beaver lodge which formed the first foundation for the great platform and causeway at Flag Fen. Archaeological finds at West Cotton near Stanwick Lakes in Northamptonshire (1280–920BC) and at Burwell Fen between 1310 and 1040BC contained beaver bones (Coles 2016). Not far from Burwell, at Haddenham, a community appears to have been specialising in the harvesting of beaver pelts and teeth, which may have been exported to other parts of Britain or even abroad.

Roman drainage and farming probably reduced the fenland population, but by the 5th century AD, finds of jewellery made of beaver teeth indicate that there had been a recovery. Two centuries later, the Sutton Hoo ship burial in Suffolk included a lyre which was contained within a beaver-skin pouch. This is not necessarily evidence that these artefacts came directly from the fens as they may have been traded from across the North Sea, but it does indicate the value placed on beaver products. Perhaps this indicates that they were becoming scarce and valuable items. Teeth and bones of Beavers were found at West Stow in Suffolk, amongst those of domestic livestock, interestingly, other remains of Hen Harrier *Circus cyaneus*, Crane, Badger, Brown Bear, Red and Roe Deer, all indicate a thriving local wetland.

Despite this exploitation, they seem to have shown remarkable resilience and adaptation to human activities and appear to have remained a relatively common inhabitant of the fens and surrounding river catchments throughout the Anglo-Saxon period. Following this, increasing demand for castoreum and the valuable pelt trade inevitably began to depress the population. No more was beaver the staple of any local economy, but by the 11th century had been elevated to the menus of monastic institutions such as the abbey at Jarrow and high-status houses like Castle Acre in Norfolk.

During the following centuries the fortunes of the beaver are traced more in art and literature than in direct observations, suggesting a decline in direct field knowledge and more reliance on myth and folklore. Legends such as the beavers biting off their own testicles to avoid capture suggest a less than accurate knowledge of the species! Until recently, it was thought that the last individuals in England succumbed sometime in the 15th or 16th centuries, but new evidence suggests that they may have survived far longer than this in some places. Beavers do not always build dams and lodges, and can live quite happily along deep-water rivers without humans being aware of their existence. How long the fenland population survived is difficult to assess, but they may still have been present until the 17th century drainage.

One action which is likely to have hastened the beaver's demise was the 1566 *Act for the Preservation of Grayne*. This gave local officials the power to grant bounty payments for 'vermin', which included the hapless beaver as well as Otter and Polecat *Mustela putorius*. Although the bounty was not large, it was clearly a welcome additional income, and in 1789 the last known beaver was presented to the Church Warden of Bolton Percy in the Humberhead wetlands in return for just tuppence (an Otter would have been worth 10 times this amount).

Action to re-establish *Castor* to its previous haunts began almost as soon as it became extinct in Britain. In 1860 the Acclimatisation Society was formed, which aimed to introduce species to areas of the commonwealth where it was thought they would enrich the native fauna. In England, a wealthy landowner, Frederick Barne, was the first to release Canadian Beavers *Castor canadensis* onto his estate in Suffolk, a few miles south of the Broads, where they survived for a few years. The Marquis of Bute made a similar attempt in 1874/5, but there is no further evidence of attempts to re-establish them until 1992, when the European

Habitats Directive urged signatory countries to investigate the possibilities of returning extinct plants and animals to the wild.

In Britain since then there has been much activity. They were first officially released into the wild in south-west Scotland but there have been small colonies living in enclosures of various sizes in Kent, Cornwall, Devon and Gloucestershire for some time. In Devon's River Otter, Beavers were discovered living wild in 2008 and although the initial government reaction was to remove them, they are now part of a trial reintroduction scheme run by the Devon Wildlife Trust. Other significant wild populations are also now established in the Rivers Tay, Tamar and Wye.

In time, there may well be opportunities to re-establish this iconic animal onto the Great Fen, where it could resume its ancient role of shaping the new wetland.

The Bittern's story

The Bittern is another fen species which has been (and still is) of immense importance and is a key indicator of a healthy wetland ecosystem.

We have little idea of how numerous Bitterns were in the days following the retreat of the glaciers, but it is reasonable to assume that early woodland clearance, grazing and beaver activity created open space for wetlands of considerable size. Later records from sites such as Flag Fen indicate that bitterns were being eaten regularly and in some archaeological finds, Bitterns were the fourth most common species. While we should be cautious about the amount of 'wild' fen in the immediate pre-drainage era of by the 17th century, it must have been the case that numbers of Bitterns were still at very high levels, despite the efficiency of 'punt-gunning'. This was the consequence of the fen people maintaining marsh and fen for their own purposes, which suited Bitterns and other marsh birds very well. As Chris Newbold (former chief aquatic scientist at English Nature) said: *the local population unwittingly sustained and managed the fens in what would be regarded today as a large nature reserve*" (Newbold 1999).

Bittern shoot

In 1819, a Mr Lubbock shot 11 Bitterns whilst out snipe shooting, and his keeper had known 20 or 30 to be killed during a morning's shoot at Downham in Norfolk, probably late in the 18th century. Other means of hunting the birds was simply to walk them through the reedbed using horses and presumably shoot or catch them at the other end.

In the 1990s, RSPB researchers copied this old hunting method so that netted birds could be ringed or radio tagged – happily they were not shot afterwards! (Gillian Gilbert pers. comm.).

Bittern *Botaurus stellaris* [GP]

Clearly, the bird was highly valued and available as a food source. Even in the more peripheral areas of breeding habitat around Eastbourne in East Sussex, a Mr Bates remarked that in the 1870s they would sell for sixpence each for eating. In the early 17th century birds were sold at between sixpence and eightpence to Lord Dacres at Herstmonceux Castle for his menu (Walpole-Bond 1938). At a banquet held for the inauguration of the Archbishop of York around 1465, the menu included over 200 Bitterns, as well as a hundred of other not so common species like Curlew *Numenius arquata*.

While many wildlife species managed to adapt to farmed habitats, wetland drainage had more severe consequences for specialists like bitterns, which had no ability to adapt to the loss of marshes and lakes. Numbers gradually declined from the 17th century as fen drainage began to transform a great wetland into a great farmland. As habitat loss accelerated with more efficient pumps in the 19th and 20th centuries, together with continued enthusiastic shooting, even the Broadland populations went into severe decline. By 1885, H. Stevenson remarked that the bittern was one of the birds: *"which drainage and enclosure have driven from their old haunts"*, in contrast to the numbers indicated by earlier accounts which he had documented.

The iconic sound of the male's booming call has had major consequences for the historic relationship between people and bitterns. It is said to have held a negative association with people because of the mystery surrounding it. It is rumoured that many marshland villagers and towns-people would drive the birds away because they were considered harbingers of doom. If you heard a Bittern – you were sure to die fairly soon after!

The last documented breeding record for Norfolk was in 1868, and although there were some 'boomers' at the turn of the century, it was not until 1911 that breeding was again confirmed – presumably colonists from the continent. For the next 30 years, breeding numbers rose, but remained largely confined to the Norfolk Broads. A peak of about 60 booming males was reached in 1954, but the combined effects of pollution, harsh winters and coypu predation and caused a new decline. Although there was a recovery to about 80 pairs by 1976 (Sharrock 1976) further deterioration in quality and loss of reedbeds put such pressure on the remaining population that there were just 11 booming males left by 1997. Compare that to the records of 11 being shot at once by the punt-gunners of Whittlesea Mere and you get a sense of how great the decline had been!

As the cause of the decline was almost entirely due to the activities of humans, so it was the painstaking research and applied management techniques on several nature reserves which led to a remarkable recovery. Scientists from RSPB, working with other organisations such as English Nature, the Wildlife Trusts and the Broads Authority and backed by EU funding, gradually began to piece together the complicated story of exactly what habitats and food they needed to survive. Such has been the success of this work, that by 2017 there were over 160 'boomers' in England, with over 80 of these in East Anglia, including Woodwalton Fen.

The Eel's story

"Eel fisherman quits amid plunging eel numbers". Daily Telegraph, January 2016.

For an area of Britain which was once renowned for its inexhaustible supply of eels, this headline in a national newspaper documenting the demise of the last eel catcher in fenland was shocking news. Peter Carter, who gave up the profession in 2016 due to lack of eel numbers, said: *"I feel I have let all the eel men of the past down – 3,000 years of Fen life has finally gone".*

Archaeological excavations at Ely have revealed eel traps from 3,000 years ago (Tsukamoto ed. 2014), and they remained an important part of the diet of kings and paupers right into the medieval period. According to Isaak Walton in his *Compleat Angler* of 1653, the Romans: *"esteemed her the Helena of their feasts"*, and they were used equally as currency and food well into the medieval period.

It is extraordinary that for such an important cultural, financial and dietary animal, the eel has remained such a source of mystery, and there is yet much to be learned. The life cycle of this most enigmatic of beasts was the source of many imaginative explanations. According to Walton: *"some say they breed of generation, as other fish do, others that they breed, as some worms do, of mud... or out of the putrefaction of the earth... others say, that eels growing old, breed other eels out of the corruption of their old age... and others say that... eels are made of a particular dew, falling in the months of May and June on the banks of some particular ponds and rivers...".*

Even today, the true nature of its extraordinary life cycle is only partly known. It is thought spawning of the European Eel takes place in the Sargasso Sea, after which the tiny larva float or are blown on currents which take them to freshwater rivers such as in fenland, where they metamorphise into 'glass' eels. They may spend a decade or more growing through a yellow stage to become mature 'silver' adults. At this stage, they make a marathon 4,000-km migration on their way back to the Sargasso, where they spawn.

Eels appear to have been one of the most successful of the fenland inhabitants, judging by their uses. Eel-rents were common at the time of Domesday, where it is recorded that up to half a million eels were used each year as currency (*Historia Cartarum*). Payments were counted in 'stitches' which were a stick of 25 eels (Darby *et al.* 1977). During the monastic heyday of post-Norman conquest, there were many written accounts of their abundance. In 1150, for example, Ramsey Abbey paid a rent of 3,000 eels to the monks of Peterborough, to quarry stone from the quarries at Barnack, whilst the Bishop of Ely commanded rents of

As old as an Eel

Captive Eels have been known to live as long as 90 years, but in 2014 one was recorded as having died in Sweden at the grand age of 155! (*The Times* 2014). [Painting: Vadim Gorbatov]

Eel weir from the 1325 Luttrell Psalter [Wiki Commons]

80,000 eels from his tenants. The Lord of the Manor of Ely, meanwhile, was paid a rent of 100,00 eels per annum by his serfs.

Whilst eels have a long history with humans as both food and financial items, they also had medicinal and other uses, and were recommended for curing warts, deafness and arthritis. Added to all that, they had been commonly used as whips since Roman times and are still valued for purses and other leather substitutes today (Schweid 2009). At the same time, they were often regarded in a more derogatory sense. The common phrase "*slippery as an eel*" denotes an untrustworthy person, and the fen people were called "*yellow bellies*" by their less enthusiastic admirers!

The story of the eel appears to be one of 'boom to bust'. Despite drainage, they appear to have remained relatively plentiful into the 20th century. The largest known catch was one caught in Hampshire in 1978, which weighed in at 5 kg, and other large ones are still occasionally found, but in recent years there has been a catastrophic decline. The centuries-old fenland eel fishing industry is now defunct and there are strict controls on private fishers.

On a brighter note, the Environment Agency has installed countless eel and fish passes to water control structures which would otherwise prevent the passage of older eels upstream. There are still very few eels, but in a press release from 2017 the EA expressed cautious optimism that they were returning to some areas where they had not been seen for decades. Since 2008, scientists have been implanting electronic tags to migrating eels in an attempt to find out more about their lives and identify possible causes of their decline.

Conclusion

Lowland peatland, with its fens, marshes and bogs, is potentially one of the richest habitats on the planet. The variety of water, vegetation and soils can provide a home for more plants and animals than an average keen naturalist could expect to see in a lifetime.

'Fenland' covers a wide variety of peatland habitats, all of which are highly dynamic, dependant on the availability and quality of water, and can be modified greatly by grazing or mowing. Fenland has not been a truly 'wild' landscape for centuries, but even in its 'managed' state is of great significance to humans and wildlife alike. The benefits which a functioning peatland ecosystem can contribute to our lives include the economy, health and well-being and resources of useful products. Storing water saves properties and farms from flooding, while opportunities for recreation feed the spirit and have proven health advantages. Reed, sedge, livestock and biomass contribute to everything from food to energy generation and preventing oxidation of peat helps mitigate the effects of climate change.

Almost all that remains of the fenland ecosystem is protected in nature reserves. Here, a nucleus of wildlife is a potential 'seed-source' for land around the reserves which is restored and so help to rebuild some of the functions of a healthy wetland.

Although many species have not survived the centuries, others have been more fortunate, and we can rightly celebrate the flowering meadows and symphony of birdsong which a visit to the East Anglian fen nature reserves like Woodwalton or Wicken Fen can provide. Bitterns, cranes and Tansy Beetles are a reminder that careful research and sensitive management can restore the fortunes of threatened species.

In the next chapter, we will explore some of these places and meet the wildlife that lives there.

Cranes returning to the fen by Vadim Gorbatov

"Once I could meet with them on every side;
But they have dwindled long by slow decay;
Yet still I persevere, and find them where I may."
(The Leech Gatherer) William Wordsworth *Resolution and Independence* 1807

We have seen how the breaking up of the once vast fen wetland impacted both the wildlife and the people who once thrived there. The founding of the nature reserves of Woodwalton and Holme Fens served to preserve two fragments of this and work has gone on ever since to conserve and improve the habitats there. Given the loss of the surrounding wetland it might seem to have been a thankless task, but perseverance, hard work and dedication have achieved a great deal.

The vision of the Great Fen is to re-connect these isolated fragments so that the next generation will inherit more, not less of the wonders of these fens. The reserves will then be recognised for what they have been – reservoirs of biodiversity which hold the key to the future.

Nature reserves are places of calm, a place to regenerate the spirit, and the fenland NNRs are no exception.

Woodwalton Fen

My first impression of the Fen when shown around by warden Ron Harold, was excitement that such a variety of habitat could exist on one site. Woodlands and bushes of sallow bordering fields of waving grasses... and water, water in the ditches, water in the meres, water in pools and puddles. Ron told me he scarcely took his boots off and over the years I was to find out why! I knew little then of buried Roman coins, monastic causeways or buried forests, just that this was an enchanted place and it was going to be my responsibility.

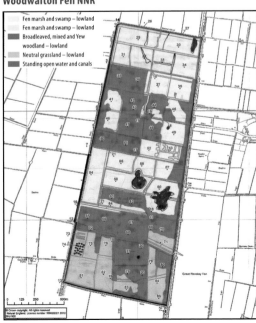

Woodwalton Fen NNR

Fen marsh and swamp – lowland
Fen marsh and swamp – lowland
Broadleaved, mixed and Yew woodland – lowland
Neutral grassland – lowland
Standing open water and canals

To cross the bridge onto Woodwalton Fen is to leave behind daily life and enter a 'Narnia' world of dazzling wildlife and reminders of human endeavour across the centuries. Is this, then, an artificial place with no real role in modern society, a museum of quaint artefacts and doomed species? On the contrary – here are the building blocks of a new landscape, lessons from the birth of modern nature conservation and innovative and bold ideas that are shaping the future outside this precious place.

History

The Fen which is now the National Nature Reserve was owned by Ramsey Abbey in the 13th century. It was then part of the mosaic of meres, bogs and reedy fens that surrounded Whittlesea Mere and its satellite lakes of Ramsey, Trundle, Ugg, Brick and Benwick. The land was probably dry enough for summer sheep grazing and mowing marsh, but most of it would have remained dominated by *Sphagnum* moss pools and wet fen, no doubt with occasional birch and willow carr in drier spots.

By 1887 the Ordnance Survey map showed much rough pasture and scrub, crossed by drainage channels which were used to take peat turves out by fen barge. Peat digging for fuel was an important activity and there are remains of a peat

Miriam Rothschild's view

"*They were still cutting peat in my day, at the bottom end of the Fen. I had a peat cutting spade, which had a square hole in the middle, but I gave it to a museum. There were no proper bridges over the dykes, only a plank, I was terrified of falling in, I got stuck one day in the middle. There was much more water then than there is now.*" Dame Miriam Rothschild, interview with Alan Bowley, 2002.

milling works along the eastern bank of the reserve adjacent to the Great Raveley Drain, which was active well into the 20th century. The site of the present Great Fen Countryside Centre along Chapel Road was a brick kiln, and it was here that some of the peat was transported by boat to fire the kilns.

Thankfully, when Charles Rothschild bought the first 342 acres of the site in 1910, there was still sufficient peat for some characteristic species to thrive, where it remained wet enough. Following the initial purchase, a lease on a further area was taken out, which was purchased in 1920. A further

Early naturalists at Woodwalton Fen in the 1930s

154 acres of heathy land was acquired in 1919, and the sum of these (514 acres or 208 hectares) forms the present reserve.

Despite the common perception that Woodwalton is like the original wetland, it is anything but. Very little of the present reserve has remained untouched by drainage or peat digging, and some areas were put under the plough in the late 19th/early 20th centuries. In the early years of Rothschild's ownership many pine trees were planted at the south end, but luckily none survived! As the farming came to an end, reed became established in sufficient quantity for it to be harvested on a regular basis, but soon the continued dry conditions allowed bushes to grow up and cover the entire site. A 1930s article in a local newspaper called it the 'Jungle' because it was so inaccessible.

These changes have had an enormous impact on the flora and fauna that we find today. Many of the special fen plants which have survived in the Norfolk Broads have been lost or are very rare in Woodwalton, such as Fen Orchid, Milk-parsley and *Sphagnum* mosses. Indeed Dr Bryan Wheeler from Sheffield University used to say *"Woodwalton has no right to be as good as it is because it has been so messed about with over the years"*. Nevertheless, much has managed to survive or has been re-established. This is one of only three sites in Britain for the Fen Violet, for example, and the recent re-discovery of the almost extinct tansy beetle shows the resilience of some animals even in this isolated fragment of habitat.

Following Charles Rothschild's death in 1923, the care of the reserve passed to the SPNR and day-to-day management was the responsibility of Charles Stuart and his assistant George Mason ('watcher under Stuart'), the first of three generations of the same family to care for the reserve. At the same time, eminent naturalists like H.M. Edelsten and Sir John Fryer also worked here and were responsible for re-establishing some of the lost plants at the fen. These included Marsh Sow-thistle *Sonchus palustris*, Marsh Pea and the enigmatic 'Rothschild Sunflower' Yellow Oxeye *Telekia speciosa*, which was planted as nectar for the Large Copper butterfly – of which more later.

Lack of resources and the intervening Second World War did little to arrest the decline of the fen into scrub. Although there were attempts to isolate the site from the effects of drainage, it was not until after the war that concerted attempts were made to stop the drying out and tackle the encroaching scrub.

Following the lease of the NNR to the Nature Conservancy in 1953, a Joint Advisory Committee was established which enabled experts from the SPNR (now the Wildlife Trust) and the Nature Conservancy (now Natural England) to jointly influence the future of the site. It is largely thanks to the knowledge and enthusiasm of the expert and dedicated naturalists of the Committee that the reserve has earned such a special place in the history of conservation in Britain. This Committee was reformed as the Joint Technical Advisory Committee (JTAC) of the Great Fen and continues to provide essential ecological advice

The Masons of Woodwalton Fen – keepers of the Fen for 90 years

Having succeeded James Stuart as keeper of the Fen in the 1920s George Mason worked on the site for 35 years, being joined by his son, Gordon, in 1936. Gordon (pictured top rightg) became renowned for his knowledge and care of the Large Copper butterfly population, with which he had great success. Gordon was so dedicated to the reserve that it was difficult to persuade him to go away on holiday. His wife, Nancy, once told me that on the day she persuaded him to take the children to the beach for the day, the naturalist in charge of supplying Large Copper larvae visited the Fen unannounced. Gordon was not amused!

He was joined in turn by his son Andrew (pictured bottom right) in 1972, and Andrew went on to work on the Fen until his retirement in 2015. I was lucky enough to have Andrew as a colleague during the whole of my time on the Fen and his instinctive connection with the reserve and his uncanny ability to solve problems made him one of the best field managers I have ever encountered.

and guidance. From 1963–68 the reserve was administered from the experimental station at Monks Wood, but then reverted to the East Anglia region of the NC.

Management of the NNR

Achieving a consensus as to the best way to manage a reserve of this type has not been easy. The site has become marooned from a once substantial area of wetland and the processes which once influenced the wetland are no longer active. It is in effect a huge 'flowerpot', a garden which needs constant tending to maintain its interest. During the 1930s, wooden dams were installed along the eastern boundary to try and maintain higher water on the Fen. This made it possible to separate the fen from the agricultural drained system, although the western ends of dykes 7 (Coleman's) and 10 remained open. This was not enough to keep the site wet, however, and scrub continued to grow unchecked. It was not until the 1960s that concrete dams with controls were introduced and scrub clearance began in earnest (the one exception was in the 'Copper' fields, where scrub had been cleared for the Large Copper butterfly introduction in the 1920s).

1970s Article in local newspaper documenting habitat management at Woodwalton Fen

An air-curtain burner kept emissions from burning scrub to a minimum

A temporary railway kept ground compaction to a minimum during scrub clearance

Volunteers cutting and carting reed in the northern reedbed

Not all management goes to plan!

It was in 1955 that the first scientific assessment of the site was undertaken, when Duncan Poore (later to become director of the Nature Conservancy) carried out his PhD into the vegetation of the reserve. Poore was one of the first to use aerial photography to describe vegetation – a technique widely used more recently in Pete Stroh's PhD study of Wicken and the Great Fen. Poore's descriptions of the vegetation and the ecological processes were influential in the formulation of the first Management Plan in 1957 – a splendid gold-embossed hardback tome which was largely compiled by staff working under Eric Duffey at the Monks Wood experimental station. The importance of the research and applied ecology which was developed at Monks Wood cannot be over-estimated. It included painstaking work by Terry Wells and others into the effects of grazing (including frequent weighing of cattle to assess biomass intake), long-term surveillance of Chinese Water Deer *Hydropotes inermis* populations by A.S. Cooke and Lynne Farrell and ground-breaking studies into dragonflies by Norman Moore. It was also at Woodwalton that Chris Newbold undertook his PhD studies in freshwater ecology and warned continually of the dangers posed by nutrient enrichment. This research and experimentation on the reserve was a key reason why NNRs had been proposed in the 1949 Act and led to formulation of the cutting and grazing regimes which are the foundation of the reserve's management to this day. Additionally, there have been many hydrological investigations carried out. Other observations and research have led to a greater understanding of the complexities of the hydrology of the reserve, ultimately leading to the 2015 Water Level Management Plan.

Scrub clearance, mowing and ditch maintenance (initially mostly by hand) became established over the next few years until by the 1980s there was a comprehensive programme of cutting, cattle grazing and mechanical ditch management. In the early 2000s, 35 ha of scrub and trees were cleared and several coppice plots established – the final step in creating an intimate mix of open fen/woodland and scrub to provide habitat for a wide range of species.

The glory of Woodwalton Fen lies in its variety, and this can only be maintained by continual management. Gardening on a grand scale it may be, but there is no alternative on such an isolated site, where extinction looms for the vulnerable plant and animal communities.

A walk through Woodwalton Fen
We may never be able to visit the ancient wetlands of Whittlesea Mere and deep bogs of Holme, but we can catch a glimpse on the NNRs, hear an echo of the life of the ancient wetland. Let me take you on a walk through the reserves where we will find excitement and wildlife at every step

North end/reedbed
It's a short walk from Jackson's bridge to the reedbed but a journey back in time of four thousand years. Neolithic seas swept in here and the retreating waters laid down estuarine mud which can still be seen, buried a few centimetres under the later peat. This soft grey 'buttery' clay is found at varying depths, sandwiched between layers of peat, but has not been found south of the modern reedbed. As the peat continued to build up, the tidal marsh became a reedy fen until Victorian drainage.

As the waters receded after the drainage, the drying fields became invaded by sallow 'carr' (scrub) until the 1980s when large areas were cleared. So dense was the smoke from the fires of cut material that local farmers raised the alarm in fear of their crops being destroyed! But soon the site was all but free of trees and bushes and for the next few years the fen workers were engaged in pumping water from the Great Raveley Drain to try and make the area wetter, but with little success. It remained stubbornly dry, and scrub began to advance once more. Investigations by the University of Sheffield (ECUS) in the 1990s revealed that the water was not penetrating into the site, and was probably seeping back into the Great Raveley Drain, so scrub was cleared once more. At the same time, oxidised peat was removed from some areas, and a windpump and reservoir installed to store water and distribute it to drier areas. One of my abiding memories of the Fen was working with Andy Mason and his father-in-law, Doug Shaw, to install huge concrete rings to line the sump for the windpump. As we worked late into the afternoon the skies changed from deep blue to peat black and we were caught in a storm the like of which only the open fen can produce! Since then, the area has been maintained as reedbed by regular reed and scrub cutting, and water control using the windpump and reservoir.

Windpump [GP]

Marsh Harrier
Circus aeruginosus
nest-building

The driving ambition behind the 1990s restoration of the reedbed was to improve conditions for that most quintessential fenland bird, the bittern. By the mid 1990s there were fewer than a dozen breeding pairs in England, so it was with help from a grant from Anglian Water that we attempted to create the right habitat. Bitterns had always been a rare winter visitor at Woodwalton, so when RSPB research detected just what habitat Bitterns needed, we were confident that they would soon colonise. Well that's what I love about Mother Nature – we think we know what to do and expect instant results, but that is not always what happens! In fact, despite regular 'booming' from the reedbed since 2009, it was not until 2015 that breeding was confirmed... and that was on the fringes of Gordon's Mere in the middle of the reserve. By 2018, though, 'boomers' were at last living within the reedbed.

The reeds have become a haven for both Hen and Marsh Harriers. That Hen Harriers should choose to winter in the Cambridgeshire fens, when they breed in the wild upland moors, is testament to the importance of different habitats for some animals at different seasons. For several winters, the abundant food of the reeds and fields of the fen supported up to a dozen Hen Harriers and were a great attraction for visitors. After the late 1990s, however, few birds were seen. This was probably due to a drastic decline in their breeding success, coupled perhaps with warmer winters making it possible to find food further north.

Contrasting with the decline of Hen Harriers has been the extraordinary increase of Marsh Harriers. This species is traditionally strongly migratory, breeding in the fens and reedbeds of Europe before travelling to West Africa for the winter. Increasingly, however, some individuals have been remaining on their breeding sites all year. This much persecuted species was absent from the fen as a breeding species until 1989, when one pair raised three young. The following year four young were hatched, but there were no further attempts for several years. During the 2000s, Marsh Harriers have become established as a regular breeding species and they are now resident across the Great Fen.

Another recent success has been the elusive and fascinating Bearded Reedling (or Bearded Tit). These extraordinary birds had first been recorded in 1981, but had only been present as fleeting visitors. Their reluctance to breed has always been puzzling. Insects and reed seeds are abundant on the fen and as the birds can take advantage of both it would appear to be an ideal habitat, as at Wicken Fen, where they have bred for many years. On my last day as warden of Woodwalton Fen in 2014, I was overjoyed to hear the distinctive 'ping' call as a small party moved through the reeds. A year or so later breeding was proven, after a wait of many decades! During my many years wardening this magical place, I often thought that my dream would be fulfilled if Marsh Harriers, Bitterns and Bearded Reedlings would find a home here... and I nearly made it!

In the late 1980s a hide was erected here to allow easy access for watching Chinese Water Deer and the harrier winter roost. This was the first place on the Great Fen where Common Cranes *Grus grus* were sighted in 2008, by Chris Gerrard, then project manager, but although there have since been sightings of groups of up to 11 birds since, they have not yet attempted to breed. The view from this hide has for many years been across the reedbed to the arable fields of Darlow's Farm. Since 2004, the farm has been owned and managed by Natural England on behalf of the Great Fen, so that visitors can now see first-hand how the wildlife of the reserve is beginning to move across to the surrounding landscape.

This is one of only two sites on the reserve where the beautiful Marsh Pea can be found. This native species probably became extinct after Victorian drainage but was re-established by H.M. Edelsten in the 1940s. There is also one of the best stands in England of the very uncommon Greater Water-parsnip which has drastically declined in England over the last few decades due to loss of habitat.

Bearded Reedling *Panurus biarmicus* [NE]

Chinese Water Deer *Hydropotes inermis* [GP]

Marsh Pea *Lathyrus palustris*

Greater Water-parsnip *Sium latifolium*

Copper fields

Let's walk south away from the open reeds to the furrowed fields (the 'copper fields') lying beyond a narrow patch of Alder and birch. It is difficult to imagine now the revolution which took place here in 1927, for this is where Captain E.B. Purefoy carried out the first attempt at re-establishing a lost butterfly species in England. Thirty-five adult Large Copper butterflies had been brought over from the Netherlands and released into cages set out on the fen. The fields had been prepared by clearing much of the scrub and planting the foodplant, Water Dock *Rumex hydrolapathum*.

For over 70 years this extraordinary attempt continued, through wars, several wardens and in the face of near extermination of the donor population in Holland. Ultimately, the introduction did not succeed, but stands as a monument to the innovative and brave spirit of dedicated naturalists to reverse the decline of wildlife in our countryside. This spirit has inspired the management of the reserve ever since and drives the Great Fen today.

A military butterfly breeder

Edward Bagwell Purefoy was an Irish gentleman and soldier who fought in the Boer war but later retired to devote his energies to butterflies. Purefoy might be considered as the father of modern butterfly conservation, and was a colleague of Frohawk. It was he who first described the intricate association of the large blue with ants and he who first attempted to re-establish the Large Copper *Lycaena dispar*. Following an attempt in 1913, he experimented with an introduction of subspecies *rutilus* to his estate in Tipperary in Ireland, but they only lasted for a few years.

In 1927 Purefoy and his associate Schofield, brought 35 individuals of the Dutch subspecies *batavus* to Woodwalton Fen and released them onto the 'Copper' fields. Never before had this revolutionary approach to reinforce or re-establish vulnerable populations been attempted.

The Large Copper

Large Copper, male, Woodwalton Fen [JA]

The 'Orange Argus of eloe' *Lycaena dispar dispar* was discovered in Dozens Bank in Lincolnshire in 1749 by members of the Spalding Gentleman's Society. Just a century later, this hapless insect was extinct, the last specimen being seen at Bottisham Fen in 1851. It was definitely known from the Great Fen at the time of the drainage of Whittlesea Mere and there was a thriving trade in larvae which local fenlanders collected and sold to visiting collectors!

Attempts to establish the similar subspecies *batavus* from the Netherlands initially concentrated on releasing 35 adults onto plants in the 'Copper' fields. These fields were divided into sections in 1932 and managed in various ways to create suitable habitat. After severe predation, however, the plants were covered with cages, a practice which ensured their survival for some years. When Gordon Mason took over the rearing programme, the breeding was confined to a greenhouse, from where the emerging adults were released onto the Fen. Annual counts of larvae were undertaken on plants in the field, led by Dr I. MacClean of English Nature, but ultimately the butterflies were never able to reach a self-sustaining population, probably due to inbreeding and lack of suitable habitat. The breeding project was terminated in 1998, but research has continued in the Norfolk Broads and the possibility remains that this beautiful butterfly may once again be seen fluttering above the waters of the Great Fen.

A research project was carried out by Andrew Pullin and a PhD student, Mark Webb, from Keele University (Webb and Pullin 1996), the results of which suggested that there were several factors which prevented the prospect of a sustainable population. This is a great example of how Woodwalton Fen has stimulated important research.

The Scarce Chaser *Libellula fulva*

This beautiful dragonfly (pictured right [DC]) was once relatively widespread but by 1980 was known only from one riverside site in Sussex and a few places in East Anglia. Since then, the species has extended its range and is now found in six main localities; in East Anglia (including Cambridgeshire), Kent and Sussex, Wiltshire/Somerset, Dorset/Hampshire. At Woodwalton it has been studied intensively by Prof. Norman Moore and has colonised from a small population along the Great Raveley drain to now being found extensively around the reserve. To walk along the dykes on a calm spring morning when thousands of nymphs have hatched is a sight never to be forgotten!

There is network of ridges in the 'copper' fields which are probably left from peat digging. The resulting wet and dry areas give rise to a diverse flora, including Common Valerian and Common Meadow-rue *Thalictrum flavum* which is the foodplant for the very rare Marsh Carpet moth *Gagitodes sagitta*. This insect owes its rarity to its demanding habitat requirements. The adult moths are active in June but the larvae do not emerge until the autumn when they feed exclusively on the seeds of meadow rue. They have extraordinary camouflage and are very difficult to see. This is a good example of how critical management can be on such a small and isolated site. Cutting before the seeds are ripe will destroy the foodplant, but later in the season may be too wet to cut and may allow scrub to invade!

Scrub and trees along the Great Raveley Drain are a habitat for Scarce Chaser *Libellula fulva* dragonflies and maintain a screen for

Common Meadow-rue *Thalicrum flavum* [PC]

the NNR. Professor Norman Moore, who worked on dragonfly research for 30 years at Woodwalton, was most insistent that this was retained as it was a key breeding site for the species. Over the years, the dragonflies have spread into the reserve from the river's edge but it does underline the need to be mindful of how a relatively small area can be of crucial importance to a rare species.

One or two fields in the western part of the reserve appear to have escaped major peat digging, leaving more of the 'red' peat which is less nutrient-rich. Little rush or reed grows here, and it is a joyous place in summer, full of wild flowers including rarities like the Slender Sedge *Carex lasiocarpa*, Purple Moor-grass, Marsh Pennywort *Hydrocotyle vulgaris* and occasional Fen Violet. There is also scattered Saw-sedge (also known as the Great Fen-sedge). This sedge had always been an important part of fen life as it is used for the ridge of thatched roofs. Native to the south end of Woodwalton, it was probably planted here in the 1940s.

Getting away from it all

The 'Rothschild Bungalow' is my all-time favourite building. In its dark recesses, shielded by thick thatch in the heart of the beautiful fen, there is peace and tranquillity, as well as history and stories of a century of caring for wildlife.

The reed for the roof came from the Rothschild estate in Ashton, and it lasted 100 years until it was re-thatched by local thatcher, Clive Dodson in 2011.

Miriam Rothschild's niece Kari de Koenigswarter (right), with husband Ruary Mackensie-Dodds (left) and Prof. Philip Corbet   Repairing thatched roof

The Rothschild Bungalow

In 1911, the Rothschild Bungalow was erected on the site of a former stackyard, for the use of the Rothschild family and their friends when visiting the Reserve. Miriam Rothschild recalled with glee afternoons spent with her father on the fen, followed by tea in the Bungalow.

There were several cottages along Bungalow Drove (now Masons Drove) including a few near the site of the Bungalow. Miriam Rothschild loved to tell the story of Mr Jackson, who lived in one of these cottages and reputedly never wore a stitch of clothing until he took peat to market once a year. A local lass thought he must have immense wealth hidden somewhere, so married him with a fortune in mind. Unfortunately for her, she died before him and now we will never know the truth! Whether or not Jackson's hoard can be found beneath the Bungalow has never been investigated.

I never tire of visiting this iconic building – the 'pride of the NNR' – which has huge historic importance. This is where Charles Rothschild and others laid down the foundations of British nature conservation. The Joint Advisory Committee always met here and I often wonder what the walls could tell us if they could talk! A decision to sell off the original furniture in the 1980s paved the way for the building to be demolished as a 'white elephant' which did not relate to nature conservation. When I arrived in 1991, I set about persuading NCC managers of the error of this decision and with help from volunteers and reserve staff set about renovating the building. A few years ago, it was re-thatched using some of the reserve's own reed and its survival now seems assured. What a tragedy its loss would have been! Many visitors including HRH Prince Charles have marvelled at its unique atmosphere and it has inspired many donors to support the work of the Great Fen.

The central area

As we walk alongside the dyke heading south from the Bungalow we can hear Reed Warblers reeling from the fields and dyke edges. Crossing Coleman's Bridge, we reach the famed 'violet' fields. There is a seam of underlying gravel here with faster drainage which represses the grown of the nutrient-demanding Common Reed and allows a varied flora to thrive.

This has been the stronghold of the Fen Violet, although it has a mighty battle with the invasive soft rush, which is a major competitor to the smaller flowers. The Fen Violet has been studied by botanists for decades trying to understand why it is not more common. Competition from more vigorous species and correct soil moisture are clearly important, but it has been very challenging to work out just how we can increase the population of this rare and mysterious creature. Recent work points towards these fen plants needing very specific conditions to germinate, flower and produce viable seed. By a strange coincidence a thriving population lives on the limestone of the Burren in Eire, not far from where Capt. Purefoy experimented with Large Copper introductions! Plants here are altogether more robust and long-lived, so we may have to accept only occasional flowering feasts of this delicate creature (such as in the

The Fen Violet

In 1958, Eric Duffey recorded plants from eight compartments. In 1972 about three hectares of scrub was removed from ct 55 (now known as the 'violet' field) by a tracked excavator and the material burnt on-site. Over the next few years, hundreds of flowering violets covered the field.

Fen Violet *Viola persicifolia* [PCu]

1980s), which must be paid for by years of famine! It is this type of applied ecology which is the heartbeat of the NNRs and together with in 'ex-situ' work such as seed storage and germination experiments by Kew Gardens will hopefully guarantee the future of such species.

The meres and ponds
After the disastrous floods of the late 1940s/50s there was a concern by the Ministry of Agriculture and the Middle Level Commissioners to better manage the flow of water down the Great Raveley Drain. Anxious to create wetter conditions within the reserve, the Nature Conservancy agreed to the idea of the fen being used to store excess flood water. Rothschild's Mere is the oldest and deepest of the two meres excavated to get the clay to seal the western and northern banks. Dug out between 1970 and 1972, the excavated clay was transported to the west bank by rail. Rumour has it that train spotters were seen lurking in the bushes waiting for the diesel locomotive to come past! Gordon's Mere was dug between 1977 and 1982 and has more shallow margins and was designed more with wildlife in mind. Although

Gordon's Mere

Rothschild's Mere is connected to the dyke system, the meres have only ever been filled by water percolating through the peat and from precipitation, so have not suffered the pollution problems of the general dyke system. Today they are a sanctuary for wildlife and people alike, as many hours can be spent watching the wildfowl and more recently, Otters, Bitterns and Kingfishers *Alcedo atthis*.

The south end

The sweet scent of Bog-myrtle meets us as we approach the south end, passing the meres and through a primeval woodland where hares and woodcock lurk among the tussocks. Bog-myrtle is an extraordinary plant and the only one I know which is equally effective as an insecticide and a rather distinctive tasting beer! This is a secretive area of wild birch woods, Alder groves, fields of Saw-sedge and marsh-orchids *Dactylorhiza* spp. Water-violets *Hottonia palustris* splash the old ditches with purple, accompanied by the whine and bite of mosquitoes!

The open fields and woodlands here were separated from the northern part of the reserve early in the 20th century by a clay bank. This kept the area drier so that it could be farmed, and now offers the chance to manage water levels differently in the two

Water-violet *Hottonia palustris* [PC]

parts of the fen. It is also home to one of the rare grassland types on the reserve which is part of its international status (with Wicken and Chippenham Fen NNRs) as a Special Area of Conservation (SAC). The Meadow Thistle *Cirsium dissectum* grows here, along with Purple Moor-grass and the tiny Spiked Sedge. One field which contains many tussocks (some undoubtedly old anthills) was, until 1968, home to a large colony of Deptford Pink *Dianthus armeria*. Efforts to create wetter conditions within the site, however, clearly did not suit this species and it has not been seen since the 1980s, although others like Devil's-bit Scabious *Succisa pratensis* and knapweeds *Centaurea* spp. thrive.

At the very corner of the reserve is the cattle area, where generations of fenmen and wardens have sweated over the care of livestock. In the 1960s cattle were re-introduced to the site and the Nature Conservancy and its successors owned beasts right up until 2015. There have been a variety of breeds, but they all had one thing in common – they were native stock. For many years these were Galloways and Belted Galloways, transported from Scotland (latterly from the West country) and kept for five or so years before being sold for slaughter. Others have included British White, Highland and Sussex. They all have their characteristics, the Galloways being rather unruly at times and could become remarkably selective in not

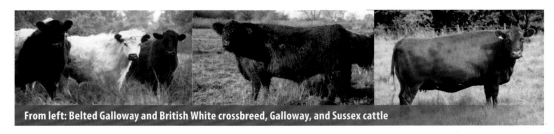

From left: Belted Galloway and British White crossbreed, Galloway, and Sussex cattle

eating soft rush! But they have been an invaluable tool at controlling the coarse vegetation, helped in later years by native ponies. It is time-consuming and hard work to own livestock but the expertise which the staff developed has been invaluable in having first-hand knowledge to communicate with local farmers and other land managers.

With the research station at Monks Wood so close it was inevitable that they would use the Fen for their work. In 1966 a series of ponds was excavated near the cattle sheds at the south end and these were used for research into water quality, dragonflies and Great-crested Newts *Triturus cristatus*.

That's the end of our walk. If we walk back along the flood-bank we can see the farmland to the south-west and the new Great Fen fields of Middle Farm. Sometimes in wet seasons these can flood and attract exciting waders and ducks.

Hydrology and the ditches

The way in which drainage has affected Woodwalton Fen is a classic example of how the ecology of a fragment of a larger wetland can become quite unlike that of the original ecosystem. Isolated from river flow, shrunk to a size where many species cannot survive, and impacted by the drainage of intensive agriculture, the modern reserves defies experts as to how its hydrology works. Add to this a legacy of impure quality of the drainage water and silt-laden floods and you have a complex problem.

As we have seen, Woodwalton dried out during the late 19th/early 20th centuries. Loss of peat and gradual enrichment by nutrients caused changes in the terrestrial flora, encouraged scrub encroachment and caused many ditches to dry out. It was hoped that by building water-proof banks to seal the reserve as part of the flood-relief scheme, this would promote wetter conditions and benefit the wildlife. Unfortunately, despite concerns raised at the time, no monitoring was put in place to assess the effect of holding water inside the reserve. In practice, this turned the site from a free-flowing 'sieve' into an impenetrable 'bucket', where water flow could only happen through ditches when levels allowed it or when pumped. In a survey of 1975, many water plants were found that indicated the ditches were in a healthy state, following widespread cleaning and re-wetting. It was not until a repeat survey some 20 years that the effects of water quality and flood storage were demonstrated; there had been a decline in open water plants rooted in the mud, in favour of floating plants like duckweeds and Lesser Water-parsnip.

Ditch at Woodwalton Fen

Silt pump

The exact process of this change may never be fully understood, but recent investigations suggest that flooding, silt deposition and the high nutrient quality of the water flowing in from the agricultural drains have been major factors in reducing species richness. In addition, more recent wetter winter /spring conditions at the south end appears to have increased the dominance of rush and reed at the expense of more varied flora. Work is now underway to remove silt, enhance the water quality and provide other areas for storing flood water outside the boundaries of the reserve – a key objective of the Great Fen.

Ditches

Once you could take a boat along the ditches, but bridges and culverts now provide the chance to walk instead. The ditch system meanders for 15 km across the Fen and is an important feature of the RAMSAR designation – an international recognition of the quality and importance of Woodwalton Fen and its special plants.

The age and original function of the ditches varies considerably. Some, like Coleman's dyke were excavated in Victorian times and were the route for drainage water running from the west of the Fen to the Great Raveley Drain, as well as providing transport for the removal of peat. Others were excavated for conservation and have a variety of aspect and depth. Whether a ditch has a clay or peat bottom has an important effect on which plants grow there, with clay generally allowing better rooting for aquatic plants. There are some wonderful sights to be seen in these narrow channels. Pink Water-violets, yellow Bladderworts and massed white blooms of the water-parsnips set the background for the dazzling colours of dragonflies such as the Scarce Chaser and the metallic blue damselflies.

Wildlife

Woodwalton Fen was originally designated as a nature reserve and SSSI because of its importance for specific insects, flowers and relict fen habitats. Management and research are still concentrated on these, of course, but Nature does not stand still and the relative abundance of species and habitats is constantly changing. It is important to be able to adapt management and expectations to make sure they have the best possible chance of survival.

Invertebrates

No less than 49 different butterfly species have been noted on the reserve, although some have been fleeting visitors. Ever since the 1970s, wardens have carried out a weekly summer count as part of the national monitoring scheme, which is now organised by the charity Butterfly Conservation.

One of the most intriguing events was the sudden appearance of the now very rare Chequered Skipper *Carterocephalus palaemon* (after which the pub in the Rothschild village of Ashton is named). In 1968, the warden reported to Miriam Rothschild that he had seen one on the fen and it was then seen in small numbers for several years, after which it disappeared. This is primarily a woodland species, but one of its main foodplants is the Purple Moor-grass which grows in isolated spots around the fen. In the mid-1990s, a plan was discussed to re-introduce the skipper to the fen but this never came to be. Interestingly, one of the main obstacles was considered to be the lack of flowering Ragged-Robin – a beautiful pink-flowered plant which is an important nectar source for the skipper. Faithful to Nature's fickle ways, within a few years they were flowering in profusion all across the site!

A butterfly which has fared better is the Purple Emperor *Apatura iris*. This elusive creature – which spends much of its time high in the oaks – was once very much confined to the southern counties, particularly Sussex, with outlying populations in the woodlands of Leicestershire. It began to appear at Woodwalton around 2012 and has been a regular feature around the Rothschild Bungalow ever since. Here, the butterflies can be seen happily feeding on the putty around the windows (it also likes dog poo, but as this is a no-dog site perhaps putty is a good alternative!)

Moths are a particularly important group. The late Victorians and Edwardians were very active moth collectors and breeders and while their more enthusiastic adventures may have caused the decline of some species, we owe them a lot in our understanding of many species. We also know how much more abundant the variety and number of these creatures were before the fen drainage and even before the effects of insecticides from the 1960s. More recently, thanks to painstaking work by lepidopterists like Barry Dickerson, we know that more than 1,000 species have been recorded since Rothschild first acquired the site – that is over one third of all the moths found in Britain. Sadly, not all of the recorded species are still with us. In the country as a whole, over 60 moth species became extinct in the 20th century and in *The State of Britain's Larger Moths* 2013 report Butterfly

Garden Tiger moth *Arctia caja*

Conservation found that the total number of larger moths recorded in the national network of Rothamsted traps decreased by 28% over the 40 years from 1968 to 2007. At Woodwalton, the Marsh Moth has not been seen for many years and there are fears that the Concolorous moth *Photedes extrema* is also declining rapidly. Despite this in one memorable night in July 2008, 272 species were recorded by Barry and his team. How sad that many people have a biased view that all moth larvae eat clothes and are unaware of the stunning colours, variety and habits of these fascinating creatures!

Of the 43 resident species of Odonata in Britain (the posh names for dragonflies and damselflies) 23 have been recorded at Woodwalton, making this one of the best sites in Britain. 'Horse stingers' and 'Devil's darning needles' are the old country names, and I once heard with dismay a scout leader telling his enthralled followers to avoid these vicious beasts because of their bite! They are quite harmless to us but the nymphs are voracious predators and spend their years underwater feeding on smaller swimming prey. The Small Red-eyed Damselfly *Erythromma viridulum* colonised England a few years ago and is now seen regularly at the fen, and the beautiful Willow Emerald Damselfly *Chalcolestes viridis* has very recently become established.

Among the often-overlooked groups of invertebrates are the beetles, many of which are fenland specialists. Several water beetles now survive only in these old fens, such as *Hydraena palustris* and *Helocharis obscurus*. As we saw in the last chapter, the rare Tansy Beetle, has recently caused great excitement. Declared as a threatened species and thought to be confined to just one short stretch of the river Ouse in Yorkshire, this metallic green beetle looked set to join many of its relatives and become extinct in England. On the day in 2013 that its Yorkshire river home was declared as a Site of Special Scientific Interest

Willow Emerald Damselfly *Chalcolestes viridis* [PB]

(SSSI), however, the sharp-eyed entomologist Peter Kirby spotted one on Woodwalton Fen and since then it has appeared in small numbers every year. This was all the more remarkable because the scientists attempting to re-establish the beetle on the Fens had declared Woodwalton as not really suitable. How inscrutable Nature is! There are times when I think we know so little of the real lives of our wild neighbours that we should do more than sit on the river bank and observe, rather than rush around thinking we know how to fix the plight of wild animals and plants which we have so sorely damaged. Why the Tansy Beetle turned up at Woodwalton after an absence of many decades is a mystery – perhaps it was there all the time, perhaps its eggs were transported on some itinerant bird. We shall never know, but it gives us hope that all is not lost in the fight to provide a secure home for a wider range of species in the future.

Flora

Many of the plants of the great wetland are no longer found on Woodwalton, but some were planted in the early years of the reserve in an attempt to re-establish them in their old haunts.

The Milk-parsley was planted in 1912, but has never been more than a very rare plant. This is unfortunate, because it is the larval foodplant of the Swallowtail butterfly. Another butterfly which did benefit from planting was the Large Copper. The 'Rothschild sunflower' was probably introduced in 1927 as part of the butterfly introduction programme and still grows vigorously around the Bungalow and along

Bog Pimpernel *Anagallis tenella* [NE]

the ditch edges there. In addition, wardens of the 1950s and 60s would regularly plant great water dock as larval foodplant.

More recently, the Fen Ragwort was planted as part of English Nature's Species Recovery Programme near to Jackson's Bridge and near the Bungalow. This plant is now only found on one roadside near Stuntney in east Cambridgeshire, and its fate is far from certain. Research has shown that in the absence of regular flooding it is unlikely to thrive.

Birds

Although not originally noted for its bird species, recent studies have shown how crucial this fen is for many birds. The reedy ditches are home to Reed and Sedge Warblers; Common Whitethroats *Sylvia communis* sing their scratchy song from bramble thickets and Bitterns boom from deep cover. But these populations change for all manner of reasons. Climate, vegetation management, water levels, competition from nearby sites, all affect both breeding and wintering birds.

Long-eared Owl *Asio otus* [DG]

David Garner ringing Barn Owl *Tyto alba* at Woodwalton Fen

Declining species

A few years ago, Willow Tits *Poecile montanus*, Lesser Spotted Woodpeckers *Dryobates minor* and Turtle-doves *Streptopelia turtur* could be regularly seen and heard on the Fen. In his *Birds of Woodwalton Fen* (Harold 1990) warden Ron Harold identified a healthy population of Willow Tits. He estimated that the breeding density was over 40/km^2 in 1981–82, but had declined to just 20/km^2 in 1987–89. A decade later there were none. Lesser Spotted Woodpeckers could still be heard at the South End in 2012, but are rarely if ever seen or heard now. The reasons for these declines are poorly understood, and are often due to factors outside the confines of the reserve. The BTO Atlas surveys during 2008–2011 showed that the decline of Willow Tits since the mid 1970s had led to local extinction from the south-eastern part of its English range since 1988–91. The UK conservation listing was upgraded from amber to red in 2002 and it is now considered as a rare species. Similarly, the Lesser Spotted Woodpecker has one of the fastest declining species in Europe since 1970 and Turtle-doves are considered by IUCN as globally threatened.

For other species, it may be a combination of changing distribution and conditions within the site. Once there were over 40 pairs of Nightingales *Luscinia megarhynchos* at both Woodwalton and Holme Fen as well as Monks Wood and Caster Hanglands NNRs. In recent years their numbers on the fens have steadily declined, and the last time I heard one at Holme was in 2014. The loss of dense vegetation under the scrub – due in large part to browsing by Muntjac deer *Muntiacus reevesi* – is almost certainly a factor in their particularly severe decline here.

Increasing species

On a happier note there have been some spectacular gains, particularly in the last few years, when it may be that the Great Fen management of fields surrounding the reserve has been of benefit. Marsh Harriers can now be seen all year round and nest in several places throughout Woodwalton Fen.

The *'chetty'* call of Cetti's Warblers *Cettia cetti* has become a more common sound in recent years and I have occasionally heard the much rarer Savi's Warbler *Locustella luscinioides*. This song can be confusing as it is much like a Grasshopper Warbler *Locustella naevia*, but at a higher pitch.

Invertebrates are also thriving in the reserves and in the wider Great Fen.

Woodwalton Fen may be the last outpost of a once enormous wetland empire, but our walk has shown what a variety of life there is in this small space and given some idea of

Barbastelle bat *Barbastella barbastellus* [HS]

the work that needs to be carried out to maintain and improve it. There are great challenges, but with the increasing area of land around the reserve coming into management where wildlife has more opportunities to expand, the future is looking optimistic.

Holme Fen

I am sitting under the birch trees at Holme Fen on a sunny May morning. Chiffchaffs and Blackcap Warblers are singing in the branches and I am gazing at the tufts of pale green Sphagnum moss which are the last of the great bog which once was here. Two centuries ago I would have sunk up to my armpits in the bog, now I sit in a woodland and dream... It is a conservation war-cry to "fell all the birches and let the bog re-grow" and one which I agree with... to some extent. For these birches have their own majesty, their own wildlife communities, and are one chapter in a long story of change. From tundra to dry plains, from forest to fen, from fen to farmland, this place is witness to the history of the fenland and the people who have lived in it.

Walking through Holme Fen is to walk through history into antiquity. Quiet grassy droves lead through birch woodland and heathy glades, past meres and rare patches of bog mosses. Deep in the trees it is cathedral-quiet, the footfall soft on the layers of decayed leaves of decades. But beneath the woodland canopy lies an ancient world – a raised bog once mighty enough to hold back the encroaching seas, a world inhabited by rare flowers and mosses, insects and birds. Drainage has changed the bog to woodland and shrunk the peat by 5 metres, but the original bog surface survives. The site is now the finest birch woodland in England, home to rare fungi and a paradise for walkers, but at the same time a precious relic of a habitat which took thousands of years to evolve – a

Holme Fen NNR

raised bog, now a dried and shrunken crust but still capable of resurrection... all it needs is water.

Most of Holme Fen escaped the post-drainage cultivation of Whittlesea Mere, but in the 1870s it is believed that several plantations were established and many of these original trees have survived today. The great oaks and pines are now in the middle of their second century.

Much of the area around the Holme Posts was clear felled during the Second World War to provide charcoal for gunpowder, but happily many of the plantation trees here were spared. During the 1950s and '60s grass and heath became established with extensive willowherb, bramble and bracken. This encouraged some spectacular wildlife. A man who once lived in the cottage near to the Holme Posts told me that he would be kept awake by the incessant warbling of the 40 pairs of Nightingales who inhabited the undergrowth and Nightjars *Caprimulgus europaeus* purred and flapped their ghostly way across the heath.

In 1964, parts of the site were leased to the Forestry Commission and the site could have been converted to conifer plantation, as the insatiable demand for home-grown timber increased. It was only the intervention of a BBC film maker, John Houlton, who saved the site from destruction. Houlton used to visit from his London home at weekends and park his camper van in the local pub. His abiding interest was fungi and the site are now famous for its number of species, some of which are scarcely known outside the reserve.

Soon woodland began to reclaim the heath, but a dense undergrowth persisted until the 1990s when increasing shade and the spread of Muntjac deer reduced the bramble and scrub considerably and changed the whole woodland structure quite significantly. Control measures since 2005 have reduced the numbers of deer and a consequent recovery in herbs and tree regeneration has occurred.

The reserve is regarded locally in different ways. For some it is the ideal place to walk the dog beneath the cathedral-like panoply of trees, to sit in the quiet of soft peat, while others watch the water fowl on the meres or the butterflies flitting among the branches. Others still yearn for the days when this was a wet and wild place.

Management on the NNR

Because Holme Fen is such a complex site, deciding on the correct management is not an easy task. In the early days of the Nature Conservancy, forestry-based management was popular and there was some clear felling to try and stimulate new growth of birch. The aim appeared to be to clear-fell whole blocks to maintain even-aged birch woodland, but this

The Holmewood Estate was purchased by John Ashton Fielden in 1902. The Fieldens had made their money in cotton and were very wealthy. He was by all accounts a benevolent landlord and helped his tenants in many ways.

The estate then employed 100 people and consisted of 680 acres of parkland, with 20 tenanted farms. In 1924, the Squire paid out of his own pocket for new pumping stations and oil-fired engines at Black Ham and Whittlesey Mere.

Among Fielden's more generous actions were financing the London Hospital from 1900 onwards, helping with Sir Ernest Shackleton's expedition to the South Pole and supplying a hospital ship in the First World War. He also played cricket for Huntingdonshire whilst living at Lawrence Court, Huntingdon, prior to his move to Holme.

During the Second World War he is best known for his donation of two Spitfires and many other contributions to the war effort. He also gave over one wing of the house to a number of women who had been blinded in the bombing of Coventry and East London. The Hall was later secretly used as a base for sending agents to France.

One of Fielden's main interests was game shooting (which is still a widespread practice in the fen today) and access to the site for the public was made very difficult. Records from this era are therefore rather sparse, but it seems that the developing woodland would have been managed primarily for pheasants and this was possibly when some areas were planted.

was only carried out in one location. Later, a non-intervention policy was adopted, with control of invasive species like sycamore. Much research in the 1990s led to the view that it was more desirable to attempt to re-wet at least a part of the ancient bog surface. As the birch woodland was one of the criteria for establishing the NNR, it was a controversial decision that some trees should be felled to create conditions which might lead to re-growth of bog mosses. But more recently, the importance of the relict bog has become more recognised. Holme Fen is at the most south-easterly edge of the range of raised bogs in Britain and until recently, the prospect of regenerating anything like bog conditions here were impossible, but the Great Fen has changed this. Re-wetting the landscape around the NNRs should slow down the seepage of water out of the site, and allow wet fen to develop. This could then lead to the growth of *Sphagnum* and so the bog might be re-born. Rymes Reedbed to the east of the reserve, on the edge of Whittlesea Mere, is already becoming wetter, as is Summer Standing to the west, so the process has been started.

Compartment 5 – Old Duck Decoy
A view of the West side. The right background is formed by the birch woodland of Compt. 4 and the left background by that of the birch woodland adjoining the railway.

Extract from Holme Fen management plan

A walk through the Holme Fen

It's a long walk through the whole of the reserve, but it is a journey worth taking. From the noise of wildfowl in the meres to the silence of the deep woodland, the heather on the heath and the assortment of strange fungi, the variety is hard to beat. We'll start our walk early on

a summer's morning in the north, then through the heathland to the open woodland and glades of the south. Bring your dog, he will enjoy the air, but make sure to keep him close to heel, for there are hares, deer and ground-nesting birds that need peace and quiet.

Northern block (Stiltons Roughs)

Turning off Short Drove just beyond the railway crossing and away from the deep roadside ditch, a long straight ride stretches away to the north. Today the ride is overshadowed by mainly birch woodland but also by Alders and a few oaks. There is a glade along the way where Common Twayblades *Neottia ovata* and the very rare Heath Dog-violet *Viola canina* ssp. *montana* grow.

After a few hundred metres, the ride opens out into 'Basher's glade', so-called because in the 1980s much woodland was cleared here to allow heath and open grassland to flourish. Ever since, the open field has needed to be cut regularly to prevent it returning to scrub woodland. In the past few years the dominant vegetation has changed from willowherb to bracken and increasingly to heath, with Cross-leaved Heath and Heather (Ling) *Calluna vulgaris* forming ever-widening patches. During the 1990s there was a strong colony of Small Copper *Lycaena phlaeas* butterflies which delighted in the swathes of Sheep's Sorrel *Rumex acetosella* which grew here.

Cross-leaved Heath *Erica tetralix*

Royal Fern *Osmundia regalis*

The reason that the relict bog survived at Holme and nowhere else on the Great Fen is because the peat here proved too difficult to drain and cultivate. Although the raised dome of the bog has collapsed, the actual acid peat surface is still there – it just needs water, but not any kind of water. Pumping water over the bog surface from surrounding meres would not be successful because it is too mineral-rich and probably contains nutrients due to the geese who live there. For the bog to have any chance of re-birth it needs three things: rainfall; fewer trees which soak up the water; and a means of retaining the rainfall when it falls. This was why areas such as Rymes reedbed have been created. These surrounding wet fields will prevent water seeping away. It's called 'lagg fen'.

Beyond the open heath is hidden one of Holme Fen's great secrets. Here, in an old duck decoy is the only *Sphagnum* bog-moss for many miles. Once there were at least seven different species but although the number of species has declined, it is still a crucial feature – the source of a bog for the future. Other interesting bryophyte flora here includes the Pointed Spear-moss *Calliergon cuspidatum* and Heart-leaved Spear-moss *Calliergon cordifolium*. The dip-wells here were installed in the 1970s to measure the water table of the area. We call this the 'bog' but it is not really a bog any more. The bog-mosses here are not the highly specialised species which grow only on raised peat, but are those which are happy in more nutrient-rich and drier fen. They are all we have, though, and the exciting re-discovery of the beautiful Lustrous Bog-moss in 2016 is an indication that all is not yet lost.

The true bog dates back to ancient days, at times being invaded by trees, at others being so extensive that it kept the Neolithic sea waters at bay. Scratch a few centimetres below the modern surface of dry and oxidised peat and you find the perfectly preserved remains of the creatures who thrived here thousands of years ago. So delicate was the bog surface in the early 19th century that a small boy from Holme sunk to his armpits until rescued by local fenmen, yet within two decades of the Mere's drainage, the bog had collapsed. Aided by some planting of oak and pine in the 1870s, the Holme Fen of the early 1900s became the Holme Woods of the turn of the century, beloved of its owner for game rearing, but banned to local people. Even years later, the redoubtable lady crossing-keeper 'Queenie' guarded the level crossing and you had to have a good reason to pass through!

Alongside the mosses lie the waters of McPhail's and Burnham's Meres, named after previous wardens. The first of these was excavated in the 1960s and was an attempt to re-create some of the lost habitats of Whittlesea Mere. I have often walked around the meres and been mystified as to where their waters come from, because no ditches drain into them and the surrounding trees drink huge quantities of water. This may the second driest place in England, but clearly there is more rainfall than you think! There are a few islands scattered across the main mere, but despite early attempts to keep these open to encourage nesting birds like terns, they are now heavily wooded. This has

Holme Fen Meres by Chris Rose

suited Cormorants *Phalacrocorax carbo* very well, and in recent years numbers of nests has grown to over 20. The young can be seen in the nests quite early in the year and when on the wing are easily recognised by their whitish undercarriage. Burnham's Mere is also home to a very sedentary flock of Greylag Geese *Anser anser* (often joined by Canada Geese *Branta canadensis*) whose world seems to revolve around feeding on the farm fields along the Yaxley road and roosting on the mere and its islands. Alongside the geese are a growing number of other wildfowl – Mallard *Anas platyrhynchos*, Tufted Duck *Aythya fuligula*, Gadwall *Anas strepera*, Teal *Anas crecca*, and Pochard *Aythya ferina* are common, and are joined in winter by Goldeneye *Bucephala clangula*. Just very occasionally you may be lucky enough to see Goosander *Mergus merganser* or Smew *Mergus albellus*. The meres are also a magnet for dragonflies and damselflies and the waters can be almost covered in late summer by thousands of Common Darters *Sympetrum striolatum*.

Crossing the ditch (Caldecote Dyke), we find scattered colonies of Bog-myrtle and occasional Saw-sedge. These are remnants of the bog-loving plants which would have been common here before drainage.

A few oaks can be found among the birch including a splendid specimen along the southern edge, near to a Rowan which I have watched grow from a tiny seedling to a fine specimen.

Following the Second World War felling, the open heath which grew up gradually became invaded by brambles. A local farmer told me that he couldn't go anywhere off the rides when he was a boy in the 1950s, and it was still very dense when I arrived in 1991. But while this was a no-go area for small boys and new wardens, it was a haven for breeding birds. Nightingales, Willow Warblers *Phylloscopus trochilus*, Common Whitethroats and Blackcaps *Sylvia atricapilla* were widespread and even Wood Warblers *Phylloscopus sibilatrix* and Redstarts *Phoenicurus phoenicurus* made a brief appearance. But the dense understorey was soon to decline, partly because the trees were growing taller and creating more shade, but mainly because of Muntjac deer. As their numbers began to increase, their browsing of shrubs and brambles began to create a very different habitat and the woodland structure became very open. While the browsing removed nesting sites for scrub warblers and nectar for invertebrates, however, it also created opportunities for other species such as *Dryopteris* ferns and Climbing Corydalis *Ceratocapnos claviculata*. The reduction of deer numbers has resulted in a resurgence of bramble, but by reducing the intensity of deer control it should be possible to maintain a balanced understorey structure.

The north and east boundaries were adjacent to arable farmland until the Great Fen acquired the land and arable farming ceased in 2012. The boundary ditch discharged directly into the IDB drain and so water levels remained low, but since the completion of the work to create higher water levels in Rymes Reedbed the ditch levels have risen.

Since 2013, there has been a hide (Trundle Mere Lookout) just off the northern corner of the NNR, to allow the public to view Rymes Reedbed. It has a grass roof and

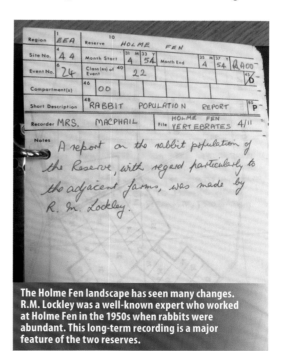

The Holme Fen landscape has seen many changes. R.M. Lockley was a well-known expert who worked at Holme Fen in the 1950s when rabbits were abundant. This long-term recording is a major feature of the two reserves.

is a testament to the enthusiasm of Great Fen warden John Smith, who sadly died shortly after his appointment.

Central block
This block stretches between Holme Lode and New Long Drove (Ladyseat Road) and is divided by the Short Drove Dyke.

Plantations
As we cross the footbridge we are immediately confronted with two iron posts.

Before the Mere was pumped dry, William Wells had the foresight to install some timber piles to record the shrinkage of the peat after drainage. It is rumoured that one of these may have survived for almost 100 years, but clearly it was thought that the timber would rot away, so a cast-iron pillar was fixed onto timber piles driven into the underlying clay in 1851/2. The post is set on oak piles driven into the

A post in dispute
It has been disputed as to whether or not this was a post from the Great Exhibition of 1851. Hutchinson (1980) thought it unlikely, as it does not appear on any plans of the structure, but it may have been from an internal exhibition and there are others still holding up roofs in barns nearby. In a spirited conversation some years ago with the son of the author, the Rev. W. Awdry (of *Thomas the Tank Engine* fame), I was informed that there was no question of its authenticity! The post still stands today.

underlying clay and has faithfully recorded the decline of the peat ever since. Perhaps one day if Holme Fen re-hydrates, the posts will begin to disappear under a bog!

Believed to have been planted in the 1870s, Ballard's covert survived the Second World War fellings and now displays some fine oak and pine trees. Although some of these have fallen in storms the block remains quite densely populated with mature oaks, while to the east is the largest stand of mature Alder coppice on the NNR. These are even-aged and are presumably regrowth from the war fellings. No management has been done here to re-coppice these trees as it is suspected that this may open up the self-protecting nature of the stand and make the more exposed trees prone to wind-blow.

Despite the rather desolate and windswept atmosphere on the Whittlesea Mere site today, there were once many cottages along here, two of which were for the game-keepers of Holme Fen. On the edge of the big Alder stand are bushes of damsons and rhododendrons which once grew in their gardens.

Along the path leading around the plantation is the remains of a charcoal kiln. This was where the trees which were felled for the war effort were made into charcoal for gunpowder. The sun is beginning to warm up now and an early Silver-washed Fritillary *Argynnis paphia* butterfly crosses our path, searching for bramble nectar. Their caterpillars feed on violet

Silver-washed Fritillary *Argynnis paphia* [NE]

White Admiral *Limenitis camilla* [JA]

plants, but bramble flowers are very popular with the adults who also feed on aphid honey dew high in the trees. If we are very lucky, we might meet a White Admiral *Limenitis camilla* butterfly later on but although there is plenty of Honeysuckle *Lonicera periclymenum* for their caterpillars to eat, they are very rarely seen these days.

Wandering along the wide ride leading south you come across one of the most interesting and important areas of Holme Fen. After a 20-year programme of clearance of small birch and control of invasive bracken large areas of acid grassland/heath have become established among the trees, with thriving populations of bryophytes (mosses and liverworts) – predominantly *Polytrichum* mosses – and also the largest population on the reserve of heathers and Wood Sage *Teucrium scorodonia*.

This is an area where an important birch surveillance project has been conducted since the 1980s (Gill 1981). This fascinating study has revealed that some of the smallest trees are in fact the oldest!

Holme Fen by Chris Rose

This special place may hold the key to the future of at least some of Holme Fen, for it is here that experimental management is aimed at establishing conditions where a future bog may be able to grow. By preventing seepage of water and clearing some trees it is very likely that some of the 'seed' species which are already here will encourage *Sphagnum* and other bog species to spread.

Further afield are some of the finest trees of Holme Fen, with stately specimens of larch, poplar and Scots Pine *Pinus sylvestris* dominating the skyline. Although these were all planted in the 19th century they remind me of the Caledonian pine forests of Scottish Highlands. Further west, are many Yew *Taxus baccata* and Holly *Ilex aquifolium* trees. Until 2013, many of the Holly were affected by deer browsing but since deer numbers have been reduced there has been a marked increase of young saplings growing through. There is an interesting comparison here with Flitwick Moor in Bedfordshire, where holly has invaded to form dense stands on the peatland.

The western edge of this block consists of relatively species-poor grassy glades which have been cut and gathered in winter for at least three decades. But look closer at this 'uninteresting' grassland and there is a surprise in store. Arriving at the fen in 1991 I was solemnly informed by Maurice Massey, the East Midlands Chief Warden, that this was the only site for many miles for the rare white-flowered Climbing Corydalis, but one effect of the deer browsing has been to provide open conditions which allowed the plant to spread throughout the reserve and it now covers many hectares!

Along the northern boundary is the largest area of Elder *Sambucus nigra* bushes with several mature oak, Scots Pine and other conifers amongst open bracken.

Short Drove Dyke (Engine Drain)
This area is bounded on the west side by the east-coast mainline railway and until 2012, land-use to the north and east was tenanted arable farmland. Caldecote drain runs west-east

through the middle of the block, where water levels have remained consistently low due to Internal Drainage Board (IDB) control, draining farmland to the west of the reserve.

This ditch was used to drain farmland until English Nature and the local drainage board cut a by-pass ditch in 2002. Since then, the ditch has come under the control of NE, although there is a need to inform the IDB before altering water control settings. New water controls here have allowed the ditch water level to be raised and re-wet some fields on the new Great Fen land at Summer Standing. It has also started the process of raising water levels within the NNR – the first step towards re-wetting the bog.

This area of the fen is quite different from where we have been before. It is open beneath the tree canopy and this is where the rare Fen Woodrush can be found. Once thought to be extinct in Britain, it was re-discovered in 1949 by the botanist Francis Rose. It a tricky species, because it does not like competition from other plants or too much shade. In the past, large numbers have been found on disturbed ground where tree clearance has taken place, but they soon become lost again when the vegetation grows up.

If we went in beneath the trees, we would find a damp area where saw sedge grows alongside Common Reed, but we'll stay on the path as there are many holes in the peat which you can fall into – as I have done!

Heading towards the road we come across a very open area which is where experimental felling took place in the 1950s. Due to the vigorous growth of bracken, few trees have grown up again.

Eastern block – Boston's Mere (compartments 42–48)

To the east of New Long Drove (known locally as Ladyseat Drive) lies one of the few places where peat was extracted on a small scale. The only evidence is now a small depression and it had nothing like the effect of the wholesale extraction at Woodwalton. The rest of the peat surface is untouched, save where the mere was excavated in the 1980s. Here and there are more Victorian plantings of oak, many of which are now of great size, although others have succumbed to the dry conditions and crashed to the ground. Around these trees is much open ground dominated by bracken, which effectively prevents any regeneration of new seedling trees.

Two Ash trees guard the entrance to the track down to the mere. When I arrived on the reserve in 1991, they were babies and I have enjoyed watching them develop into fine mature trees over the years.

Many of the dry ditches have been colonised by Alders, some of which have been cleared in the last few years to encourage the ditch to hold water. During the 1990s there was a lot of die-back amongst the Alders and there were fears that many would be lost, but this threat now seems to have passed.

For some years there was a heronry here, with up to 11 nests, but in recent years the Grey Herons *Ardea cinerea* have completely deserted the area, preferring instead to establish a smaller colony in Stilton's Roughs. This is where they were when I saw the first nests over 25 years ago!

The Mere

Boston's Mere (named after previous warden, Roger Boston) was excavated in the 1980s and is bordered on its eastern edge by a deep dry dyke. Although a water control was constructed at the northern end of this dyke, it has never held more than a few puddles of water, which may explain why the mere has not achieved as high a level as was intended. It was also hoped that fen vegetation would develop at the southern end of the mere, but this has not happened as it has never become wet enough. A tower hide here was burnt down early in the 1990s and has been replaced by an open shelter at the eastern edge.

This mere attracts a different community of wildfowl than at Burnham/McPhail's, with diving ducks such as Tufted Duck more common. This was a breeding site for the introduced

Heron Disturbed
by Carry Akroyd

Ruddy Duck *Oxyura jamaicensis* in the early 2000s but they have not been seen for many years. At that time there was a controversial plan to prevent these birds breeding in Britain because of their habit of migrating to Spain, where they inter-bred with the threatened White-headed Duck *Oxyura leucocephala*. Happily, no nests were found at Home Fen. Greylag Geese and Canada Geese often congregate in large numbers around the island at the northern end.

West of the mere (compartments 43–45) the vegetation is dominated by bracken with scattered mature birch in compartment 43 and smaller trees more densely packed elsewhere. There is a denser stand of Alders at the south-eastern edge of the mere, which was one of the last strongholds of Nightingales. There is a stand of Saw-sedge in compartment 44, west of the mere.

The open field near to the old railway crossing cottage at the north-west corner of this area is known as the 'poor fen'. This has been mown for many years but is extremely uneven, so more recently it has been grazed by sheep, cattle and ponies. The flora is not species-rich, with the exception of Common Meadow-rue, the foodplant for the rare Marsh Carpet moth. Larvae were seen here in the 1990s but grazing initially suppressed the plants. In recent years the remaining plants have been protected by electric fencing and perhaps the moths will return to bred here in the future.

Otter *Lutra lutra* [ML]

Wildlife

The wildlife of Holme Fen is quite different from that at Woodwalton, as the site is much drier, but it has some very special and exciting species.

Holme Fen is a classic example of a complete replacement of one habitat with another. The raised bog and fen which was sustained by the surrounding mere and wetland, has been succeeded by dry birch woodland entirely because of drainage. Ironically, the woodland itself is considered important in its own right because it is such as large expanse of birch woodland. Where Whittlesea Mere was the largest lake in lowland England, Holme Fen is now the largest birch woodland!

Invertebrates

Of the many invertebrates on the reserve, over 20 are so rare that they are included on the UK Red Data Book (RDB) lists.

Before the drainage of Whittlesea Mere, Holme Fen was legendary amongst moth and butterfly collectors. Not only was the Large Copper butterfly found here, but also moths like the Gypsy Moth *Lymantria dispar* and Rosy Marsh Moth. Many of these could not survive the drainage and have not been seen for very many years, but even now the effects of the isolation and drainage of this place is affecting its inhabitants. The RDB Marsh Carpet moth, for example, has not been recorded here since 2008, although thankfully it has colonised new habitats in the wetland around the nearby Hampton nature reserve.

Almost 850 moth species have now been recorded from the reserve. Walking along the rides in early Spring, you may see what appear to be butterflies dancing along the edge of the woodland. In fact, these are Orange Underwing moths *Archiearis parthenias*, a day-flying species which is dependent on the birch trees for its larval food.

It is often the rarest species which are most easily overlooked. In the 1990s there was concern that the Jumping Weevil *Orchestes testaceus* was becoming very rare. Consequently, researchers from the University of Leeds embarked on a study to see if it could be found on the reserve. Equipped with climbing ropes and harnesses, they scoured the tops of tall Alder trees and found several living happily on the leaves and branches.

There are some wonderful butterflies at Holme Fen. Apart from the ones we saw on our walk, the Speckled Wood *Parage aegeria* is often seen in the shady glades, while in the open heath the Small Copper has been

Marsh Carpet *Gagitodes sagittata* [RL]

It is thought that the Great Green Bush-cricket *Tettigonia viridissima* has its most northerly colony in Britain at Holme Fen.

extremely common in some years. This small butterfly is found mainly in the north of the site, where the larva feeds on Sheep's Sorrel. For some years Holme Fen was the Huntingdonshire headquarters of this butterfly with up to three broods being produced each year.

Mammals

The mammals you are most likely to see at Holme Fen (apart from humans and their dogs) are Muntjac deer. Brought into to Woburn Park in Bedfordshire from China in the early 20th century, these deer have now become widespread across much of central England. Muntjac can breed all year round and so have the ability to rapidly increase their population. They are quite tame and I have often seen them wandering along the lanes of Holme village as well as in the reserve. Their characteristic bark can often be heard – a much shorter and dog-like sound than the hoarse grunt of the Chinese Water Deer. Perhaps it is their ability to live alongside humans and their ability to breed so quickly which as led to their rapid increase at the expense of the more timid water deer. The native Roe Deer *Capreolus capreolus* has become more common in recent years.

Chinese Water Deer have been seen less often at Holme Fen as numbers of Muntjac have increased

Browsing by Muntjac *Muntiacus reevesi* has had a major effect on the ground flora [GP]

After an absence of many decades, there has been the very occasional sighting of Otters around the meres, and Water Voles *Arvicola amphibius* are not uncommon in the field ditches on Summer Standing, adjacent to the reserve. It is hoped that when ditch water levels within the reserve increase due to reduced drainage in the surrounding fields, that the voles will return to Holme Fen itself.

Birds

The birdlife of the reserve has changed as the vegetation has changed. Before drainage, this was the haunt of waterfowl, cranes and Bitterns, but as the trees invaded, different species replaced them. In the years after war-time birch clearance there were Nightjars here, Woodcock *Scolopax rusticola* and the occasional Wood Warbler and Redstart. In the last three decades, these have been replaced by tits, Wrens *Troglodites troglodites* and Robins *Erithracus rubicula*, with Common Whitethroats in the brambles along the dyke-sides. Among the raptors, Long-eared Owls occasionally nest among the birches and the first Red Kite *Milvus milvus* nest was discovered in about 2008.

Conclusion

Woodwalton Fen and Holme Fen NNRs may be very different from the wetland which once surrounded Whittlesea Mere, but they have retained an extraordinary variety of wildlife. You only have to walk in the countryside outside the reserve to appreciate just what astonishing places they are. Where much of the 'wider countryside' is all but devoid of colour and birdsong and beauty, the reserves are a reminder of what it once was and could be again.

Common Whitethroat *Sylvia communis* [NE]

Long-eared Owl at Holme Fen by Vadim Gorbatov

Huge effort from reserve staff, ecologists and volunteers has achieved some magnificent results, but the yawning gap between these two outposts of biodiversity has remained a serious obstacle to many plants and animals for over a century. The shadow of loss lies all around; potatoes and sugar beet occupied spaces which more sedentary species could never hope to cross; the reserves are simply too small, too isolated and ill-equipped to withstand the old effects of drainage and the new challenges of climate change. Additionally, no matter how much habitat is created and maintained within the reserves, the effects of global influences (such as conditions in bird wintering areas) and climate fluctuations and longer-term climate change can make life very hard for some species. The future of the 'Nature in a flowerpot' is far from secure.

People of the fenland NNRs

Many people have been responsible for the protection, research and management of the two national nature reserves.

In the early days, colleagues of Charles Rothschild, Sir John Fryer and H.M. Edelsten took a keen interest and helped with experiments like the Large Copper introduction and the re-establishment of lost fenland plants. Captain Purefoy was charged with the breeding of the Large Copper and left a legacy of suggestions as to how best raise the larvae. Duncan Poore's PhD research laid down the foundations of an understanding of the ecology of Woodwalton Fen and others such as

Don and David Garner erecting a bird hide in 1995 [SS]

Rachel Hamilton, Andrew Pullin and Brian Wheeler increased species and habitat management knowledge.

The Joint Advisory Committee (JAC) was an important feature ever since NC took over management of the reserve from SPNR. Chaired for many years by Ted Smith and latterly John Redshaw, many scientists and other experts guided the development of the reserve, including Terry Wells, Norman Moore and Chris Newbold. The Great Fen is now advised by a successor to this body (Joint Technical Advisory Committee) which relies heavily on volunteer wildlife specialists.

Volunteers have been hugely important. Don Garner and his son, David, began working under warden Ian McPhail at Holme Fen in the early 1970s, and became 'official' voluntary wardens in 1978. Since then they have contributed outstanding research into Long-eared Owls, being the first to tempt them to breed in willow baskets and adding greatly to the understanding of this scarce and secretive bird (Garner and Milne 1998). David continues to carry out ringing of Barn Owls *Tyto alba* across the fenland, and to date he has ringed over 800 of them. Others have been no less active. Barry Dickerson and his team have spent many nights at both Woodwalton and Holme recording moths and Barry's inexhaustible enthusiasm has included research into historical records and an inspiration to people who wanted to learn more.

Arnold Cooke and Lynne Farrell started work recording the ecology of Chinese Water Deer in the 1970s and Dr Cooke has become a leading expert on this species. The results of this work have recently been published (Cooke 2019).

The Mason family have worked on the Fen for generations, but other long-serving wardens were: Ron Harold (13 years) and Alan Bowley (24 years), helped by talented estate workers, assistant wardens and scientists from throughout Natural England and its predecessor bodies. Early Holme Fen wardens were: Ian McPhail, Roger Boston and Paul Burnham.

It is for those reasons that it became essential to provide a long-term solution, to allow wildlife to have bigger areas to colonise and to allow more variation of habitat to develop. The conversion of the wet fens to arable agriculture was carried out with noble intentions and the skill of farmers in producing the nation's food has been admirable, but the underlying effects have been slow to be recognised. As the agricultural peat resource declines, it presents an opportunity to regenerate the fenland for its deeper value. Larger areas will allow us humans (who have been part of the story of these fens for thousands of years) to re-discover the value of a landscape where Nature is not confined to small pockets, but is part of the 'every-day' space where we live our lives. The creation of a new ecosystem crafted from the existing reserves and restored farmland offers benefits for wildlife and for people.

The Great Fen and Wicken Fen were the first of these new landscape-scale initiatives, and we will visit the Great Fen in the next chapter.

The Great Fen

There is an animated film on the Great Fen website (www.greatfen.org.uk/heritage) which was made by local youngsters. It shows how the wetland around Whittlesea Mere contracted after drainage, and how the surviving wildlife retreated to the fragments of wetland which lay beyond the reach of the thirsty pumps. These fragments are now Woodwalton and Holme Fen National Nature Reserves – survivors of a once-great wetland, but now struggling to survive into the future.

Why do we need a 'Great Fen'?

Our story has followed the changes from a world which was once mainly wild with few humans, to one which is mainly tame, and highly modified by humans. The modern fen landscape is dedicated to food production, which has consumed so much of the peat soil that many areas can no longer support this level of productivity. 'Wild Nature' is confined to tiny pockets of nature reserves or ditch edges.

A century and a half ago, William Morris described his view of a utopian world centred around two guiding principles: nature as the aesthetic guide for society, and work seen as necessary and pleasurable.

He proposed a way of living where:

"… indeed, we should be too ashamed of ourselves if we allowed the making of goods… to carry with it the appearance, even, of desolation and misery."

Morris was not an advocate for wilderness, but rather for a cultural landscape where natural forces and human endeavour existed side by side. While some people might dismiss this as a utopian dream, in reality it addressed two fundamental principles: the dangers of ignoring the effects of economic growth and industrial activity on the natural world, and the way in which that affects human society. There is now ample evidence of the consequences of ignoring Morris's vision and the Great Fen offers an example of how we might turn the tide and use the resources of the world around us in a better way.

A new millennium – a new direction

As we have seen, fenland hasn't reached its present condition by chance. It has been a 12,000-year story, through ice and flood, fish and birds, grazing, war and drainage.

The families who walked across the Doggerland of pre-history, the Saxon farmers, monks, drainage adventurers and modern farmers have all left their mark. As their societies became more sophisticated, their once-close relationship with nature became blurred, then increasingly opaque. It might be argued that it is now almost completely eliminated. At the same time, the peat resource built up over 6,000 years has become depleted to the extent that most of the soils which are now exposed are those of the Bronze Age, and few people venture out onto the black peat fields.

Something of the ancient world has remained in the current nature reserves, but despite escaping physical destruction they are but shadows of the original wetland, and separated from the lives of ordinary folk. By the turn of the 20th century the area of Woodwalton and Holme Fens represented just 13% of the original Whittlesea Mere wetland, but retained few of its features. River flow, open water, raised bog and its surrounding fenland had been replaced by drying grassland and scrub. A succession of wardens and naturalists since 1912 have laboured at 'gardening' these flowerpots to maintain a home for the special plants and animals which survive there, and to a remarkable extent have been successful. Woodwalton, in particular, remains an oasis of a stunning variety of insects, birds and flowers. Yet in the long-term, even this reduced variety of life will be difficult to sustain. Water quality has declined, flood storage and silt deposition has caused changes in the ditch and meadow ecology, and aquatic plants struggle to thrive. Add to that the threats from a rapidly changing climate and the future the wildlife of these sites seems bleak indeed.

It is not just fenland which has been damaged, of course. In my years as warden of downland and wetland nature reserves in Sussex, the same process of isolation of chalk grassland fragments reduced their resilience to change and diversity of wildlife. Also, the isolation of these places was not just geographical; they were fading from the consciousness of society as a whole. When I came to the fens, I realised that I was not alone. Maurice Massey,

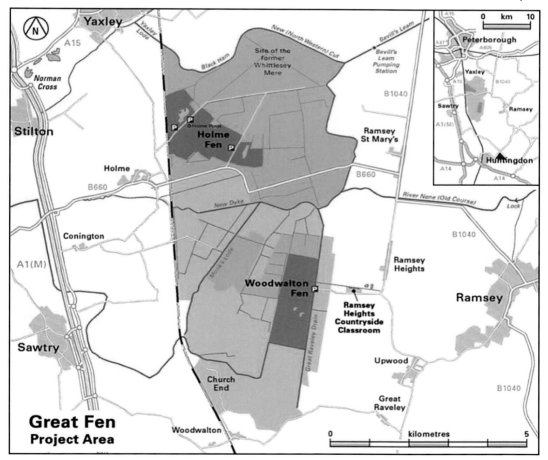

English Nature's chief warden in the 1990s, held the same view and Miriam Rothschild had spoken of it frequently. Classic studies like Norman Moore's work on the effects of pesticides and Chris Meade's studies of farmland birds at the British Trust for Ornithology, demonstrated how changes in agriculture were having catastrophic effects on farmland birds like Yellowhammer *Emberiza citrinella*, Grey Partridge *Perdix perdix* and Lapwing. Bitterns, Otters, and Water Voles were disappearing fast. Yet these were issues which no amount of management within the tiny nature reserves could hope to influence. When the Large Copper butterfly breathed its last on Woodwalton Fen, the need for 'joined up' landscape became ever-more pressing.

By the early 1990s, more people had become convinced of the need for a major change of approach if the accelerating losses of 'wild' countryside were to be stemmed. In 1996 the 'Wet Fens for the Future' project enlisted the co-operation of several organisations to investigate how this trend might be reversed. Despite continued arguments to maintain maximum production from the declining peat, the scene was set for a bolder approach... in an entirely new direction.

History of the Great Fen

Early days
Following a visit to the Oostvaarderplassen wetland creation in the Netherlands, the Wildlife Trust for Bedfordshire, Cambridgeshire, Northamptonshire and Peterborough (BCNP, now BCN) launched their 'Big Idea' for an area of wetland in the west of the fens in the mid-90s (Colston 1997). The project was abandoned after opposition from fen farmers, and its chief proponent, Adrian Colston, moved to Wicken Fen NNR, where the National Trust launched its '100-year Vision'. This would extend the reserve towards Cambridge city via a vast wetland of more than 5,000 hectares. At the same time, risking the outrage of my superiors, I submitted a proposal to English Nature outlining a process to link Woodwalton Fen and Holme Fen NNRs (Bowley & Willott 1997). The official policy at the time was that sites could only be acquired if they were already of nature conservation value and were under threat. To buy arable land to create new habitat was considered unworkable at least and preposterous in the extreme. Despite the doubters, I persuaded the leader of the Wet Fens Project, Robert Oates, to chair a meeting between English Nature, the Wildlife Trust and the Environment Agency to discuss how we could work together to join up the two NNRs. Nine decades had passed since Charles Rothschild held the first meeting of the SPNR at the Natural History Museum to think the unthinkable. In a small room at the Nene Valley offices of English Nature early in 2001, we took the next great step...

There were some lively characters involved. Tom Tew was the current team manager for EN and was an enthusiastic and innovative leader. Nick Hammond was Director of the local Wildlife Trust and Martin Slater represented the Environment Agency. The atmosphere was electric – feathers flew as differing opinions were expressed, but the result was life-changing... the Great Fen was born! Within a short time, a project officer, Chris Gerrard, was appointed through generous funding from the Garfield Weston Foundation and we were on our way!

There began a period of immense creativity, coupled with luck and good powers of persuasion. The Wildlife Trust commissioned studies into the tenure of the surrounding land and also the state of the soil (Smiths Gore, Duncan 2002). At the same time, Chris Gerrard visited many people and farms in the area to chat about what the future might hold for them. I went with him on several of these visits and reactions were varied. Some saw that a different future to arable farming might be beneficial, given that inputs for intensive farming were increasing and profits decreasing. Others were suspicious, fearful, or felt that the whole idea was nonsense and would never be realised.

At this crucial point, when the idea could have remained just that, salvation came in two forms. In the year 2000, English Nature was awarded government funding for its 'Capital Modernisation' scheme. Backed by fenland specialists such as Roger Meade, we were assigned £1 million to carry out extensive remedial works on the NNRs, and (after much persuasion) to purchase land. At the same time, the Heritage Lottery Fund (HLF) had agreed to put some funding into the Great Fen. Just before Christmas 2001, Chris Gerrard and I met Stuart Papworth, owner of Darlow's Farm adjacent to Woodwalton Fen, and discussed his impending retirement and plans to put the farm into contract management. After lengthy discussions we went away for Christmas. The New Year brought the best Christmas present of all, when Mr Papworth agreed to sell the farm to Great Fen. Far from being a 'pie-in-the-sky' idea, the dream was about to become a reality, and by the end of the year the sale was complete.

The process of converting the farm to pasture was carefully planned to take advantage of the farmer's knowledge and allow him to get some benefit from carrying out the works. Mr Papworth was given a short lease to continue farming, whilst reducing fertiliser inputs; he was then contracted to re-seed the land in preparation for new management. This approach would be repeated over the years and gave re-assurance to farmers that working with the project could have benefits.

The next few years were some of the most exciting and creative times in nature conservation. A small band of people began to do what they had been told could not be done – create a new landscape for wildlife and for people, with no pre-conceived ideas of how it might develop. The three founding partners worked closely together and shared many ideas and initiatives. In the Wildlife Trust, fund-raisers like Jane Cabutti did sterling work in getting potential funders to visit. The rest of us just showed them the reserves and the potential for the surrounding farms, and the land spoke for itself.

The Rothschild Bungalow on Woodwalton Fen was always particularly successful in this respect, because of its history and its 'feel' it always enthuses visitors. One important visit was from Huntingdonshire District Council (HDC). Although the Council might at first have seemed an unlikely partner, they became enthusiastic supporters after an inspection

Darlow's Farm plot

by two senior officers in 2002. HDC shortly became a full partner and their input changed the course of the project. The Great Fen vision was originally one of an ecological solution to the problems of the isolated nature reserves, but HDC had different ideas. The general economy of the fens outside farming was at a low ebb, with several areas where families were not thriving, and the Council saw the Great Fen as a perfect solution. Not only would it create areas for recreation and contribute to a healthy environment, but it could also regenerate a rural economy based on tourism and pastoral farming.

The Government also saw the advantages of creating 'green initiatives'. As part of relief from the huge development proposals for this part of East Anglia, funds were provided in 2006 to purchase Middle Farm, adjacent to Darlow's. The relationship of Great Fen with

A farmer's view

"I'm a fourth generation farmer and home is Middle Farm. As a family we got involved some years ago, we sold the Great Fen some land and have been working with the Great Fen to convert that land from arable. It's been a big change for my family and for our staff and for everybody we work with. We've gone forward and embraced change; our business is actually bigger now, we employ more staff, we do more different and varied things. We've gone from basic arable farming to managing an awful lot of grass and we have created a hay forage business. The cows are a new enterprise, we have been able to use some of the farming practices we had already intermingled with habitat management and grass management. We do an awful lot of contract work for the Great Fen, that can be anything from ditching, building roadways, to car parks and picnic areas. The latest project we are working on is to convert a build for holiday accommodation for people to come and stay in the Great Fen and hopefully enjoy the wildlife and habitats around us. I am helping people get close to wildlife and its something I didn't think I'd be doing a few years ago but now I am definitely working with nature.

We are making it work for us, as a partnership as well and working with some great people. All of the work we do is within five miles of where we are, so we employ lots of local people, everything is local and it's sort of creating a bit of a circle of life.

My vision for the future is that this massive environmental project will create opportunities like the tourism and, and that's where I think we've got to concentrate. There will still be ongoing management here for years and years to come and hopefully we'll be involved in it".

Jonathan Papworth

the owners, Messrs John and Jonathan Papworth, had developed over some time. They had closely scrutinised the restoration work at Darlow's and having been convinced of our abilities, had the confidence to sell the farm to the Wildlife Trust (on behalf of the Great Fen partnership). The family then entered into a long-term tenancy with the Trust and a Higher-Level Stewardship Agreement with Natural England to provide the finance for conversion and future management of the land (English Nature became Natural England in 2006).

It was at this point that Barbara (now Baroness) Young became involved. As a previous Chair of English Nature and in her role as Chief Executive of the Environment Agency, she brought the new ideas of landscape and wildlife conservation to the attention of people who could make a

Great Fen landscape **detail by Carry Ackroyd**

difference. The Secretary of State for the Environment, John Gummer, had been an early visitor and was impressed with the vision and magnitude of the scheme and the solutions it offered to the conflicts between agriculture and conservation. A reception in the House of Lords in 2007, and a later one in the House of Commons (hosted by local MP, Shailesh Vara) were key moments in encouraging major stake-holders to take an interest in our proposals.

One of the most important landowners attending these events was the Crown Estate, who owned the 1,300-hectare Holmewood Estate around Holme Fen. This land originally belonged to William Wells, drainer of Whittlesea Mere, but had been owned by the Crown since 1949. They decided to dispose of their interest early in the 2000s, and after much negotiation between tenants, landlord and the Great Fen partners, the sale of the greater part of the estate to the Great Fen was completed in 2008. A successful bid to the HLF for £7.2 million provided much of the funding, matched by other donations and fund-raising.

This purchase confirmed in no uncertain terms that landscape-scale conservation was the path to the future. It sent shock waves through the conservation world, and was to prove a catalyst for other landscape-scale ventures. At the time of going to press, there are now over 150 landscape initiatives across England. Many are championed under the Wildlife Trust's 'Living Landscapes' banner; the RSPB has its 'Futurescapes', and there are several exciting private schemes such as the Knepp Castle Estate in Sussex, and Wild Ennerdale in Scotland.

The work proceeds

This drive for a new direction to the way we regard wider landscape management was given a boost in 2008 by the launch of the National Wetland Vision. The idea of grand-scale wetland creation and protection had become a national policy, was widely supported and describes a more strategically planned future for wetlands. Flood events over the past few years have given this new

Wetlands for all

The National Wetland Vision is delivered by five organisations: the Environment Agency, Natural England, English Heritage, the Wildlife Trusts and the RSPB, with the Wildfowl & Wetlands Trust and National Parks supporting the steering group. The Vision sets out guidelines for England's wetlands over the next 50 years.

impetus and there are increasing examples of wetlands being used to mitigate the effects of uncontrolled flooding.

Back on the Great Fen, the conditions of the HLF grant required a five-year restoration programme for the Holmewood Estate. Working with local contractors, particularly Fen Ditching (now Fen Group), who had been carrying out ditch management for both the Drainage Board and Natural England for many years, a variety of habitats was created. These included Rymes Reedbed on the edge of Holme Fen, the sinuous water channels of Kester's Docking and the pools and meadows of Engine Farm. The vegetable crops raised within the bed of Whittlesea Mere for 150 years have now given way to livestock, wildflower meadows and access for people. A small mere on Engine Farm provides a home for amphibians, and the marshy meadows have begun to ring with sounds of wetland birds.

Research and experiments are also continuing on how to develop 'wetland agriculture' amongst the new habitats. In 2019, Great Fen, together with partners Cambridgeshire ACRE, the University of East London and the Centre for Ecology and Hydrology, received funding from the Dream Fund bid (People's Postcode Lottery) for its 'Water Works' project. The fund will finance new research and experimental management to develop ways of producing crops like *Sphagnum* moss, biomass for energy generation and withies for basket-making.

One important result of the restoration work has been to slow the seepage of water from Holme Fen; the possibility of re-growing at least a portion of raised bog in the reserve is one step nearer.

Support

Funding

None of the aims of the Great Fen would have been possible without financial backing, and this has come from a variety of sources.

The HLF grant for the Holmewood Estate purchase and restoration was the largest ever offered for an environmental scheme (a further grant of £1.89 million was received in 2014 for the restoration of Engine Farm). Whilst being a fantastic opportunity, this also presented a challenge for the infant Great Fen. Firstly, there was a short time-scale in which to make crucial decisions about which areas of land and farm buildings to purchase. Secondly, the terms of the offer required that a large area of land should be restored within five years – a testing target when the obstacles were virtually unknown.

The decision to accept HLF funding was not taken lightly, because it introduced an element which had previously been blissfully absent from the Great Fen. While the Steering Group members did represent their

The objectives of the HLF grant

- Purchase and restoration of 747 hectares of land.
- Provision of public access and interpretation.
- Delivery of community and education activities.
- Widening the audiences engaged with the natural heritage of the Great Fen.

organisations, decision-making had been largely driven by the enthusiasm of the individuals acting as the Great Fen. It was freedom from the bureaucracy and hesitation of corporate bodies which had allowed the partners to make bold decisions, but an alliance with HLF would introduce a degree of control. The imposition of targets and desired outcomes had to be balanced against the ability to purchase large blocks of land. In reality, it was not a hard decision, the grant was agreed and the change of emphasis which HLF introduced proved to be a catalyst in broadening the scope of the project. Encouraging more local involvement through history, education and volunteering revealed much interest from people who might otherwise not have engaged with a wildlife project. This area of fenland had been a part of the lives of successive generations for thousands of years, and the new approach by the Great Fen was intended to re-kindle that. It was not to be 'wildlife or people' but 'wildlife AND people'.

Other funders have also been crucial, and include charitable foundations, the general public and direct funding through the project partners, either in kind or financially. Individuals, including the Rothschild family, have also backed their commitment by supporting specific projects or with general funds.

A bumpy ride

It is a small miracle that we ever received support from HLF. When their senior officer visited Woodwalton Fen to look at the project, Chris Gerrard and I took her across the fields to see the cattle. I was driving them in an amphibious vehicle, but I had forgotten that we had dug shallow channels across the field. We hit the first one with a bang! As she rose gracefully into the air, missing the windscreen by a fraction, and landed back in her seat with a gasp, we both thought it was the end of our bid for funding. Happily, she thought it was great fun, and the rest of the story is history!

People

Without money from the funders, the project may have taken much longer to make progress, but without people it may never have happened at all. From the first stirrings of discontent which created the original idea 20 years ago, to the enthusiasm of the countless staff and volunteers who have worked so diligently, the Great Fen has had the best that people can offer. I cannot remember a time in my life when there has been such consistent passion and expertise, such dedication and co-operation, as on the Great Fen. Science, art, interpretation, planning and physical labour have come together to create an extraordinary amalgam of positivity which has been responsible for the progress of this great ideal. Many inspiring people have helped bring the new landscape to fruition. A Campaign Executive Group was formed in 2007 and included such inspirational figures such as Sir Charles Chadwyck-Healey, Stephen Fry (president), and Tim Smit from the Eden Project. In the same year HRH the Prince of Wales visited Woodwalton and gave his royal patronage. This was renewed in 2013 and was celebrated by the attendance of some members of the team at the Prince's 70th birthday garden party at Buckingham Palace in 2018.

It has been an enormous privilege to work with people who have been so inspiring. When Stephen Fry visited in 2006, we walked along Bungalow Drove discussing the reserve and he posed for a photograph, hanging on for dear life to some reeds just above a deep ditch! Tim Smit spent a short time on the Fen one evening and left us buzzing with new ideas. Ray Mears quietly made a fire to cook some reedmace pancakes and paddled his long red canoe across the meres!

One of our patrons, the Right Honourable Sir John Major, described the Great Fen as:

"… *a project that is close to my home as well as my heart. One can seldom find space in our busy and crowded world, but the Great Fen Project delivers that in triplicate: space, tranquillity and the sheer beauty of the landscape and its native habitat. We should treasure this, alongside encouraging more people – young and old – to enjoy the experience, thus improving the local economy through tourism*".

Rangers

In 2012 the Great Fen voluntary ranger service was created. Each weekend, they are on duty to help the public and to keep an eye on the wildlife. This has become a valuable activity for many of the rangers who gain experience and are able to get to know local people and visitors alike.

Not all inspiring people have the high profile of princes and actors. It has been the volunteers and staff who have created the success of this project and it is their work and dedication which has produced the results on the ground and in the hearts of the public.

The commitment of HLF was primarily through funding, but also highlighted the importance of the social benefits of a new landscape ideal. This led to the creation of an Education and Visitor section of the Great Fen, based at the old brick-kiln at Ramsey

Facts and figures

since the project began
514 volunteers

- Over 22,000 children have been involved with activities on the Fen.
- Over 500 volunteers have given their time, 21 of whom have contributed more than 100 days each. (Two volunteers looked after Darlow's Farm two days each week for several years!)
- Trainees have, in most cases, gone on to jobs in conservation after working with the team.

A long walk

In 2011 the Great Fen Local Group was formed and they have sinced raised £14,000 for various projects. One of their members, Adrian Kempster, proposed the idea of a long-distance path from Woodwalton to Wicken Fen, linking two of Charles Rothschild's original nature reserves. On a day of continuous rain in 2014, several hardy walkers completed the 39 miles of this Rothschild Way route. It was hard going, but the welcome from the team in the dark night at the Rothschild Bungalow was an event not to be missed – even my dog got a medal!

Pioneer walkers – the Rothschild Way

Some Great Fen people – heroes of the new ideal

I have had the privilege of working alongside some inspiring characters.

The Steering Committee has been chaired by some very able people. **Tom Tew**, **Sarah Fendley** and **John Orr** drove the project through some of its more challenging years. Director of Planning for HDC, **Malcolm Sharp** became a key player early on in the Great Fen story. Although the original concept was to improve conditions for wildlife, his vision was for a closer engagement with local people and opportunities to improve lives by boosting the local economy, creating jobs, and putting fenland on the map.

Chris Gerrard had worked for the Wildlife Trust for some time before the project came to be. As the first project officer he met countless people from all walks of life to explain, enthuse and bring an idea to a reality. His successor, **Kate Carver** has guided, coaxed and inspired partners, staff and the wider public to achieve extraordinary progress. **Brian Eversham** is another Wildlife Trust champion whose knowledge of wildlife and dedication to the Great Fen has been hugely significant.

As Chief Engineer of the Middle Level drainage authority **David Thomas** had the foresight to understand that the answer to effective flood protection of farmland and communities lay in the Great Fen.

Paul Jose and **Helen Smith** (later to be Chair) both represented the Environment Agency and succeeded in maintaining the Great Fen as a major initiative within the Agency. Other notable members have included **Nick Hammond**, **Catherine Weightman**, **Derek Langslow**, **John Torlesse** and **Stewart lane**.

Working on the land, successive rangers have achieved remarkable results. **Tim Sutton** and an able band of volunteers transformed Darlow's Farm as the first Great Fen land holding. **Jon Smith** (pictured right) had all the enthusiasm and skill that has driven this idea to such success, and his early death in 2013 was a major blow to morale. Others though, have taken up the cause with equal effect and **Helen Bailey** and **Mark Ulyett** are now putting ideas into practice.

The scientific input has been no less important. **Paul Tinsley-Marshall**, **Josh Hellon** and **Henry Stainier** have ensured that rigorous research and monitoring has been developed to provide a sound basis for assessing the impacts of the changing land and water on wildlife and people.

The early years of the project were characterised by an enthusiastic group of people whose job it was to bring the ideal to the notice of politicians, financiers and others. **Kelly Dickson** and **Tanya Mercer** helped arrange and conduct numerous visits to Woodwalton Fen at this time. Education, heritage and community involvement has been crucial – thanks to the effort of dedicated staff and volunteers, among whom are **Helen Moore**, **Louise Rackham**, **Sue Wallis**, **Lauren Stonebridge**, **Barbara Cracknell**, **Rebekah O'Driscoll** and **Mandi Corney**.

The Joint Technical Advisory Committee (JTAC)

The technical knowledge of amateurs and professionals alike has been key to ensuring that the Great Fen has good scientific credentials. **Chris Newbold** and **Owen Mountford** have chaired a committee which has included professional naturalists like **Pete Kirby**, **Phil Grice**, **David Gowing**, and **Lesly Saint**. **Mick Burton** joined the Great Fen volunteers to pursue his keen interest in birds and since then has collaborated in a major report on the bird populations since the project began. He trained as a botanical surveyor and is now an expert in bryophytes. He is a perfect example of how people giving their time voluntarily to this new idea are so important.

Heights. Working with youngsters and with older generations who had laboured in the fields through good times and bad, the work of the team helped to reveal a rich history of fenland life, and created much support for the project. Their contribution to the success of the project has been immeasurable, because it has gained the trust and support of many people who may otherwise have been nervous about the great changes which are happening in their immediate environment.

The challenges of change

The progress of this great undertaking has not always been smooth, particularly in the first few years. While the initial purchase and restoration of Darlow's Farm was relatively straightforward, taking on the huge area of the Holmewood Estate put a great strain on staff and the partners.

It also raised disquiet amongst some of the local community. Concerted opposition from some of the tenant farmers, the local Internal Drainage Board and some local Councillors made these the most difficult years we experienced. The spectre of the fen gallows with which the 17th-century 'fen tygers' threatened the drainers sometimes felt uncomfortably close! I was shunned by some villagers, and there were many acrimonious meetings and conversations. Opposition from within the ranks of one of the partner organisations almost led to their departure from the steering group, and the Drainage Board simply could not accept why the work of years in draining the fen should be reversed. How could it have been otherwise? The proposed changes were a huge departure for families who had spent two or three generations working in the pump-dried fens. It was bound to cause unease, particularly when agricultural policy and the global economy were undergoing huge changes.

The disapproval was not helped by local and national media, who announced with misguided enthusiasm that the whole area was to be taken out of food production and flooded. This caused immense and lasting damage to people's perception of the scheme; in reality, the Great Fen was not an attack on the safety and food source of local people, but the re-balancing of the fenland ecosystem into one which offered an improved environment, protection from flooding and long-term economic opportunities. The case is clear – the remaining peat is a precious resource where our history is preserved and where a unique wildlife community hangs on by the skin of its teeth. A newly invigorated landscape based on the surviving peatland has immense advantages for people from all walks of life. For centuries people made their living from an environment which was also rich in wildlife; the wildlife itself enriched the lives of the people, while at the same time preserving the essential functions of the ecosystem. There is no reason why this should not be true in the future, if we take an informed and enlightened view of what can be achieved.

We took comfort from the fact that the great campaigners of the past also met with stiff opposition, but they knew what they stood for was right and this is still true today. Creating better harmony in the way that fenland is used and appreciated is a major process which will ultimately bring

The Great Fen Partners

The Great Fen is overseen by the Great Fen Project Partnership. The founding partners were the Environment Agency, Natural England and the Wildlife Trust for Bedfordshire, Cambridgeshire, Northamptonshire and Peterborough (now BCN), all of whom were primarily concerned with the ecological aspects of joining up the NNRs of Woodwalton and Holme Fens. Huntingdonshire District Council joined in 2004, while the Middle Level Commissioners took an active part, but did not become a full partner until 2010. The strength of the project lies in the skills and diversity of approach which the partners and their staff provide.

A further partnership is provided through the involvement of volunteers, whose varied skills have been decisive in making the progress that has been achieved so far.

The strategic aims of the Great Fen

Aim 1. Natural and historic environment
To create a new resilient fenland landscape which delivers major wildlife and heritage benefits and achieves high standards of sustainability in all respects.

Aim 2. Social
To create an accessible, inspiring and tranquil environment for recreation, education, health and well-being.

Aim 3. Economic
To contribute to diversification and development of the local economy, consistent with environmental and social objectives

Aim 4. Climate change
To plan, design and manage the Great Fen to benefit climate change adaption and mitigation.

Great Fen Masterplan

March 2010

ENV/03

benefits which will far outweigh any initial difficulties which major change always brings. It will take time, patience and good powers of persuasion, but has already begun to prove its worth.

Planning for change

It was never intended to formulate detailed plans for the future landscape, but pressure from planners and funders soon made it necessary to present at least some outline of how the project might evolve. It was also important to make sure that the ambitions of the Great Fen were considered early in the planning process. Too often, aspirations of local people are considered only after major plans have been approved. If projects like the Great Fen are to reach their full potential, it is essential that they are considered as an integral part of any proposals, and not as a 'bolt-on' gesture such as creating greenspace or a cycle path.

It was a great fortune that HDC could bring their expertise to the master-planning process, and that their officers such as Director of Planning, Malcolm Sharp, were far-sighted and understood the ethos of the scheme. After many hours of debate, which allowed us to clarify the direction we wanted to take and how we could go about it, an indicative Masterplan was published in 2010. The Masterplan describes a vibrant landscape where birds, plants and animals can flourish in safety within and between the two NNRs; where people can enjoy natural beauty, new opportunities for leisure, learning, and making a living; and where nature and humans alike can benefit from living and working within a 'natural' environment. Initially, a period of 60 years was stated as the life of the project, but this was an entirely arbitrary timescale. In reality, this is an open-ended scheme, which will twist and turn depending on a wide range of factors, many of which are yet to be discovered.

The Masterplan set out where new physical features could be established and where existing ones could be retained. It states four strategic aims, parts of which were revised in 2017 to reflect changes both within the fen and in wider society (Williams, J. Ed 2017). The Plan is unique because it embraces ecological, economic, social and climate change aspirations – all of which have equal importance and are inter-connected.

Access to nature

Much of the Masterplan concentrates on access. With few existing footpaths or other access routes, we had the opportunity to plan access as an integral part of wildlife habitat, rather than having to fit one around the other. In this way we hoped to avoid conflict between activities like walking, riding and, in some areas camping, and the needs of sensitive species like cranes or otters. Of course, it is not a simple task, because it can be difficult to predict where wildlife will decide to settle, and people are keen to have as close contact as possible with beautiful creatures.

By 2015, there was a comprehensive system of paths where people could visit parts of the land which had been inaccessible for generations. One of these is the 'Last of the Meres' trail, where not only can people walk around the old Whittlesea Mere, but can get a commentary via an app on their mobile phone! Future plans may include a water taxi, canoe routes and camping areas.

Access is not confined to the physical. The website has been carefully developed to include a wide range of historical and topical subjects, including film and the opportunity to submit ideas and wildlife sightings.

A changing landscape – wilderness or restoration

Stepping out in a new direction of how we perceive and manage the landscape involves difficult decisions, not the least of which is the definition of 'wild' and 'wilderness'. Assessing an area as 'wild' suggests that there will be no interference from humans, but even the decision to use native livestock – or no livestock at all – are human decisions which affect the very concept of 'wild'. Perhaps we would do well to remember that humans are as much a part of the natural world as beavers or butterflies – it is just that centuries of thought and cultural development have persuaded us that we stand apart from the normal processes of Nature.

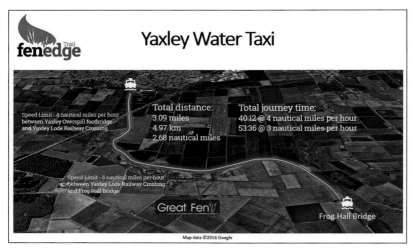

A water taxi could provide an exciting access to the fen without increasing motor traffic

When the ideas for a new wetland around the fenland NNRs first emerged, they were influenced by new thinking about ancient landscapes. Oliver Rackham had begun to question the extent of the wildwood and this query had been expanded by Frans Vera. Although not without its critics, the fresh research argued that the dense post-glacial 'wildwood' might not have been so dense after all. Instead, the activities of large herbivores like Aurochs and Giant Elk, beavers and geese fashioned a 'kaleidoscope' of moors, heath and grassland amongst the admittedly huge areas of woodland.

We wondered whether these wilder landscapes could be replicated in the English fens; could they be 're-wilded'? The ancient oak and pine woodlands here had been replaced by saltmarsh, reed-fen and grazing pasture at various times, managed by sea, wild animals and man. Could it be possible or even practicable to allow natural processes and extensive grazing to re-mould a wilder landscape? This raised further questions. What is 're-wilding' anyway;

when were the fens really 'wild'; how big an area is needed; how will local people react; and is it a worthwhile goal?

It is not always clear how much influence humans had at any particular time, and lack of evidence of human intervention does not necessarily mean that there was none. No doubt at some periods, fen land was 'wilder' than at others, but we need to be cautious about assuming that until recently there were vast areas of unmanaged habitat here. Human intervention has been a dominant feature at least since the Roman era, and the three or four millennia before that saw increasing human impact, first from hunting wild animals and then from domestic livestock.

Steve Boreham has summed up the results of his borehole studies as:

"... taken together, these survey boreholes describe the changing palaeoenvironments across the Rymes Reedbed site for at least the past 6,000 years. It is quite clear that very few locations... have remained unchanged during that time, and that most have experienced rising and falling water levels of various kinds. The concept that this landscape must have been a constantly changing mosaic of different vegetation types is an important one when the significance of these 'heritage' sediment sequences is considered.

There is also a: *"compelling environmental and archaeological story of lakes, reedswamps, woodlands, heathlands, raised bogs and marine inundation".* (Boreham 2013)

The 20th century saw the confinement of wildlife in protected areas reserves, where 'desirable' species were prioritised and the suitable habitat created and managed to meet their needs. This achieved some very successful results, but ultimately had failed to protect much of Britain's wildlife outside the confines of nature reserves and other 'protected areas' such as Sites of Special Scientific Interest (SSSI). I believe it is this emphasis on 'micro-management' which has fuelled the desires for a re-incarnation of the 'wild' – even if it has not existed for such a long time.

The debate on the value of this more 'naturalistic' approach to landscape management is not entirely new and can be described as having three differing aspects: Re-wilding, Restoration and Abandonment (of farmland).

Re-wilding

John Muir and others had established the first North American National Parks in the 19th century because of their value as large and wild areas of great grandeur. Their biological

Re-wilding can take many different forms. This fenland landscape is managed for wildlife but retains its 'wild' feel

importance became evident later on, and was followed by the realisation that if protected areas were too small, the principles of 'island biogeography' came into effect. This is what the problems of small nature reserves are all about – small size, genetic isolation and 'un-naturalness'.

In the 1990s, Michael Soulè put forward the concept of 're-wilding' as: *"the scientific argument for restoring big wilderness based on the regulatory roles of large predators,"* whereas previous interest had been more concentrated on the moral and aesthetic aspects (Foreman and Wolke 1989, Fox 1981). The scientific case for re-wilding was based on three arguments (Soule and Noss 1998):

- large, strictly protected, core reserves (the wild)
- connectivity
- keystone species (such as Beavers) and top predators (such as Wolves).

While he emphasised a scientific foundation for case, Soulè did not deny other important features of wilderness. There are, he adds: *"two non-scientific justifications: 'the ethical issue of human responsibility,' and 'the subjective, emotional essence of 'the wild' or wilderness'."*

The current desire to progress from the confines of nature reserves to landscape-scale management brings all these issues together. If carefully planned and executed, it has the potential not only to provide a truly sustainable solution to the problems of small-site conservation, but also to bring to an end the separation of people from Nature. Whether or not the grand-scale ideas of Soulè and others are manageable on a relatively small scale, however, is debatable. In the fens of East Anglia, two of the basic factors for re-wilding are missing – size and top predators. 3,500 hectares is certainly large in comparison to the existing NNRs, but the whole of that area is not fully functional (it will still contain farmsteads, houses and roads). Secondly, it is impractical to re-establish top predators such as wolves to control herbivore numbers in a small area of lowland England. Even the release of beavers as a keystone species would have to be very carefully planned and managed. Re-wilding in its purest from, therefore, may have to be consigned to the grand-scale upland moors and mountains than lowland England, but that certainly does not mean that a modified approach can achieve extremely beneficial results.

If there is neither the room for, nor cultural acceptance of, top predators, then introducing large herbivores which have at least a degree of autonomy could at least re-

Native cattle at the Knepp Castle re-wilding project in Sussex

establish one crucial aspect of a 'wild' landscape. This is being done in some large European projects and also at the Knepp Castle re-wilding project in Sussex, where 1,400 hectares of ex-farmland are now being grazed by native cattle, ponies and Wild Boar (Tree 2018). Here, as would have to be the case at Great Fen, the place of top predators in controlling herbivore numbers will be taken by humans. This is what ecologists call the 'trophic cascade', whereby the structure of the vegetation is directly influenced by the activities of the predators which control the numbers of grazing animals. In the case of landscape-scale conservation in lowland England, human culling of deer or harvesting cattle for meat replaces the balance achieved by wolf pack or roaming bears.

Restoration

So much for re-wilding – what other method can transform a disjointed landscape? This is a topic which has been debated in relation to the built environment for a long time, and perhaps we can draw some comparisons with Nature's environment. In his essay *Seven Lamps* of *Architecture*, John Ruskin considered: *"Neither by the public, nor by those who have the care of public monuments, is the true meaning of the word restoration understood. It means the most total destruction which a building can suffer… Do not let us deceive ourselves in this important matter; it is impossible… to restore anything that has ever been great or beautiful in architecture."*

By contrast, the French architect, Viollet-le-Duc, considered that restoration is a *"means to re-establish [a building] to a finished state, which may in fact never have actually existed at any given time"*.

Turning to the landscape, the social enterprise 'Future Terrains' defines restoration as: *"The improvement of degraded land on a large scale that rebuilds ecological integrity and enhances people's lives"*.

It considers that landscape restoration activities should include:

"… reintroducing missing or declining biodiversity; connecting disconnected landscape elements; involving a mosaic of ecological habitats, communities, land uses and interest groups; ensuring that communities and habitats are enhanced by the restoration programme; and stimulating development of a self-sustaining system".

They also recognise that these initiatives should be on a large scale, although this could embrace several smaller projects, which are easier to conceptualise, fund and deliver.

Restoration at Rymes Reedbed (Great Fen) [WTBCN]

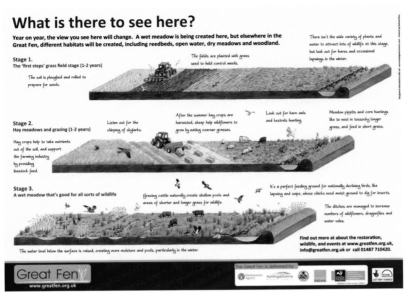

These aspirations do not imply 're-creation' of a past landscape – which is neither possible nor desirable. Instead, it is a re-assembling of the ecological processes which have been removed (for whatever reason) in order that a novel, healthy and functioning ecosystem can begin to evolve.

The process of landscape restoration is initiated by removing some of the limiting factors (such as drainage) and 'kick-starting' new habitats. For example:

1. Arable land will be converted to an undrained pastoral system, with limited habitat creation such as scrapes and pools. Seeding ex-arable can help prevent further peat loss and limits the immediate flush of competitive species which can severely delay the establishment of a more diverse vegetation. The result is that essential biological and physical features are re-established, and connected to existing high biodiversity areas (such as the fen NNRs).

2. A more relaxed approach can then be followed, and the grazing animals can begin their task of moulding an entirely new landscape.

3. Static areas of 'grassland', 'scrub' or 'open water' are not the normal state of Nature, so after this initial 'restoration' phase, there should be very limited pre-planning of where specific habitats might develop. Extensive grazing, climate, water control (including absorbing excess floodwater), or the effect of wildlife itself, such as deer – or (one day) Beavers – will be more influential than detailed management decisions. This has the potential to allow vegetation and its wildlife to be in a constant state of flux. With the larger land area and lack of pre-conceived targets, a dynamic landscape could evolve, where species and habitats have the space to adapt to circumstances such as climate change.

The mechanics of how this naturalistic approach can be achieved will be a challenge, but remaining faithful to the original principle is essential.

Abandonment

There is a final, and ostensibly easier, way to develop a more natural landscape. Removing all human interference and simply allowing Nature to re-assert itself would seem to be an obvious and cheap solution. Provided there was access to areas of higher biodiversity, natural balances would be restored and wildlife hotspots would soon emerge. In his review of re-

Restoration in action – the grazing conundrum

The debate over re-wilding was in its infancy when early decisions were taken about management of the new lands. These were initially guided by assessments from the Centre for Ecology and Hydrology (CEH) at Monks Wood. We asked them to consider three scenarios:

What might happen if:
Scenario 1: the current drainage regime continued;
Scenario 2: drainage was halted and basic grazing and mowing introduced; or
Scenario 3: a controlled water management regime was introduced, creating water storage for habitat creation.

After much discussion, Scenario 2 was adopted as being the most pragmatic approach and one which would not involve intrusive engineering and cost. This allowed for a mosaic of habitats to develop whilst still providing opportunities for access and other activities. It was accepted that this provided a useful starting point which allowed maximum flexibility as ideas and the physical environment itself changeover time.

The shift away from 're-wilding' to an initially more engineered landscape meant that Great Fen began to diverge somewhat from the National Trust's image for Wicken, where Konik ponies and Highland cattle have created vegetation mosaics which may mimic those of roaming Mesolithic herbivores. Natural England had for many years run its own herd of native Highland and Galloway cattle, as well as native ponies, which both offered staff valuable experience of livestock and complete control of when and how they grazed. Following a change of personnel on the NNRs, however, the cattle were disposed of and Great Fen became reliant on livestock owned by others. Not ideal, perhaps, but it did present the opportunity to encourage farmers both to switch from arable to livestock and to extend existing grazing onto the new land. Some payments were required to induce the first few tentative pioneers, but today there are several enthusiastic farmers with native livestock on the new lands who pay an economic rent.

This approach demonstrates that the Great Fen is not another isolated nature reserve but a landscape where commercial farming can co-exist with vibrant wildlife habitats. A 'wilder' approach will evolve later.

Restoration methods were initially trialled at Darlow's Farm. In order to prevent thistles and ragwort causing a nuisance to surrounding farms, all the boundaries were seeded with a wild grass mix. On other fields, regular mowing sought to control the thistles which emerged from the nutrient-rich soils of the old arable, but eventually we had to resort to targeted chemical control. While it might be argued that thistles and ragwort were a natural response, and would have declined over time (and been a great source of nectar), we had to consider the longer-term objective. This was to win over our neighbours to the prospect of a different land-use than growing potatoes and sugar beet, without causing problems for existing farming enterprises. In the first few years of raising water levels, there were spectacular wildlife gains. Wading birds came to visit, Lapwings and Snipe *Gallinago gallinago* bred, harriers and Short-eared Owls *Asio flammeus* hunted the fields. Plants like Golden Dock *Rumex maritimus* and the wonderfully-named Trifid Bur-marigold *Bidens tripartita* (pictured [PC]) appeared after an absence of many decades. The

raising of the water level was not without its problems, because it created ideal conditions for unwelcome species such as Soft Rush *Juncus effusus*. Several fields became dominated by huge tussocks which broke both machinery and the will of the hapless staff and volunteers, who gave so much of their time and energy to the restoration work. Eventually the issue became so intractable that it was decided to just lightly graze some fields and observe the result. That is the essence of the Great Fen approach. It is not about 'micro-management'; it is about initiating the transition from arable to pasture and then experimenting with various degrees of intervention as necessary.

wilding, Graham Lawton suggested that 'passive rewilding' as the result of abandonment of farmland across Europe may affect 300,000 square kilometres of land by 2030 (Lawton 2018). This might at first seem to be the perfect opportunity for this 'eco-balance' to be restored, but current evidence suggests that this may not be the case; in some situations, it is the invasive species which gain the upper hand and the variety of wildlife which had been benefitting from low-intensity farming has been reduced. A similar process has been suggested for the Saxon and medieval landscapes of England. Until the great drainage of the fens in the 17th century, the mosaic of habitats maintained by water control, grazing and scrub control, created ideal living conditions for birds, Beavers and Otters, and a bewildering array of invertebrates. The resulting biodiversity may well have exceeded the variety of species which inhabited the tundra or wildwood before humans began farming the land.

The principles of restoration, then, appear to offer the best chance of creating a new fenland landscape, but if this is the case, what of wilderness? How can we experience any sense of the wild, of a world removed from the interference of humans? I believe that while we may not be able to replicate the 'wild' of our forefathers, we can still have an increased sense of closeness to the natural world by careful use of different landscape zones. There is already an atmosphere of peace beneath Holme Fen birches and in the whisper of the Woodwalton reeds, but the new cry of Curlews *Numenius arquata* across the Kester wetlands are a suggestion of an altogether wilder feel to the nascent Great Fen. A land which was once half sea, then a freshwater lake, then arable farmland, is once again stirring with the sights and sounds of untamed nature among the agriculture and townships which surround it.

It is impossible to predict what it will look like in 10 years, let alone a century, and perhaps that scarcely matters. What does matter is that a large wetland of unknown character is emerging from the intensive farmland of East Anglia. That is at once exciting and challenging, and promises enormous benefits to society.

Despite the intention to make the great Fen as 'naturalistic' as possible, with few specific targets, it soon became clear that some form of model was necessary – at the very least to ensure that successive managers don't keep initiating random ideas. In 2013, a Management Plan was compiled for Natural England for Darlow's and Middle Farms, but was entitled a 'Development Guide' so as not to suggest a rigid management regime.

In 2016, a Management Plan for the wider Great Fen was produced as part of the HLF restoration work on Holmewood Estate. Early management here has been driven by habitat targets, which, as already stated, may not be ideal, but does have the advantage that there is now a wide range of habitats on the Estate which are attracting much wildlife.

Excavated scrape at Rymes Reedbed

Much of the restoration management has been discussed and formulated within the Joint Technical Advisory Committee (JTAC), which developed from the Woodwalton Fen Joint Advisory Committee (JAC). This panel of experts from across the spectrum of wildlife species and management, have contributed a series of guidelines within which land managers can operate. These include predator control, introductions of species and vegetation management.

A changing landscape – assessing the effects

Science underpins the Great Fen. Whatever the outcomes from the land-use changes which we have initiated, it is essential to record their effects on wildlife, on people and on the landscape as a whole. Without an accurate record, future generations will not have the information to decide whether or not the project has been an overall benefit. Most nature reserves have a system for assessing the results of land and water management. Sites are protected for their pre-existing wildlife or geological interest, and there are various ways of measuring changes to wildlife communities against the work being done for their benefit. This may involve 'in-situ' work on the sites themselves or 'ex-situ' breeding in zoos or botanical gardens for later field trials or re-establishment in the wild. This is why nature reserves are important – they can offer facilities for field experiments which are not available elsewhere. Conservation management of reedbeds is a good example. Intensive research by RSPB on surviving populations of Bitterns provided management prescriptions which, when activated on Woodwalton Fen, created the right conditions for Bitterns to breed again after many decades of absence.

On a landscape-scale, the situation is rather different and the experts on the JTAC have developed some novel strategies for formulating management principles and how to record the results. In addition, research by Francine Hughes and Pete Stroh at Anglia Ruskin University (Hughes *et al.* 2011, 2016) has developed and tested methods of surveillance which can be applied to large-scale land and water areas. They describe how the 'traditional' approach of habitat manipulation to achieve a pre-defined end cannot be applied to 'open-ended' landscape-scale. Here, the evolution of novel habitats progresses from an initial 'blank canvas' and may involve uncertainty, long time-scales and unproven methods of 'restoration'. With no specified end-point, it becomes difficult to conceive how success can be measured. The answer lies in replacing measurement of 'success' with an acceptance of the unpredictability of the future, abandoning any idea of adaptive management to shift habitats towards a desired goal. Instead, the emphasis is on long-term surveillance of a range of parameters, which can illustrate the changes which are occurring and how wildlife

Monitoring station

communities are responding. On the Great Fen this includes water level measurements, vegetation mapping by remote sensing and quadrat analysis, fixed-point, drone and infra-red photography, statistical analysis, and mapping.

More traditional species counts are also important, but careful choice of species is needed because some are more indicative of change than others. Additionally, some birds and mammals may appear to be of greater significance because they are readily observable, whereas the activities of other less obvious species, like saprophytic invertebrates, may be far more significant on the overall health of the ecosystem.

For example, if we are hoping to measure the development of the Great Fen against the records of wildlife in pre-drainage times, then monitoring eels, cranes, beavers and waterfowl may be relevant, but could prove difficult in practice. Eel numbers now appear to be extremely low but are difficult to assess accurately, and beavers are no longer present. Common Cranes *Grus grus*, by contrast, have recently re-colonised unaided and provided that disturbance can be minimised, they have a good chance of breeding, as they have on the nearby Nene Washes. For that species, there is a high probability of accurately recording their progress.

Deer populations are likely to have a significant effect on other future wildlife due to their role as 'keystone' species. Assessing numbers of Muntjac Deer and their effect on vegetation structure at Holme Fen has already led to the decision to control this alien species because of the effects the change in vegetation is having on numbers of breeding warblers. Further monitoring will reveal whether or not the control policy has been effective. Monitoring the effects of native Roe Deer will be carried out in order to better understand how their browsing influences other species. The effectiveness of this has already been demonstrated by the long-term monitoring of Chinese Water Deer at Woodwalton Fen by Dr A.S. Cooke and Lynne Farrell (Cooke and Farrell 1998).

In 2011, Hughes summarised some of the difficulties of developing new monitoring techniques:

"Open-ended approaches do not lend themselves to conservation evaluation methods established in the UK that rely on an image of success defined by specified species or habitats... Open-ended, large-scale restoration projects emphasise the importance of natural processes and are characterised by uncertain outcomes. Many stakeholders find them difficult to engage with as they represent a departure from the conventional conservation philosophy of limiting ecosystem change to deliver tightly defined conservation objectives". (Hughes *et al.* 2011)

Hughes further warns that:

"Over time, landscape-scale wetland restoration projects can expect biodiversity and ecosystem services delivery to change in response to both endogenous and exogenous factors. Any project, however well-defined its targets, is on a trajectory of ecosystem change. These changes need to be factored into project expectations and to any Payment for Ecosystem Services... It is important that projects do not attempt to create static ecosystems... since this would not only have detrimental effects on many wetland species and habitats but also be unsustainable in the long term". (Hughes *et al.* 2016)

Assessing the effects of the changes is not confined to the biological or physical world. The response of people is crucial, and has been recorded through interviews, the Developing Audiences Project (DAP), data analysis, questionnaires and events such as Project Partners' evaluation workshops.

Changing landscape, changing wildlife
There are too few records from the infant Great Fen and similar schemes to make any informed statement as to their effectiveness in improving either the current state of wildlife

populations or the impact on human well-being. Twenty years is a short time in the grand scheme. There have been lessons to learn, but the early signs of a blossoming of wildlife and its appreciation by people are encouraging. It may take many decades for some wildlife species to respond to the newly developing ecosystem, but several species have already shown interest in the new habitats.

Early raising of water levels and re-seeding of the fields at Darlow's created conditions which were quickly discovered by wild plants and animals which had not been seen for many years. Lapwings and a few Snipe managed to breed among the tussocks of rushes, and Common Cranes were soon feeding frequently in the more secluded fields. Water Voles thrived, and dragonflies previously confined to Woodwalton were soon spotted flying over the ditches.

An example of the results of changing conditions around Holme Fen occurred during the winter of 2015–16 when the Cambridge Bryology Group (mosses and liverworts) surveyed the area. The Marsh Bryum moss *Bryum pseudotriquetrum* var. *bimum* was one of the most unusual finds, as there have only been three previous records of this variety, while other acid-loving species including Small-bud Bryum *Bryum gemmiferum*, Crimson-tuber Thread-moss *Bryum rubens*, and Lesser Potato Bryum *Bryum subapiculatum* were new to the area. In addition, the Juniper Hair-cap *Polytrichum juniperinum* was found at the edge of one of the new meres and had probably migrated from Holme Fen, which is its only known locality in Huntingdonshire.

Crimson-tuber Thread-moss *Bryum rubens* [PC]

Juniper Hair-cap *Polytrichum juniperinum* [PC]

In the spring of 2016 Common Toads *Bufo bufo* were heard calling for the first time at Kester's Docking. In July of the following year, Barbastelle, Common Pipistrelle *Pipistrellus pipistrellus*, Soprano Pipistrelle *Pipistrellus pygmaeus* and Noctule bats were recorded there, while a pair of Little Grebes *Tachybaptus ruficollis* bred on the new mere at Engine Farm. Several species of wading birds dropped by on spring migration, including Bar-tailed Godwit *Limosa lapponica*, Black-tailed Godwit, Black-winged Stilt *Himantopus himantopus* and Garganey *Anas querquedula*. Some which stayed for the summer included Lapwing, Oystercatcher *Haemantopus ostralegus*, and Redshank *Tringa totanus* all benefitting from the higher water levels.

Otters are now regularly recorded by infra-red cameras.

Oystercatcher *Haemantopus ostralegus* [PG]

The role of ecosystem services

"The restoration of ecosystem services is now recognised as an important conservation goal, alongside the restoration of biodiversity and ecosystems (Paetzold et al. 2010, Bullock et al. 2011). This reflects a utilitarian turn in conservation, an emphasis on use values as well as intrinsic values in nature (McCauley 2006, Kallis et al. 2013, Mace 2014) and an increasing recognition of the importance of links between the state of nature and human well-being (IPBES 2014, Kenter et al. 2015)" Hughes *et al.* 2016.

The economic and social benefits to wider society and the environment which 'joined-up' landscapes can achieve have been given the title of 'ecosystem services'. Most people have probably never heard of them, and yet they play one of the most important roles in Nature.

An integrated landscape contains many differing habitats and features which function together to provide these services. Water provision and absorption, soil health and carbon sequestration are all good examples. As large ecosystems are broken up, however, such as in the fens, their ability to provide these services is degraded and may become completely destroyed.

Because drainage has removed the ability of the land to absorb water, it has become essential to maintain continuous pumping to evacuate water draining from land both within and beyond the fen. Water from fields of the 'Highlands' to the west, and from the A1 motorway, flows into the Great Raveley Drain. From here it is pumped all the way to the North Sea, but in times of high flow it can over-top the banks and cause serious flooding. For 50 years, some of this has been diverted into Woodwalton Fen, such as in 1998 when the reserve was flooded from bank to bank one metre deep! This has not only damaged the reserve's biodiversity but also will fail to confront predicted increases of flooding in the future. Transforming the large area of peatland across the Great Fen to a more 'natural' state of grass and fen will enable large quantities of floodwater to be stored safely. As the area is of such a large size and has little pre-existing biodiversity, occasional floods can be tolerated and are likely to beneficial.

In short, making the Great Fen available for flood storage and the contribution it can make to a reduction in CO_2, are services to wider society which bring both economic and wildlife benefits.

"... the value of projects and land such as this to the wider community is not in rare and rarefied species or arcane plant communities, to which most people cannot relate. Conservation will engage with general audiences much more effectively if it delivers outcomes that are more relevant to individual lives. ...Great Fen is perfectly suited to provide such outcomes in two main areas: ecosystem services and health and well-being." Mike Harding, Great Fen HLF Monitor – February 2017.

The Holme Fen bog – once the heart of the wetland

The Holme Fen bog thrived because it was supported by surrounding wet fen, which trapped water and so enabled the bog to grow for thousands of years. Whereas the wet fen and bog together had the effect of absorbing huge quantities of rainwater, draining the fen led to the destruction of the bog. This removed a natural 'sponge' and water from rivers and land drainage was forced to flow into artificial drains, or flooded onto farms and villages.

The drainage was essential for growing arable crops, but had a negative effect on wildlife, which only survives in the risky location of small nature reserves. Exposing the peat by drainage and ploughing has also released CO_2, which contributes to rapid climate change. Keeping it wet and covered with vegetation, on the other hand, may help slow the rate of climate change by 'locking up' the CO_2.

Words, pictures and music... and Lego

We have already seen how the importance of the natural world was revealed in the 18th and 19th centuries through the work of poets, artists and writers. The role the Arts can play in people's lives is also central to the vision of the Great Fen. The transformation of this landscape is not just about ecology, it embraces the whole rainbow of human experience and expression.

It was a more than lucky chance that the Artists for Nature Foundation (ANF) agreed to make their first UK visit to the Fen. Thanks to the efforts of the Wildlife Trust's Nick Hammond, 28 artists from around the world camped at the Ramsey Heights Countryside Centre for two weeks over two years in 2004–05 and roamed the woods, fields and ditches for inspiration. In a remarkable period of creativity, they brought the atmosphere of the fen to life. The resulting artwork was presented in a book (Gerrard 2006) which became very popular. This torrent of artistic expression illustrated graphically the beauty of the land and water. It also demonstrated the possibilities for the future and the potential of inspiring people to visit, treasure and hopefully wish to protect what they had seen.

Alongside the role of art in revealing the landscape changes is photography, which has recently become a major activity. Volunteers have captured in stunning clarity many events and wildlife spectacles, and the recent use of the drone has captured valuable aerial video

Lego model of the Great Fen 2017

'Fen Friends'
created by Mandi Corney

images. Films and animations are a further illustration of the power of different media to convey the message of optimism for the future of this land.

While some messages can be conveyed through visual images, music is also a powerful medium. In 2008, Peterborough Cathedral and King's College Cambridge hosted the premiere of an orchestral composition by John Woolrich called *Whitel's Ey*. The Britten Sinfonia also gave performances of *The Lark Ascending* by Vaughan Williams and *Scene with Cranes* by Jean Sibelius. Hosted by Paul Gambaccini, there was not an empty seat and the event introduced the landscape to a whole new audience.

The fens have always attracted storytellers, and this tradition is being continued. A native of Ramsey, Sybil Marshall wrote several books about fenland life in the Edwardian era, such as *Silver Knew Nothing* and *A Pride of Tigers*, while Edward Storey recounted his life on the fens in *Call it a Summer Country* and other titles. More recently, Mandi Corney (whose great-grandfather was present at the drainage of Whittlesea Mere) has created four characters whose adventures are intended to engage youngsters with the life of the fen around them. Luna, Squadron Leader Swoop, Newton and Verity have taken on a life of their own and hopefully will all flourish in their new homes and enthuse the new generation to learn about their surroundings.

While Great Fen owes a great deal to the past, it is not defined by it, and introducing new ideas is part of its lifeblood. It should come as no surprise, then, that an event to build the entire landscape from Lego bricks was held in 2017. The brainchild of Natural England's Catherine Weightman, half a million bricks were used by the public to build a 10 x 5 metre model of the fen.

Wider aspirations – heritage, visitors and dark skies

The importance of the local landscape to daily life cannot be overestimated. The current condition of the land is due to centuries of human endeavour, whether in wetland or post-drainage times. It is local people through the ages who made this landscape; this is their history and to ignore it would be folly indeed. A Local History Group (now Heritage Group) was formed in 2011, and has been involved in a great deal of work with the local community. One of the major projects was to assist with the excavation of a crashed spitfire in 2015. Working with the MoD and Oxford Archaeology East, this received wide media coverage and is now used by Historic England as an exemplar of this type of excavation. Several

Dark skies over the Great Fen

local people had witnessed the crash in 1940 and were pleased to re-live old memories and contribute to an important part of local history. It also was important for the family of the pilot, Harold Penketh, to take part in a memorial service.

One of the enduring features of the farming period were the cottages and farmsteads which once dotted the area. One of these was at Darlow's Farm, where not only was there a small cottage, but also outbuildings which housed prisoners-of-war who worked on the farm in the 1940s. Although too dilapidated to be renovated on-site, the cottage was dismantled by volunteers and re-erected at the Ramsey Rural Museum. Local school children made a film of the lives of the people who had lived in cottages like this.

It is sometimes debatable whether or not a conservation project needs a visitor centre. They can overshadow the very attraction itself if not carefully created and managed. Great Fen policy has been to provide visitors with the facilities that they need on an incremental basis, but has also planned for a centre in the future. In 2012–13 an outline design was selected through a Royal Institute of British Architects (RIBA) 'Open Ideas' design competition, which attracted 200 entrants. The winning design carefully blends the flat landscape with sympathetic materials.

The daytime fen has many features to celebrate, but at night it becomes a different place. Despite its location within crowded middle England, the Great Fen is remarkably free of artificial light and the deep blackness of the night sky is a mirror of the black peat. When I discovered the existence of an organisation devoted to the preservation of our views of the night, I asked the partners to consider how our area might be included. Natural England's communities officer agreed to take the project on, and Great Fen is now an official 'Milky Way' stargazing location, certified by the Science and Technologies Facilities Council. Regular events are held to introduce people to the wonders of the night sky and efforts made to reduce unnecessary lighting around the area.

Faith, spirituality and the human/wildlife connection

Ecology is the scientific investigation and explanation of how biological organisms work within a defined 'ecosystem.' Chapter 6 explained how the Great Fen is a remnant of a wetland ecosystem, but this is not a single-issue story. Its importance lies not just in the ecological transformation of a landscape, but also in its relevance to the relationship of humans with the natural world. The role of Christian thought was very influential in the medieval management of the fen, and was part of the development of new attitudes to Nature following the Reformation. This eventually led to the development of the 'natural theology' of John Ray, which was so influential on the work of Linnaeus, Darwin and others.

In his dissertation to the 'A Rocha' project (Harper 2017) the Rev. John Harper maintains that the Christian Gospel reveals that: *"the human condition is inter-connected with the rest of creation in such a way that it realises the infinite value and purpose of both"*. This has been a recurrent theme of this book – humans have become increasingly distant from the natural world which supports them. It was a cornerstone of Wordsworth's poetry, which so influenced 19th century thought, and was the background to William Morris' campaigns against the excesses of Victorian industry. Reverence for the environment became so absent from much of 20th century thought, however, that short-term economic gain appeared to be society's only template.

All the main world religions support a policy of more reverence and care for the way in which we exploit our world today. As Harper points out, the restoration of degraded ecosystems such as Whittelsea Mere embodies a sense of 'healing'.

"the Great Fen Project is a rewarding example of human responsibility being acted out in partnership with the workings of nature. It carries with it the prospect of capturing the public's imagination and enthusiasm in such a way that faithful stewardship of the earth leads to healing – healing within nature and in terms of humanity's use of God's resources".

One step towards this 'healing' which the Great Fen partners are taking is the proposed 'Nature's Therapy' programme, whereby staff bring Nature to groups of people who can't get out and about in the countryside. There are seasonal, natural objects to view and hold, as well as natural items for activities, such as bark rubbing and wool teasing. People are encouraged to talk about their experiences and memories of Nature and their lives on the fen.

Faith and conservation

A Rocha is an international Christian organisation which engages communities in nature conservation. Its response to the global crisis of biodiversity loss is to carry out community-based conservation projects. This includes; ecological monitoring and research; spearheading practical measures for conserving and restoring habitats and species; encouraging appreciation of nature and its conservation through education and community outreach; providing a forum for understanding the relevance of the Christian faith to environmental issues.

Conclusion

In his *History of the Countryside*, Oliver Rackham summed up the consequence of the process of our 'divorce' from the natural world. He describes modern fenland as: *"... a somewhat precarious triumph of technology over a deteriorating situation, made possible by vigilance, expensive repairs and an ever-increasing input of energy"*. It is exactly that process which the work of Great Fen is attempting to address. Rather than energy-intensive pumping and engineering to support an ultimately unsustainable way of life, it advocates a system whereby economic activity can exist within a vibrant landscape.

Careful planning and execution have been essential features in the process. When Anthony Seldon wrote his essay on post-war Britain (Marquand & Seldon 1996) he described the pre-requisites for a successful transition of ideas into action as:

- they should be perceived as benign or positive;
- circumstances for their propagation should be favourable; and
- they need powerful advocacy.

All these have contributed to the progress of the Great Fen. It has been an extraordinary liaison between individuals and organisations, where a spirit of positive action and widespread support has achieved the beginnings of an enduring landscape transformation.

By inspiring decision-makers and humbler folk alike, it has awoken a desire for change which will lead to a closer connection with the land.

At times it has been stressful and confrontational, at others inspirational and enjoyable. It has unlocked co-operation between organisations and individuals, who had been set against each other for decades, whilst at the same time revealing opportunities and discoveries which had lain buried. Not all suspicions and oppositions have been overcome yet, but there is increasing support and enthusiasm for what has been achieved so far.

There is no end date to the Great Fen, neither is it a project with the commensurate goals and targets. The Wildlife Trust movement has chosen to label this type of landscape initiative (of which there are now many) as a 'Living Landscape', and this gives a sense of the open-minded and open-ended approach to the environment. The new millennium has witnessed a change in the pace and attitude to nature conservation, and its role in human existence which was scarcely glimpsed for much of the preceding century. What is important about the Great Fen is that whatever its degree of 'wildness' or 'restoration', the new approach is radically different from the principles of 'gardening' isolated nature reserves. It is re-establishing many of the necessary functions of a wetland which will lead in time to the emergence of a rich biological and cultural waterscape.

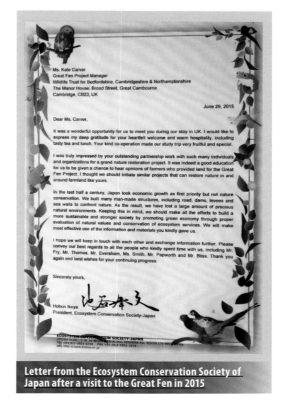

Letter from the Ecosystem Conservation Society of Japan after a visit to the Great Fen in 2015

The Great Fen has embraced ecology, music, art, literature and story-telling; it has unlocked almost forgotten memories of past life, and offers hope of a future where participation, economic aspirations, and flexibility of approach offer a wide spectrum of benefits for wildlife and for people. Spiritually, the proposed transformation of the landscape has the ability to 'heal the Earth' and rekindle the essential link between ourselves and the natural world around us.

Whether from the standpoint of ecology, faith or economics, the practical effects of the new chapter in our relationship with the natural world remain valid. Co-operation, clear and far-sighted thinking and the willingness to take bold decisions are the inspiration for the future, and are being demonstrated on the Great Fen.

1999 • First grant received from the World Wildlife Fund

2001 • The Great Fen partnership and Steering Group is formed

2002–04 • Darlow's Farm is purchased next to Woodwalton Fen and restoration begins. It enlarges the existing nature reserve by 40%

2003 • Funding from the Garfield Weston Foundation to support 5-year appointment: the Great Fen Project Manager

2004–05 • International Artists for Nature (ANF) visit the Great Fen

2005 • First formal public consultation
• Launch of the Great Fen fundraising campaign
• Sir John Major becomes a Patron of the Great Fen
"Unique is a word that is used too frequently, but this really is a unique project and landscape." Sir John Major
• Summer Standing next to Holme Fen purchased (33 hectares) and restoration begins
• Funders: Biffaward, Charles Hayward Charitable Trust, Esmee Fairbairn Foundation, Natural England, Tubney Charitable Trust.

2006 • Stephen Fry becomes President of the Great Fen
"I can't remember a more inspiring day than the one I spent being shown round the Great Fen at Woodwalton." Stephen Fry
• BBC Radio 4 broadcast about the Great Fen
• Middle Farm purchased (183 hectares) next to Woodwalton Fen and restoration begins. Funders: Communities and Local Government fund.

2006–07 • Fen Artists for Nature book and art exhibitions launched

2007 • 'Fens through a Lens' photography competition
• Consultation to develop plans for new community and visitor services
• The Great Fen is featured on BBC's "The Nature of Britain" (Alan Titchmarsh)
• Great Fen Campaign Executive Group formed, led by Sir Charles Chadwyck-Healey and Baroness Barbara Young
• House of Lords Reception
• Prince Charles visits and becomes a royal patron
• Tim Smit, co-founder of the Eden Project becomes a patron
• Beth Rothschild, great granddaughter of Sir Charles Rothschild, becomes a patron
• First Lapwings start breeding on Darlow's Farm
• Avocets are seen on Darlow's Farm in early summer

2007–08 • Ramsey Heights Countryside Classroom refurbished (now called the Wildlife Trust Countryside Centre). Funded by Communities and Local Government and Grantscape.

2008 • £7.2 million Heritage Lottery Grant for the purchase and restoration of the 1,300 hectare Holmewood Estate with match funding from many organisations, and more than 1,200 donors
• Great Fen President, Stephen Fry, hosts a black-tie dinner
• House of Commons Reception, hosted by local MP Shailesh Vara
• National launch of the Wetland Vision on national television and radio
• Common Cranes spend late spring and summer on Darlow's Farm and Middle Farm

2009 • Great Fen Concerts in Peterborough Cathedral and King's College, Cambridge. Paul Gambaccini / Britten Sinfonia
• Television presenter, Nigel Marven, becomes a patron
• Restoration of 109 hectares of land on Corney's Farm and New Decoy Farm begins
• Survey of Old Decoy and Corney's Farms finds Water Voles in 50% of the ditches
• Fen Soundscapes project with local schoolchildren.

2010
- Great Fen Masterplan is published and wins Royal Town Planning Institute's overall top award
- Great Fen features on the BBC's 'Escape to the Country'
- Natural England Senior Reserves Manager, Alan Bowley, gives presentation at international conference in Brussels
- The first commercial hay crops are harvested from newly-seeded grassland
- Rare wildlife begins to successfully spread from Woodwalton Fen and Holme Fen, including Golden Dock *Rumex maritimus*, Marsh Dock *Rumex palustris* and Orange Foxtail *Alopecurus aequalis* grass. Rare water beetles found
- Restoration of New Decoy Farm begins
- Local History Group formed
- 'Local Memories Day' event launches oral history project

2010–11
- 100+ Whooper and Bewick's Swans spend winter on farmland around Darlow's Farm
- Great Fen Memories booklets and albums produced

2011
- Defra Minister, Richard Benyon, visits the Great Fen
- 'Memories from the Fen' film

2011–12
- Restoration of Rymes Reedbed begins (200 hectares east of Holme Fen)
- Funders: HLF, WREN Biodiversity Fund and the Environment Agency.
- Great Fen is part the national 2020VISION project
- Great Fen Information Point with straw bale bird hide.

2012
- Volunteer Ranger scheme begins
- Plans for a new visitor centre. Winning design exhibited at the Royal Academy Summer Exhibition in 2013: Royal Patronage Extended for further 5 years

2013
- £1.89m Heritage Lottery Fund Grant for purchase and restoration of Engine Farm.
- Launch of the Great Fen Appeal for Engine Farm
- Major new ditches and drains constructed at New Decoy Farm
- Trundle Mere Lookout built to give views over Rymes Reedbed
- Construction and excavation begins at Rymes Reedbed
- New scrapes for wetland birds created
- Trundle Mere Lookout opens
- A tower hide on the northern edge of Holme Fen opens and gives visitors the opportunity to watch the major changes to the landscape that are being made to recreate Rymes Reedbed on the site of Trundle Mere, an offshoot of Whittlesea Mere before it was drained.

2014
- Kesters Docking Restoration. Funder: WREN Biodiversity Action Fund – £249,600
- Rothschild Way created. Woodwalton to Wicken
- Communities Trust) £70,603
- Local Archaeology Group launched
- Great Fen wins Sandford Award for Heritage and Learning

2015
- Last of the Meres Trail opens. Funder: Biffa Award – £49,756
- Great Fen App launched
- Dark Skies Designation received
- Spitfire Excavation
- Newt ponds and hibernaculum built at Engine Farm courtesy of Froglife

2016
- Last of the Meres Northern Loop opens
- Little Bugs Club launched
- Great Fen Quest App launched
- Spitfire Memorial
- New Decoy and Corney's Farms wet grassland established
- Funder: Viridor Credits £50,000
- First hay cut and sheep grazed at Engine Farm
- New Decoy derelict bungalow demolished

2016/17
- Connection of the hydrological units at New Decoy and Corney's Farm

2019
- £1million grant for 'Waterworks' scheme for new wetland agriculture

Standing on the Brink

Carl Sagan (and a few others) famously said: *"you have to know the past to understand the present"*.

Our journey through time has been an extraordinary one. Through the millennia, waves of migrants have crossed the land and sea to exploit the rich resources of this land. Neolithic and Bronze Age boat people, Saxons Vikings and Normans – all have left their legacy. It was they who drained the marshes and fens, felled the woods and created productive farms and towns. Today, human and wild migrants alike are still crossing the stormy seas in search of a better life, and the east coast remains a major attraction. Some wildlife species have managed to survive because they have been able to adapt to the conditions created by humans – others have not been so adaptable. Many species have become extinct and are doing so at an ever- increasing rate.

Adapt to survive

It was the ability of the people of the past to comprehend the vagaries of the water and the weather which enabled them to adapt and thrive. It was also their actions which resulted in the confinement of wildlife to tiny nature reserves, the pattern of drainage dykes and Washes and the wastage of the peat. Understanding how they responded to flood and drought, disease and changing agricultures may help us to make decisions which will ensure a healthy landscape, wildlife and society into the future.

The purpose of this book has been to examine the history of our relationship with the natural world and fenland in particular, how this is relevant to the creation of the Great Fen and how this might lead us to a more sustainable future. Past events have had consequences for wildlife and people and successive generations have responded accordingly. How we might use that knowledge to create a better future for ourselves and the coming generations is our challenge for the future. Let's look back and think about the influence of the past and what lessons we have learnt – or forgotten.

The lessons of the past

In the course of our journey through time, we have learnt how landscapes have changed and the role that humans have played. The 'wildwood' was not quite as dense as once thought; there was careful management of the supposedly abandoned post-Roman fens; the Victorian Whittlesea Mere may have been more a muddy pond on its last legs, than a 'silver sea' with butterflies and birds. Despite archaeology and modern research, we may never know the full story, but we do know that this has been an ever-changing story, where human influence has been paramount.

These ancient bog oaks have been revealed by peat wastage. They represent a landscape which was once very different to that of today

The Roman occupation was relatively short-lived, but heralded farming and industrial production in the fens which transformed lifestyles and the landscape in which people lived. While much of post-Roman life is still little known, we do know that it became much wetter and led to an increase in fenland. People adapted and became skilled in gaining a living among the marshland and mere and this grew into a sophisticated system of management which would last a thousand years. From the perspective of today, anything before the

Changes through time

There were certainly immense vistas of untouched Nature as the glaciers retreated, but it was not long before the hand of humans began to be felt. Mesolithic hunter-gatherers made shelters among the dry plains and encroaching woodland; Bronze-Age people had to adapt to increasing water levels, and their villages and causeways were in turn buried by Saxon peat. A medieval wetland of immense proportions was obliterated by drainage.

17th century may seem to have been a semi-wilderness, but it was far from being untamed. Surprisingly, what evidence there is suggests that some wild plants and animals fared rather well under this regime. It was not until the lure of profit from external markets and the rising demand of the late medieval period that wildlife harvesting began to reach unsustainable levels.

Fenland life in the post-Norman monastic era may have been rather more stable than in the troubled centuries of the Viking conflicts. When they weren't squabbling among themselves, the monks and priors were skilled farmers and knew how to exploit the fen wildlife. Their meticulous record-keeping chronicles an abundance of wildlife, which suggests that the human and the natural world maintained a rough balance.

We should not overlook, though, that among the vast wetlands, the bird-filled skies, the moths and butterflies, there was a darker world – one of disease and hardship. It was with astonishment that Fiennes and Defoe viewed the fenlanders and marvelled at how they could survive under conditions where malaria was only kept at bay by poppy tea (a Roman introduction). It is testament to the determination of the people that they both sustained themselves and maintained a fierce independence for many centuries.

It was the shift in attitude towards the fenland after the dissolution of the monasteries that started the process of re-modelling the whole region. Drainage, new farming techniques, and profit-driven investment replaced reverence for, and careful manipulation of, the abundance of the reeds and water. The skills and knowledge of countless generations were

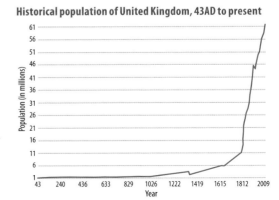

St Germans pumping station

largely forgotten, and an entire way of life abandoned. The new drainers learnt the hard way about the silting of outfalls to the sea and peat wastage; efforts to pump water faster and faster presented immense challenges, and many an investor was ruined. But the transformation of the landscape and a way of life was comprehensive.

The immediate post-drainage era coincided with a revolution in thinking about science, religion and how people related to the natural world. The old order whereby humans were regarded as entirely distinct from the other creatures began to be confronted by new ideas which recognised the connection between all species. By the time concerns were raised as to the 'collateral damage' of the drainage, however, it was too late. When the Appold pump was employed on Whittlesea Mere, the waters had already been depleted by successive by-passes of its feeder streams, and by 1852 the last great water body was no more. In 2011, St Germans pumping station was almost doubled in capacity, at a cost of £38 million. It is now the biggest facility of its kind in the UK and can pump 100 tonnes of water every second. It protects 70,000 ha of land and more than 20,000 properties, valued at £3.6 billion.

The intuition and energy of the 18th and 19th thinkers and campaigners may have been too late to save the Mere, but it started a process that ultimately developed into modern conservation. This movement has achieved spectacular successes in the face of immense pressures from 20th century lifestyles, but nevertheless wild – or even tame – Nature has retreated at an ever-increasing rate in the scramble for economic prosperity.

A consistent theme of all these changes, particularly technological advances in agriculture and the move to urban living, has been the demands of a growing population. In the 20th century, the effect of isolation caused by the two World Wars was a catalyst for successive governments to support increased agricultural and industrial production, while the growing affluence of the population led to demand for housing and transport infrastructure. Victorian objections to the early railways seem rather ironic when compared to the impact of the modern road network. Whilst creating freedom of

Historical population of United Kingdom, 43AD to present

Population (in millions) — Year axis: 43, 240, 436, 633, 829, 1026, 1222, 1419, 1615, 1812, 2009

movement it has simultaneously penetrated every corner of our lives through habitat destruction, noise and pollution. The most recent example is the massive road building programme on the A14 trunk road near Huntingdon. Vast areas of land are being consumed to construct a larger motorway close to small villages, including enormous bridges which are visible for miles around.

These past events, and the lessons we have or have not learnt illustrate how our forebears adapted to the challenges of their time. Right into the medieval period, their clever manipulation of hydrology, grazing patterns and harvesting natural resources ensured their survival. The drainage enabled a significant increase in food production, but this has proved to be relatively short-lived. The peat soil upon which it depended has been consumed and an entire ecosystem with its potential benefits has been destroyed. Nature has ended up in tiny 'protected areas'.

The problem with protected areas

Wetlands rely on connectivity and large size to provide a sustainable environment where wildlife (and ultimately people) can thrive. The consequences of reducing these self-regulating systems of life to fragmented nature reserves are illustrated by their restricted range of wildlife, the degree of intervention required to sustain it, and the separation of people from the natural world. They are too small, unnatural, and expensive to maintain. The wider countryside meanwhile, has lost much of its diversity and resilience and become uniform.

The right place, the right time

Society's approach towards transport infrastructure, industry or housing development is important. Concern for the effect of economic development on the environment upon which we depend, should not be confused with 'nimby-ism'. Population growth necessitates change to ensure a decent life for all, so some developments are inevitable. It is the location, purpose, design and proper consideration for the wider world which must concern us, rather than a knee-jerk reaction to change.

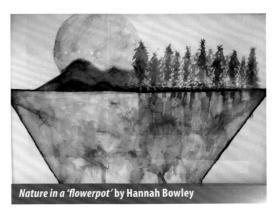

Nature in a 'flowerpot' by Hannah Bowley

I call these isolated sites 'flowerpots', Bill Adams sees them as 'postage stamps'. Whatever the description, we need a comprehensive re-think:

"The future capacity for natural ecosystems to persist in UK will depend on the success with which our protected areas can knit together into a functioning whole" W. Adams 1996

The events of the distant past and the 20th century conflict between concern for the natural world, agri-business and economic growth are the context to the events of the 1990s which led to the Great Fen.

Back from the brink
Changing perceptions
The battle for the countryside and wildlife over the last two centuries has been intense. Greenbelts around towns, wildlife legislation and the establishment of protected sites have all been hard won. At times, individuals have towered above others in their achievements.

Woodwalton Fen is isolated amongst a wider landscape of pump-drained farmland

Fen blow near Woodwalton Fen. When peatlands dry out the soil can become vulnerable to strong winds and blow away

Gilbert White woke the world to the marvels of natural history; John Clare railed against the Enclosures which destroyed open countryside and denied access to the people; William Morris challenged the destruction of the Victorian Age. Charles Rothschild, Arthur Tansley and Max Nicholson carried the fight into the 20th century; David Attenborough and others have alerted the public to the effects of over consumption and climate change in the 21st century. There has also been an increasing awareness by ordinary folk, that our wildlife and wild places may not survive in the face of population growth and consumption, demands for a constantly expanding economy, and political disinterest.

This book has traced how families of hunter-gatherers, peoples of the water, drainers and farmers have shaped the rivers and creeks, reedbeds, and arable fields of the fens. We might ask the question that if the events of distant and recent history have created the fenland we now live in, why try to change it? If the people of the past survived, why shouldn't we?

I believe the answer to these questions lies in the scale and pace of change which the last few decades have brought. Not just a change in the physical landscape, but in the perception of society as a whole – the 'landscape of the mind'. There has been a growing sense of detachment from the world outside our immediate concerns of job and home and economy. Many parts of the world have suffered immeasurable deterioration of wetland habitats. In its recent report on the state of global biodiversity, the Worldwide Fund for Nature (WWF) found that:

"*Freshwater species numbers have... declined dramatically, with the Freshwater Index showing an 83% decline since 1970*". (WWF 2018).

Nowhere is this more evident than on the East Anglian fens, where the extremes of landscape change have revealed the need for a new direction.

The benefits of landscape-scale
Our story has identified the many ecological benefits of moving beyond discrete protected areas and developing landscape-scale management. Large size and site connectivity increase the chances for wildlife to be resilient to change; prevention of soil erosion, flooding and

carbon emissions are vital services which small sites cannot hope to achieve. There are also other advantages which a more naturalistic approach to landscapes can bring. A recent WWF report underlined the essential wider role which Nature plays in our lives:

"*The spiritual, intrinsic, aesthetic and scientific cases for the protection and restoration of nature can seem remote or to have little immediate relevance. But as it becomes more widely recognised that natural systems underpin our health, wealth and security the impetus to protect and restore nature is much more powerful. If successful, we would be the first generation to accomplish such a change in direction.*"

Little Egret *Egretta garzetta* – some species have benefitted from the warming climate and wetland creation projects [ML]

Ecosystem services

We have already seen how crucial the role of Nature is in regulating our environment. The WWF Report warned of the state of global ecosystems: "*All economic activity ultimately depends on services provided by nature, estimated* (globally) *to be worth around US$125 trillion a year.... Nature, underpinned by biodiversity, provides a wealth of services which form the building blocks of modern society*" (WWF 2018).

The conflict between concern for the natural world and economic development has been fuelled by the mistaken view that ecology and wildlife conservation are largely irrelevant in modern society. Economic prosperity has been elevated to position of apparently unassailable dominance, ignoring the collateral effects on the natural systems which ultimately support it.

Happily, this view is gradually being overtaken by the acceptance that a healthy environment is not only desirable, but is essential to our long-term survival. 'Ecosystem services' are what Nature was delivering to us all the time, but we have only recently become aware of it, as failing systems have caused havoc. The disastrous fenland floods of the 1940s and 1950s were early warnings and led to great improvements in drainage, but events across England in the last decade have emphasised the need for wetlands which can alleviate the threat to communities from flooding. They can also help improve water quality and provide recreational and learning opportunities for people, while at the same time creating space for wildlife. All of these can also support economic activities such as grazing and tourism and 'wetland agriculture' such as biomass production and thatching reed.

The enormous amount of carbon dioxide which is emitted from exposed peat soil is a major factor in human-induced climate change. Converting the land from arable to pasture will alleviate this. The soil itself is also crucial to our long-term survival. Successive studies around the world have been warning for years about the impacts of forest clearance, drainage and peat exposure, but only very recently has the public realisation of the consequences of sudden climate change and abuse of both natural habitats and farmland caused this

to become a major issue. Fenland peat has been disappearing for generations, but no-one thought to ask why.

Other factors

Ecological factors are an essential feature of landscape restoration, but it would be folly indeed if we ignore the many other benefits. Feeling part of a 'natural' environment is a key factor in promoting public health and well-being and I have argued that ignoring this may be partly responsible for the lack of concern for the natural environment during much of the 19th and 20th centuries. People need more than science to awaken their connection with the world of soil, plants and animals which support them – you don't have to know the name of a plant to appreciate its beauty (although it does help!).

Mental health

It is only in the last few generations that humans have lived their lives largely isolated from Nature, and a daily encounter with wildlife is a now rarity for many people. Living in more urbanised communities has undoubtedly brought enormous benefits, but it has also eroded our relationship with the non-human world. Extensive research has revealed that Nature is essential for healthy psychological functioning.

In a ground-breaking study, it was found that: *"People with access to nearby natural settings have been found to be healthier overall than other individuals. The longer-term, indirect impacts (of 'nearby nature') also include increased levels of satisfaction with one's home, one's job and with life in general"* (Kaplan and Kaplan, 1989 p. 173 – cited in Maller *et al.* 2005).

Water Vole *Arvicola amphibius*. The opportunity to see beautiful wildlife can enhance people's lives [DK]

In a further review of research on mental health and access to the natural world, they revealed that: *"It is clear that nature and natural environments relate to human health and well-being. To seek human health and sustainability **without** considering the importance of environmental sustainability is to invite potentially devastating consequences for the health and well-being of whole populations.*

Natural areas can be seen as one of our most vital health resources. In the context of the growing worldwide mental illness burden of disease, contact with nature may offer an affordable, accessible and equitable choice in tackling the imminent epidemic, within both preventative and restorative public health strategies".

One particularly welcome initiative of the last few years has been the increase in 'forest schools' where children gain a first-hand experience of nature in the great outdoors.

The potential benefits of Nature on mental health were accented by the Great Fen Education and Community Manager, Louise Rackham, in her submission to the HLF Final Report. There is, she said: *"a growing problem, particularly in young people, of 'Nature Deficit Disorder'. This is triggered by extended alienation from the natural world, leading to a diminished use of the senses, attention difficulties and higher rates of physical and emotional illnesses".*

Wildlife Trust BCN 2017

In a further discussion, she maintained that many people appeared to sense a disconnection between their engagement with local expressions of nature, such as the Great Fen, and global environmental concerns, such as climate change and the significance of water. A key element of the Great Fen is *"to so enthuse visitors by positive experiences that they choose to incorporate the insights they gain into a more eco-friendly and sustainable lifestyle for themselves, and hopefully to influence others to do the same"* (cited in Harper 2017).

Citizen science

'Ordinary' people are also becoming more involved with amassing the scientific rationale for changing the way we use our natural resources. Recently, for example, the British Trust for Ornithology launched its *'Agenda for Change'* – a 10-point plan to broaden their operations to involve more people and be more effective on spreading the message that the health of our wildlife affects everyone. *"Where there is a lack of understanding, there is a risk of a lack of support"* BTO 2018

Environmental philosophy

The discipline of environmental philosophy arose out of the growing awareness in the 1960s and '70s of the lack of value placed on non-human Nature. The anthropocentric view (which had characterised human attitude to the natural world before the 18th century) was that the value of the natural world lay only in its usefulness to the human race, and was not valued in its own right.

One of most influential arguments of the 1970s was James Lovelock's 'Gaia' hypothesis. Lovelock's theory proposed that the biosphere acts like a living organism, that self-regulates to keep conditions just right for life. The theory explains that life on Earth depends on the interaction of living forms, especially micro-organisms, with inorganic elements. Thus, the global ecosystem will remain in balance by the very activities of biotic and abiotic factors. Although its validity is increasingly questioned, the Gaia hypothesis was a significant factor in raising awareness of our effect on the planet's natural systems.

In the 1990s, Richard Routley (he later changed his name to Sylvan) proposed 'a new ethic' with regard to our approach to nature. It had at its root:

1. respect for the needs of future generate
2. the rights of non-human animals
3. the intrinsic value of Nature.

The ethics of conservation

With others, Sylvan went on to propose a cultural shift in the attitude to the environment, including:

- teaching environmental ethics to children;
- a stronger emphasis on ethics and ethical practice;
- change individual behaviour: responsible consumption, simple living, recycling, activism;
- promoting and educating the general public on a deeper environmental ethic;
- control of the human population – based on education, not coercion; and
- government policies that encourage environmental protection.

His fundamental message was that human happiness lies in our ability to live in symbiosis with nature, through understanding and preserving it:

"*Human creatures, like others, depend on a satisfactory environment for their well-being and their very survival. But in their dealings with it, so-called developed societies have learned hubris, not wisdom,*" (p.6).

Spiritual

Richard Bauckham suggests a deeper value of restoring natural habitats: "*we have an '**ultimate hope**' of God's unconditional restoration of creation in the fullness of time, and we also have a '**proximate hope**' that human beings can be effective instruments of re-creation and restoration within each generation*". (Bauckham 2013). While these ideas are based on the Christian faith, they remain valid whether or not an individual has any particular faith or philosophy. The point is made that there is value in the work of Great Fen and other similar projects 'restoring balance to a damaged landscape' from which humans have become increasingly isolated. Treating the Earth with reverence and restoring balance between our needs and the health of the landscape in which we live, is also as much to do with healing ourselves as healing the Earth itself.

Other religions and philosophies such as Islam, Buddhism, Hinduism and Jainism, also place great emphasis on our relationship with Nature. They all see an interconnected world where we have a place alongside other species. Jains, in particular, follow the practice of *ahimsa* (doing no harm).

The arts

It is only by communication that new ideas can be made available to wider society. It was artists, philosophers and poets who first recognised the value of wild Nature and told the

Ploughing with lapwing and hares by Jonathan Yule

Jon's hide on the Great Fen made of compressed straw bales demonstrated that local materials could be put to good use

world; it has been literature, art, photography, film, TV and music which has sparked public interest in the environment in the last few decades, rather than the forebodings of ecologists.

Current initiatives

The physical world is changing, and how we respond to that change will influence our planet for generations. While nation states have struggled to agree on the causes and consequences of climate change, ordinary people have a growing sense of the need to change the way we relate to our environment. Across the globe, citizens are becoming aware of the damage to the global ecosystem and are prepared to do something about it.

International

The first global initiative to address the impact of climate change and the effect it may have on the 'natural capital' which we rely on, was the Rio de Janeiro Earth Summit in 1992. This was followed in 1997 by an 'Earth summit' of many nations in Kyoto, Japan, to agree a programme for reducing carbon dioxide (CO_2) emissions. Achievements were limited by the refusal of the United States to sign-up and continued high emissions from China, and a further conference in Copenhagen also failed to create positive action.

Between 2001 and 2005, the UN commissioned *The Millennium Ecosystem Assessment* (MEA) to: '*assess the consequences of ecosystem change for human well-being and to establish the scientific basis for actions needed to enhance the conservation and sustainable use of ecosystems and their contributions to human well-being*'. This was a significant step by the international community to address concerns at the effects of human actions on the wider environment. The MEA found that many ecosystems had degraded to such an extent that they no longer delivered services at all to society. The decreasing ability of natural habitats to provide flood prevention was a prime example.

In 2015, representatives from 196 states met in Paris in an attempt to rejuvenate the process, and 181 countries committed themselves to the agreed actions, known as COP21. This differs from the previous agreements in that at least some of its protocols are legally binding on the signatories. In late 2018, countries met again in Poland to take forward and ratify some of the actions arising from the Paris meeting, but there remained several conflicts of interest.

This coincided with the publication of the WWF report referred to earlier, which catalogued the degradation of habitats across the planet and called for urgent action to reverse the decline and ensure a healthy and happy future for all. It recommended a similar declaration by governments to the COP21.

In May 2019, the Intergovernmental Science Policy Platform on Biodiversity and Ecosystem Services (IPBES) left the world in no doubt – unless immediate and direct action was taken, the world could lose up to one million species and life for humans could become untenable. Maybe at last the message has got through – Nature is not just for ecologists; it is for life itself.

Europe

The European Union *Building a Green Infrastructure Strategy* (EU 2013), identified the challenges both within the EU and beyond. The study identified areas for further research and proposed alternative ways of, living which could be more sustainable.

The 'Wild Europe' programme was conceived in 2005 and ratified as an EU project in 2009. Initially, the project set out to enthuse the general public by a rolling programme of stunning photographs entitled 'Wild Wonders of Europe', which has been touring Europe for some years. It has more recently developed policies on protecting the last wilderness areas of Europe and restoring degraded habitats.

National

While the Great Fen was developing its novel approaches to landscape restoration, there was increasing interest and concern about our abuse of the 'natural capital' that surrounds us. This growing awareness took a significant turn when the government-sponsored Lawton Report 'Making Space for Nature' was published (Lawton 2010). This highlighted many uncomfortable facts about the state of our natural environment and stimulated a positive response from across society and from Government itself. In effect, it marked a turning point in the way in which the environment was viewed by politicians and the public.

John Lawton and his team made a thorough audit of the state of the conservation effort in the UK and its effectiveness. The report argued that Britain does not have a coherent and resilient ecological network, and that:

"we need a step-change in our approach to wildlife conservation, from trying to hang on to what we have, to one of large-scale habitat restoration and recreation, under-pinned by the re-establishment of ecological processes and ecosystem services, for the benefits of both people and wildlife.... It is a long-term vision, out to 2050, and defines a direction of travel, not an endpoint. This vision will only be realised if, within the overall aims, we work at local scales, in partnership with local people, local authorities, the voluntary sector, farmers, other land-managers, statutory agencies, and other stakeholders."

The Government's response to the Report appeared to suggest that politicians took his recommendations seriously, with successive Secretaries of State for the Environment making encouraging statements:

"Sir John Lawton is right to challenge us over what it takes to address the loss of biodiversity but he is also clear this cannot be done by Government alone. Everyone from farmers, wildlife groups, landowners and individuals can play a role in helping to create, manage and improve these areas, so if ever there was a time for the Big Society to protect our natural environment, this is it... we will follow this through with the first Natural Environment White Paper for 20 years in the UK."

Caroline Spelman – Secretary of State for the Environment 2010

The White paper was duly launched in 2011 with participation from over 15,000 people. It followed the publication of the 'National Ecosystem Assessment', which was the attempt to review the consequences of 20th century development. The Assessment concluded that

Lawton and the new direction

One of Lawton's key objectives was to: "*To restore and secure the long-term sustainability of the ecological and physical processes that underpin the way ecosystems work, thereby enhancing the capacity of our natural environment to provide ecosystem services such as clean water, climate regulation and crop pollination, as well as providing habitats for wildlife.*"

The Lawton Report made 24 recommendations for actions to improve conditions for wildlife and people. These included:

- improving protection and management of our designated wildlife sites;
- establishing new Ecological Restoration Zones;
- better protection for non-designated wildlife sites;
- society's need to maintain water-quality, manage inland flooding, deal with coastal erosion and enhance carbon storage... could help deliver a more effective ecological network;
- Government should produce a strategy to ensure that we protect and secure multiple benefits from our carbon-rich soils and peatlands, and maximise their contribution to ecological networks; and
- habitat creation requires greater focus on the needs of ecological networks, in particular the need to contribute to Ecological Restoration Zones.

Active restoration on the Great Fen

there had been too much focus on the market value of natural resources that can be sold (e.g. timber and food), and not enough consideration of 'natural capital' during decision-making. Far from being an impediment to economic growth, the authors concluded that: "*...if the UK's ecosystems were properly protected and enhanced then they could add an extra £30 billion to the UK economy. Neglect and loss of ecosystem services may cost as much as £20 billion to the economy per year.*"

The White Paper has been regularly reviewed and has made some progress, particularly in highlighting the need to reduce friction between farming and the environment and the setting of a 2020 target for biodiversity.

In his speech to the Oxford Farming Conference in 2018, Environment Secretary, Michael Gove said:

"... if we try to avoid change, hold the future at bay and throw up barriers to progress then we don't stop change coming, we simply leave ourselves less equipped to deal with change as it arrives.

If we want to preserve that which we cherish – a thriving agriculture sector, a healthy rural economy, beautiful landscapes, rich habitats for wildlife, a just society and a fair economy – then we need to be able to shape change rather than seeking to resist it. I want to ensure that we build natural capital thinking into our approach towards all land use and management so we develop a truly sustainable future for the countryside".

Meanwhile, in 2018, Natural England launched its 25-year strategy to safeguard and improve both natural environment, for both Nature and society as a whole. The natural world, the report says: "underpins out nation's prosperity and well-being. We often talk of being 'enriched' by our environment. In recent years we have come to realise that the environment does indeed deliver calculable economic benefits". The Strategy is published alongside two other initiatives: the Industrial Strategy and the Clean Growth Strategy, both of which aim to stimulate economic growth while at the same time mitigating the effects of climate change.

Putting words into practice

We have had similar initiatives before, but such is the interest and concern amongst scientists and the general public alike that maybe this time it will make a real difference.

One practical way in which change might be achieved is housing and infrastructure development. It is often stated that only a small proportion (10.6%) of England is non-rural,

Artist's view of future Great Fen

and much of this is devoted to parks and gardens. But this is not the whole story. A Council for the Protection of Rural England (CPRE) survey showed that in the 1960s, 25% of the country could be classified as subject to disturbance from the noise of transport and industry. The most recent figures suggest that this proportion is now 50% and is rising every day. Flying in to England at night reveals not only just how widespread is the network of roads and urban conurbations, but also the amount of energy required to keep the lights burning.

The Great Fen partners have involved the Local Planning Authority at every stage. Too often, consideration of the impact of development on local human and wildlife communities come at the end of a development process. In East Anglia, tens of thousands of houses are being constructed, all of which need supporting infrastructure such as water and drainage, and transport links. There is no question that there is a need for good quality housing, but the way that housing projections are calculated do not always seem to be based on carefully thought-out strategies for the whole environment in which people will be living. The Government's National Planning Policy Framework highlights the need to protect open land from building and to designate and protect green space, but too often, these requirements appear to be over-ridden to meet short-term targets, which are in themselves sometimes puzzling. In 2018, for example, the Office for National Statistics downgraded the number of new homes needed by 25% due to population projection errors.

By considering the landscape as a whole, the Great Fen approach proposes another way, which can both identify land and redundant buildings to provide a high quality of life for all sections of the community, without compromising the environment in which will subsequently live.

Other landscape projects

Several voluntary wildlife organisations have embraced the ideas of large landscape areas. The RSPB has its 'Futurescapes' project, the Wildlife Trusts now have many 'Living Landscapes', and the National Trust have several large-scale landscape estates.

Following the publication of George Monbiot's book *Feral* in 2013, 'Rewilding Britain' was formed in 2015. This charity hopes to see at least one million hectares in Britain supporting natural ecological processes for the benefit of people and nature, and they have recently joined forces with 'Rewilding Europe'.

While true 're-wilding' operates on a huge scale, smaller projects are also supported by this charity, as they can also offer considerable benefits. Among these is the Knepp Castle Estate in Sussex, which is an attempt to show that not only can re-establishing elements of a wild landscape be ecologically beneficial, it can also be economically viable.

How can the Great Fen make a difference?

The key to the Great Fen vision is not just an ecological solution to a fragmented wetland, it is changing the hearts and minds of people to value the world around them and re-discover how to live in harmony with it.

History has taught us a great deal about the consequences of our actions and their effects on both our long-term well-being and the natural environment. More recently, ecological and agricultural knowledge has provided us with intimate and current knowledge of the state of our soils, drainage patterns, agricultural methods and wildlife management. Armed with this knowledge, we have few excuses to repeat the mistakes of the recent past. Vested interests may be reluctant to abandon the old ways, but change is inevitable, is necessary, and offers tremendous hope for the future.

Current predictions of damage to our life support system have caused world-wide alarm. The 2018 WWF report emphasised this: "*We are the first generation that has a clear picture of the value of nature and our impact on it. We may be the last that can take action to reverse this trend. From now until 2020 will be a decisive moment in history*".

The Great Fen's contribution to this global concern is summed up in their final report to HLF on the Holmewood Estate restoration. The legacy of the project so far was described as:

"... the restoration and monitoring legacy will shape this landscape and the wildlife that is rapidly populating it for decades, possibly even centuries to come. The education and community legacy will continue to shape imagination, and enjoyment and that unique sense of fulfilment that successful partnerships and volunteering bring... the nascent plans for a Cambridgeshire Fens Biosphere Reserve are a truly thrilling prospect for what will undoubtedly be a bright future".

The challenges

There are great challenges, but a new approach may help us to meet them. There is an irresistible energy across society for change, but for it to succeed, the old rivalries between agriculture, business and nature conservation need to be healed. Bitterns and business can live together.

We have seen how each generation has dealt with the issues of their time, in our generation it is the Great Fen and other landscape-scale projects which hold the key to the future. Like it or not, the human race is part of the natural world, so it not just emissions of CO_2 which should concern us, but our relationship with that world. I would argue that we need to open our eyes to what is around us; we are part of a world which is full of wondrous life, but in the pursuit of our own interests we have neglected it, ignored its essential role in our existence, and become the poorer for it. Ultimately, the penalty for rapid climate change caused largely by our own activities will not just be paid by plants and animals, but by ourselves – particularly those who already live in difficult circumstances.

This new approach must be more than a fashionable exercise which comes and goes on a whim. Writing of the 2014 floods, George Monbiot claimed that the people often only become aware of the natural world when there is actual and acute danger to ourselves from natural disasters. Apathy soon returns, and the causes of the disaster are not considered (Monbiot 2014).

Looking across the Great Fen from the bank of Woodwalton Fen NNR

I think we do all care, but often we don't know how to affect change. In a UK government survey (DEFRA 2014) the public were asked about their attitude to human impact on the environment. Asked whether "we are close to the limit of the number of people the earth can support", 48% agreed and 29% disagreed; 23% agreed and just 8% disagreed when asked whether: "A major environmental disaster is imminent"; 10% of all respondents agreed that they would like to do a lot more to help the environment.

In 2018, the 'People's Walk for Wildlife' took to the streets of London, and was followed in 2019 with 'Extinction Rebellion' campaigns across the country. This is not 'normal' British behaviour, and underlines the degree of concern which is now felt amongst ordinary people.

A final word

One of my abiding memories of Woodwalton Fen is walking across the reserve and climbing up onto to the western flood-bank. Less than 20 years ago, the last echo of a great wetland lay behind me, while in front was a 'fen blow' – a smoky curtain of peat blowing across the land. The Great Fen partners acted to ensure the future of the reserve by breathing new life into its surrounding fields. Today, the fields are grazed by native livestock and are home to wetland plants and animals. Better access and new rural enterprises like wetland farming provide recreation and employment for increasing numbers of people.

I believe we are standing on a similar bank in the wider world today and we have a choice. We have the knowledge and skills to act, but if we do nothing, the legacy of the past and the hope for the future will be squandered. It is late - but not too late. The Great Fen has replaced apathy and short-term thinking with innovation, inclusiveness and action. By valuing the natural world and accepting our place within it, we can create a new future for ourselves and for wildlife. It is for each of us to decide, and persuade governments, planners and economists to act. We have but one Earth, so we need to pay attention to our present and create our own legacy for the future.

Adams, W.M. (1996) *Future Nature.* Earthscan.

Baldock, D., Cox, G., Lowe, P. and Winter, M. (1990) Environmentally Sensitive Areas: incrementalism or reform? *Journal of Rural Studies* 6: 143–62.

Balmford A. (2015) *Wild Hope: on the front lines of conservation success.* Univ. Chicago Press.

Bauckham, R. (2013) – cited in Harper 2017 Ecological Hope in Crisis *Anvil* 29 (1).

Boos, F. (1996) *An aesthetic eco-communist, Morris the Red and Morris the Green.* In: Papers from the Morris Centenary Conference at Exeter College, Oxford, 30 June–3 July 1996.

Bowley, A.L. & Willott, K. (1997) The Southwest Fens Linking Project Report to English Nature (unpub).

Camden, W. (1637) *Britain, or, a Chorographicall Description of the most flourishing Kingdomes, England, Scotland, and Ireland 1586.* Translated by Philemon Holland. London: Printed by F. Kingston, R. Young and I. Legatt for George Latham, 1637.

Chambers, R. (1844) *Vestiges of the Natural History of Creation and other Evolutionary Writings.* Ed. James Secord, London, 1994.

ChartsBin statistics collector team (2009) *Historical Population of United Kingdom, 43 AD to Present* (Online) www. ChartsBin.com/view/28K

Chesterton, G.K. (1911) *Alarms and Discursions.* Dodd, Mead and Company.

Childers, J.W. (Ed) (1868) *Lord Orford's Voyage round the Fens in 1774.* Bodleian Bibliotecha (online) www.Bodleian.ox/ ac.uk

Clare, J. (1820) *Poems Descriptive of Rural Life and Scenery.* Kessinger Publishing 2008.

Coles, B. (2016) *Beavers in Britain's Past.* Oxbow Books.

Colston, A. (1997) Conserving wildlife in a black hole. British Association of Nature Conservationists, *Ecos.*

Cooke, A. & Farrell, L. (1998) *Chinese Water Deer.* The Mammal Society and The British Deer Society, London and Fordingbridge, UK.

Cooke, A. (2019) *Muntjac and Water Deer.* Pelagic Publishing Limited.

Crane, N. (2016) *The Making of the British Landscape.* Weidenfeld and Nicolson.

Cumulus Consultants (2012) Socio Economic Study of the Great Fen. Final Report for Huntingdonshire District Council (unpub).

Cumulus Consultants (2014), Great Fen Socio-economic and Funding Strategy. Report to Wildlife Trust BCN (unpub).

Darby, H.C. (1977) *Domesday England.* CUP.

Defoe, D. (1724–27) *A Tour in Circuits through the Island of Great Britain.* London: JM Dent and Co 1927.

Duffey, E. (1977) The re-establishment of the large copper butterfly *Lycaena dispar batava* obth. on Woodwalton Fen National Nature Reserve, Cambridgeshire, England, 1969–73. *Biol Cons.* 12 (2):143–158. Elsevier.

Duncan, N. (2004) Report on Soils to Great Fen Wildlife Trust BCN (unpub).

Evans, A.H. (1903) *Turner on birds; a short and succinct history of the principal birds noticed by Pliny and Aristotle*, first published by Doctor William Turner, 1544. CUP.

Evans et al., (2017) *Lowland Peatland Systems in England and Wales – Evaluating Greenhouse Gas Fluxes and Carbon Balances.* Contract report to Dept of Environment Food and Rural Affairs (Online) http://oro.open.ac.uk/50635/

Gerrard, C. (2006) *The Great Fen / Artists for Nature in England.* Langford Press.

Gill, A.S. (1981) Variation in Genus *Betula.* University of East Anglia PhD (unpub).

Gilpin, the Rev. W. (1809) *Observations of several parts of Cambridgeshire, Norfolk and Suffolk and Essex relative chiefly to picturesque beauty made in 1769.* London. Printed for T. Cadell and W. Davies, Strand.

Gilpin, the Rev. W. (1792) *'Three essays on Picturesque Beauty on picturesque travel and on sketching landscape'*. London. Printed for R. Blamire in the Strand.

Godwin, H. & Vishnu-Mittre (1975) Studies of the post-glacial history of British Vegetation XVI Flandrian deposits of the fenland margin at Holme fen and Whittelsey Mere, Huntingdonshire. *Phil. Ray. Soc. Lond.* B270: 561–604.

Godwin, H. (Ed.) (1978) *Fenland: Its Ancient Past and Uncertain Future*. CUP.

Gottlieb, R. (1993) *Forcing the Spring – The Transformation of the American Environmental Movement*. Washington DC. Covelo, California Island Press.

Hamilton, R. (1946) *W.H. Hudson – The Vision of the Earth*. J.M. Dent and Sons Ltd. London.

Harold, R. (1990) The Birds of Woodwalton Fen NNR 1978–1990. English Nature report (unpub).

Harper, J. the Rev. (2017) In what ways can the Great Fen Project inform and motivate the general public to engage more fully with ways of sustainable living? Dissertation for Cert. Christian Rural and Environmental studies (A. Rocha UK) (unpub).

History of Huntingdonshire website (Online) www.huntingdonshire.info/history.asp

Holman, IP. (2009) *An estimate of peat reserves and loss in the East Anglian Fens*. Cranfield University / RSPB.

Hudson, W.H. (1910) *A Shepherd's Life – Impressions of the South Wiltshire Downs*. Methuen & Co.

Hutchinson, J.N. (1980) The Record of Peat Wastage in the East Anglian Fenlands at Holme Post, 1848–1978 AD. *J. Ecol.* 68 (1): 229–249.

IPBES (2019) *Global Assessment Report on Biodiversity and Ecosystem Services*. United Nations.

Keegan, B. & McKusick, J.C. (2006) *Learning to Love the Fens: Romanticism, Ecology, and Pedagogy*. Creighton University, (Online) www.romantic-circles.org/pedagogies/commons/ecology

Lambert, D. (2006) The History of the Country Park, 1966–2005: Towards a Renaissance? The Parks Agency, Wickwar, Gloucestershire, UK. *Landscape Research*, 31 (1): 43–62.

Lawton, Sir John CBE FRS (2010) Making Space for Nature: A review of England's Wildlife Sites and Ecological Network. Submitted to the Secretary of State, DEFRA.

Mabey, R. (1980) *The Common Ground: a Place for Nature Conservation in Britain's Future?* Hutchinson, Nature Conservancy Council.

Mackay, T. (Ed.) (1908) *The Reminiscences of Albert Pell sometime MP for South Leicestershire*. John Murray, Albemarle Street, London.

Marren, P. (2002) *Nature Conservation: A Review of the Conservation of Wildlife in Britain 1950–2001*. Collins New Naturalist.

Marquand, D. & Seldon, A. (1996) *The Ideas that Shaped Post-War Britain*. Fontana Press.

Marshall, S. (1987) *The Silver Knew Nothing*. Penguin.

Marshall, S. (1992) *A Pride of Tigers*. Penguin.

Matthew, J.W., Cock, J., Biesmeijer, C., Raymond, J.C., Cannon, P.J., Gerard, Gillespie, D., Jimenez, J.J., Lavelle, P.M. & Raina, S.K. (2012) The positive contribution of invertebrates to sustainable agriculture and food security. *CAB Reviews Perspectives in Agricultural Vetinary Science Nutrition and natural Resources* 7. 1–27.10.1079/PAVSNNR20127043

Mitchell, J. (1970) *Big Yellow Taxi* on *Ladies of the Canyon* album. Reprise Records.

Mossman, H.L, Panter, C.J. & Dolman, P.M. (2012) *Fens Biodiversity*. Audit School of Environmental Sciences, University of East Anglia, Norwich.

Natural England (2008) *State of the Natural Environment 2008* (Online) http://publications.naturalengland.org.uk/publication/31043?category=118044

Newbold, C. (1999) *Historical changes in the nature conservation interest of the fens of Cambridgeshire*. In: H. Cook and T. Williamson (Eds), *Water Management in the English Landscape: field, marsh and meadow*. Edinburgh University Press, pp. 210–26.

ONS/UK Gov (2018) *Indication of the future number of households in England and its regions and local authorities*. (Online) www.ons.gov.uk/peoplepopulationandcommunity/populationandmigration/populationprojections/bulletins/2016Household projections in England: 2016 – based ONS.

Oosthuizen, S. (2017) *The Anglo-Saxon Fenland*. Windgather Press.

O'Sullivan, P. (2011) Morris the Red and Morris the Green. Review in *The Journal of William Morris Studies*. Winter 2011: 22–38.

Oxford Archaeology East (2013) Archaeological Preliminary Evaluation Report Rymes Reedbed, Holme Huntingdonshire – Wetland re-creation project. Report to Wildlife Trust BCN (unpub).

Page, W. (Ed) (1932) *A History of the County of Huntingdon*: Volume 2, London (British History Online) http://www.british-history.ac.uk/vch/hunts/vol2

Pullin, Andrew S. (2002) *Conservation Biology*. CUP.

Pryor, F. (2010) *The Making of the British Landscape*. Penguin.

Rackham, O. (1976) *Trees and Woodland in the British Landscape. Archaeology in the Field Series* (First ed.). London: J.M. Dent & Sons Ltd.

Rackham, O. (1986) *The History of the Countryside*. Dent.

Rhode, C.L.H. & Kendle, A.D. (1994) Human wellbeing, Natural Landscapes and Wildlife in Urban Areas. Report to English Nature prepared by Univ. of Reading, Dept. of Horticulture and Landscape, and the Research Institute for Care of the Elderly, Bath.

Rotherham, I. (2013) *The Lost Fens: England's Greatest Ecological Disaster*. The History Press.

Rothschild, M. & Marren, P. (1997) *The Rothschild Reserves – Time and Fragile Nature*. Balaban/Harley Books, Colchester.

RSPB (2016) *State of Nature report 2016* (Online) www.rspb.org.uk/globalassets/downloads/documents/conservation-projects/state-of-nature/state-of-nature-uk-report-2016.pdf

Salway, P. (1993) *A History of Roman Britain*. OUP.

Salway, P. (2002) *The Roman Era (Short History of the British Isles)*. OUP.

Sawtry History Society (Online) www.sawtryhistorysociety.btck.co.uk/

Schama, S. (2000) *A History of Britain: at the Edge of the world? 3000BC–1603AD*. Talk Miramax Books, London.

Schweid, R. (2009) *Eel*. Reaktion Books Ltd, London.

Sheail, J. (1998) *Nature Conservation in Britain – The Formative Years*. HMSO.

Sly, R. (2002) *From Punt to Plough – a History of the Fens*. Sutton Publishing Limited.

Smiths Gore (2004) Report to Great Fen. (unpub).

Spelman, Sir Henry (1664) *Glossarium Archaiologicum Aliciam*. Warren, London.

Stevenson, H. (1887) Ornithological notes. *Transactions of the Norfolk and Norwich Naturalists Society*. 4:125–39.

Storey (1978) *Call it a Summer Country*. Robert Hale Ltd.

Thomas, K. (1983) *Man and the Natural World: Changing attitudes in England 1500–1800*. Allen Lane.

Tree, I. (2018) *Wilding – the return of Nature to a British Farm*. Picador.

Tsukamoto, K. & Kuroki, M. (Eds) (2014) *Eels and Humans*. Springer.

Turner, W. (1544) *Avium praecipuarum, quarum apud Plinium et Aristotelem mentio est, brevis et succincta historia* (The Principal Birds of Aristotle and Plinythe). CUP 1995.

Ulrich, R.S. (1984) View through a window may influence recovery from surgery. *Science* 224: 420–421.

UN (1994) *United Nations International Conference on Population and Development, Cairo, Summary of the programme of Action*. UNFPA.

Vera F.W.M. (Ed.) (2000) *Grazing Ecology and Forest History*. CABI Wallingford.

www.ramseyabbey.co.uk (Online).

www.crowlandabbey.co.uk (Online).

Waine, P. & Hilliam, O. (2016) *22 Ideas that Saved the English Countryside*. CPRE, Francis Lincoln.

Walter, D. (2000) Holme Village The Lowest Village in England – Probably (unpub).

Wells, T. (1980) The Marchioness of Huntley: the written record and the herbarium. *Biol. Journal Linn Soc.* 13: 315–330.

Wells, W. (1860) The draining of Whittlesea Mere. *Illustrated London News* Vol. 21.

Wells, W. (1860) The Drainage of Whittlesey Mere. *Journ. Royal Agric. Soc.* (1st series) 134–153.

Whitehouse, N. & Smith, D. (2009) How fragmented was the British Holocene wildwood? Perspectives on the "Vera" grazing debate from the fossil beetle record. *Quaternary Science Reviews* (Online) www.sciencedirect.com/science/article/abs/pii/ S0277379109003552

White, G. (1789) *The Natural History of Selborne*. (Penguin English Library Ed: Mabey) 1977 Mass Market Paperback.

Williams, A. (1995) *The English and the Norman Conquest*. Boydell.

Williams, J. (Ed) (2017) The Purchase and Restoration of the Holmewood Estate 2008–2017 – An Evaluation Report for the Heritage Lottery Fund. Wildlife Trust BCN (unpub).

Williams, T. (2012) *Environment Society and landscape in early Medieval England*. Boydell.

Williamson, T. (2013) *An Environmental History of Wildlife in England 1650–1950*. Bloomsbury Publishing.

Worldwide Fund for Nature (2018) *Living Planet Report – 2018: Aiming Higher*. Grooten, M. & Almond, R.E.A. (Eds). WWF, Gland, Switzerland.

Index

Species

About the author

Having grown-up within sight of the South Downs, Alan Bowley started work as Nature Conservancy Council warden of the East Sussex chalk grassland national nature reserves (NNR) in 1978, after two years at Tring Reservoirs, and a spell travelling across Africa. For 24 years until 2014, he was then senior reserves manager for the Cambridgeshire fenland NNRs of Woodwalton Fen and Holme Fen, where he oversaw major restoration and research programmes. He also advised on the management of wetland Sites of Special Scientific Interest such as Nene Washes and represented Natural England on the Wicken Fen Management Committee, during the development of the 'Wicken Vision'. He initiated the Fen Management Network across a range of conservation organisations in East Anglia and gained a Diploma in Ecology and Conservation from the University of London in 2010. In 2001 Alan was responsible for co-founding the Great Fen project with the Wildlife Trust and Environment Agency and has worked closely with all partners throughout the life of the project. He has represented the Great Fen at World Wetlands day in 2008 and the 2009 conference of 'Wild 'Europe' in Brussels, and has made wildlife management study tours of the Netherlands, Belgium and Germany. He has written widely about conservation management and the Great Fen and given many talks and lectures on wetland management. Alan moved to Dorset in 2016, where he continues to be involved in conservation and promoting closer links between people and the natural world.